Charles Ebbets

Charles Ebbets

*The Man Behind the
Dodgers and Brooklyn's
Beloved Ballpark*

JOHN G. ZINN

McFarland & Company, Inc., Publishers
Jefferson, North Carolina

ISBN (print) 978-0-7864-9973-1
ISBN (ebook) 978-1-4766-3033-5

LIBRARY OF CONGRESS CATALOGUING DATA ARE AVAILABLE

British Library cataloguing data are available

Front cover: Brooklyn Dodgers majority owner and president
Charles Ebbets, circa 1913 (Library of Congress)

Printed in the United States of America

*McFarland & Company, Inc., Publishers
Box 611, Jefferson, North Carolina 28640
www.mcfarlandpub.com*

To Henry George Zinn,
born June 25, 2015.
And in memory of
Paul A. Shubnell, 1936–2016

"Through my entire career I have believed that if I did what was right and endeavored to deliver the goods the Brooklyn Public would stick to me."—Charles Ebbets, May 10, 1913

Table of Contents

Preface and Acknowledgments

For the past decade the focus of my research, writing and lectures has been two distinct, but not unrelated, topics, the Civil War and baseball history. Ironically, I'm frequently asked about the origin of my interest in the Civil War, which is a question I can't answer, but seldom get the same query about baseball history, a question I can answer almost without thinking about it. My interest in baseball's past goes back over 60 years to when I was ten years old, growing up in northern New Jersey. At the time baseball was truly the national pastime, with other sports bridging the gap between one baseball season and another. While I didn't get interested in baseball as early as some of my peers, once I did, I wanted to spend every waking moment playing, watching or, and this was perhaps unusual, reading about baseball.

Fortunately my father was a teacher and would regularly bring home books from the school library in a vain attempt to satisfy my almost insatiable appetite. One book stood out—*My Greatest Day in Baseball* as told to John Carmichael and other noted sports writers. While I didn't realize it at the time, the book is a collection of articles, published in the *Chicago Daily News*, in which famous players told the stories of their most memorable games. The book anticipated the much better known *The Glory of Their Times*, Lawrence Ritter's classic collection of baseball oral histories from the first decades of the twentieth century. Although the accounts were far briefer than those in Ritter's book, Carmichael was able to include all-time greats like Babe Ruth and Ty Cobb who had died before Ritter began his epic journey through baseball's past.

While *My Greatest Day* included games through the early 1950s, for some reason what made a lasting impression on this 10-year-old were stories from the Deadball Era (1901–1919), beginning with Mordercai "Three Finger" Brown's account of the final game of the epic 1908 National League pennant race. Vivid descriptions of legendary players such as Evers,

1

Speaker and Mathewson playing "inside baseball" in ballparks where fans actually watched from roped-off sections of the outfield were so fascinating that my interest in the period has never faded. It's no wonder, therefore, that when it came time to write a book about baseball history, there was no question it would be about the Deadball years. Since I had grown up as a Dodger fan, it was also clear that the team from Brooklyn had to be a focal point of the story. I eventually co-wrote, with Paul Zinn, *The Major League Pennant Races of 1916*, the story of what to my surprise was, other than 1908, the only close National League pennant race of the entire Deadball Era.

With that project complete, it was only natural for us to move on to a book about Brooklyn's much-loved, now lost ballpark. Titled *Ebbets Field: Essays and Memories of Brooklyn's Historic Ballpark*, it brought together essays by baseball historians and reminiscences by the people who knew it well. Telling that story required writing about the man whose name was on the building, Charles Ebbets. Researching Ebbets' career for an essay confirmed beyond any doubt that there was more than enough material for an in-depth treatment, leading to this full-length biography of the Brooklyn magnate. From the outset it was an intimidating prospect, since Ebbets was not only president of the Dodgers for 27 years, he had been with the team almost from its creation, for a total baseball career of over 40 years. It's a story well worth telling and, I hope, worth reading.

The job of a baseball club owner has changed significantly since Ebbets' time, but even 100 years or so later, owners or magnates still have three major responsibilities—providing an attractive and accessible venue, building winning teams, and working with other owners to govern and improve the game. Almost always hampered by limited funds, Ebbets built not one, but two new ballparks in Brooklyn, both times significantly upgrading the quality and accessibility of the facility. On the field, Ebbets' teams lost more than they won, but over the course of his more than 25 years as club president, he put together four pennant-winning teams, a better record than the majority of his fellow National League owners. In addition, perhaps to a degree unequaled by his peers, Ebbets was so deeply involved in his local community that he helped build a strong and lasting relationship between Brooklyn and its ball club.

Less visible to the public was the club owner's responsibility to be a steward of the game, a role carried out in league meetings where representatives of the eight clubs gathered to make decisions about the game. Charles Ebbets took that responsibility very seriously, seldom, if ever, missing a meeting. But Ebbets didn't just attend, he made multiple suggestions and recommendations to improve the game he loved. Perhaps his most important contribution was to continually push efforts which would make the game more competitive, ranging from cost or revenue sharing to giving second-division clubs the first chance to improve their rosters. In a business environment which favored unrestricted competition, such initiatives were not always welcome, but Ebbets was persistent and succeeded more often than not. By the time of his death in 1925, Major League Baseball was a far better game and business than it had been 40 years before.

Considering the challenges in researching and writing this book, I fortunately had no shortage of help. The process began by consulting with Ellen Snyder-Grenier, contributor to the Ebbets Field book, former curator at the Brooklyn Historical Society and, more importantly, a friend who got me pointed in the right direction. Although Ebbets' over-four decades in baseball is the focal point of this book, his early life and his family history shaped his career as a baseball executive. Researching that part of Ebbets' life would have been far more difficult were it not for the incredibly detailed and thorough research done by Edward "Ted" Steele on the Ebbets family, especially his book *Ebbets: The History and Genealogy of a New York Family*. Ted was also extremely helpful in a series of follow-up e-mails, and I am very grateful for his assistance.

Historical newspapers are an essential source for Deadball Era research, beginning, in this case, with the *Brooklyn Daily Eagle*. For my previous Dodgers books, I accessed the *Eagle* on microfilm at the Alexander Library at Rutgers, which while effective for those projects, would never have worked for researching Ebbets' four decades in baseball. Fortunately, before I began my research, the Brooklyn Public Library finished digitizing the complete run of the *Eagle*, which is available for free on the Internet, making it far easier to work through 40-some years of Dodgers history. Far less well known than the *Eagle* are the other Brooklyn newspapers of the day, the *Standard Union, Brooklyn Citizen* and *Brooklyn Daily Times*. While detailed investigation of those papers wasn't possible, I was able to consult them on a few major topics, especially the construction of Ebbets Field.

When it came to archival collections, I was already familiar with the August "Garry" Herrmann papers held by the Baseball Hall of Fame and Museum in Cooperstown. Covering Herrmann's career as president of the Cincinnati Reds and head of the National Commission, the Herrmann papers are a vast collection (the finding aid alone runs 151 pages) of important primary source material about the business and governance of baseball. Previously unknown to me, and, I think, less well known to researchers in general, was the Hall of Fame's collection of the minutes of National League owners meetings. Although described as minutes, for most of Ebbets' tenure as a baseball magnate, the documents are a verbatim transcript, providing an invaluable opportunity to "hear" Ebbets and his fellow owners speak in their own words. Thanks to the Hall of Fame for preserving this vital original source material, and especially to Cassidy Lent and Matt Rothenberg for making the process of accessing hundreds, if not thousands, of pages of material so user-friendly. Working with the owners' minutes was also made far easier through the assistance of Michael Haupert, a professor of economics at the University of Wisconsin—La Crosse, who graciously shared copies he had made for the period 1899 to 1908. Michael also provided me with historical salary data that was very helpful in exploring Ebbets' salary negotiations with some of his top players. Thanks also to John Thorn and Steve Steinberg for assistance with pictures to better illustrate Ebbets' story.

Considering the slope of the project, it was essential to have knowledgeable readers to review the manuscript. I could not have found two people better qualified than Bill Lamb and Andy McCue. Bill and I have an interesting connection in that he played junior high school basketball for my father, Hank Zinn. Bill has an encyclopedic knowledge of the early history of New York Giants and baseball club ownership in the Deadball Era which made him especially qualified to review the manuscript. I knew Andy McCue through his definitive biography of Walter O'Malley and then, one overcast October morning, our paths crossed at the Hall of Fame library. Andy's in-depth knowledge of the Dodgers and his unique perspective on the club's ownership offered invaluable insights. Bill's and Andy's frank and insightful comments saved me from numerous errors and made this a much better book than it otherwise would have been. I am also grateful to Lyle Spatz for providing a cover blurb and to my sister JoAnn LaConte for proofreading the final proofs. Needless to say, the opinions and any errors in the book are my responsibility alone.

My interaction with Bill and Andy led to two editorial decisions to avoid confusion in the text. It's widely known that from the Brooklyn club's inception in 1883 through 1957, the team was known by multiple names, including Bridegrooms, Superbas and Robins, not to mention, of course, Trolley Dodgers or just plain Dodgers. For clarity's sake and following Andy's example in his O'Malley biography, I decided it was best to use the name Dodgers throughout rather than try to move through multiple names as the story progressed. Similarly, I decided to use World Series to describe the Fall Classic rather than the contemporary "World's Series," although the latter name is sometimes found in quotations. Also, unless noted, all of the statistics and player transaction information come from the invaluable www.retrosheet.org.

As always, friends and family played an invaluable part in the creation of this book. Longtime friend Stuart Grant supplied me with some important books and, as a former Brooklynite and Dodger fan, maintained an active interest throughout the project. Special thanks also to Brad Shaw and the rest of the Flemington Neshanock vintage base ball club for putting up with me and listening to far too many stories about Ebbets and the Deadball Era. About five years ago, when I wanted to start writing about early baseball in New Jersey, I decided to experiment with a blog called "A Manly Pastime." Since then the blog has expanded to a broader focus on baseball history, and I am very grateful to all those who take the time to read and comment.

No one could be more blessed than I am in terms of family. Carol and I have been married for over 43 years and since, as I've written before, unconditional love is a rare commodity, receiving it for more than four decades makes it even more special. While Paul Zinn couldn't work with me on this project, there was good reason due to his increased responsibilities for the two youngest baseball fans in the Zinn family, Sophie and Henry, six and three years old respectively. Visits to Massachusetts to see Paul, his wife, Sarah, and our grandchildren were welcome respites from long days of grappling with issues of baseball club ownership.

Spending so much time working on baseball history makes one even more mindful of the many generations who love and care about the game. Multiple generations means periods of transition, and the creation of this book saw two such changes. Leading off was the arrival of Henry George Zinn on June 25, 2015, named after his great-grandfather, a former college baseball player. Henry is already showing an aptitude for throwing a ball which his father and I are doing everything possible to encourage. No baseball fan, of course, lives forever, and sadly, Paul A. Shubnell, beloved husband of my cousin, Peggy, died on November 18, 2016. As Paul well knew, he was extremely fortunate in his wife, especially because of the love they shared for baseball, to the point that they visited over 50 major league stadiums together. His passing will leave a gap in every baseball season hereafter, perhaps gradually filled by young Henry and future generations of baseball fans who enjoy the great game for which Charles Ebbets did so much. It is a pleasure to dedicate this book to Henry and Paul.

Chapter I

"Where I learnt the first rudiments of baseball"

When Brooklyn baseball fans filed into Ebbets Field on May 19, 1925, to watch their Dodgers take on the visiting Pittsburgh Pirates, the baseball season was, in Charles Ebbets' words, still in its infancy. It was also, however, a day to honor the past, specifically the National League, baseball's senior circuit, which had just begun its 50th season. Special guests included Major League Baseball commissioner Judge Kenesaw Mountain Landis, National League president John Heydler, and Brooklyn baseball royalty ranging from Jack Burdock and Tom "Oyster" Burns of the 19th century to more familiar names like Bill Dahlen and Wilbert Robinson. As the group assembled near home plate, Shannon's Band, understandably caught up in the moment, played "Cheer, Cheer, the Gang's All Here." But as M. W. Corum wrote in the next day's *New York Times*, "They were not all there." Especially noteworthy by his absence was Charles Ebbets, the man who, according to Corum, guided "the Brooklyn club from nothing into one of the most valuable properties in baseball."[1]

Ebbets' death a month before the ceremony at the ballpark which bore his name marked the end of a baseball career of over 40 years. When the native New Yorker became what he himself described as a baseball handyman in May of 1883, Chester Arthur was president of a country guided by conservative Victorian manners and morals. At Ebbets' death, more than four decades later, Calvin Coolidge, another accidental president, led a country coping with the rapidly changing mores of the Roaring Twenties. Not surprisingly, baseball, like the country, also experienced dramatic change throughout those years. Over the course of Ebbets' baseball career, no less than four new leagues challenged the National League, provoking destructive baseball wars, with one upstart circuit, the American League, successfully forcing the older league into a somewhat uncomfortable partnership. Even when new leagues failed, the competition for players drove up salaries, an increased financial burden for club owners, but a pittance compared to the amount of money Ebbets and his peers needed to build a new generation of ballparks in the early 20th century.

Baseball wars and expensive new ballparks are just two examples of the challenges which made an already demanding job even more difficult. A successful owner had to field competitive teams, provide an attractive, accessible venue, and operate on at least a break-even financial basis. Financial solvency was essential because a club awash in red ink could never accomplish the first two objectives unless the owner had other sources of money, a luxury Ebbets never enjoyed. Always limited financially, facing multiple challenges, Charles Ebbets successfully built ball clubs and ball parks, including one so legendary it lives on in fans' collective memory. Baseball was Ebbets' business, and like Ebenezer Scrooge in Dickens' *A Christmas Carol*, it occupied him constantly almost literally until his dying day. But unlike Scrooge (before he encountered the ghosts), Ebbets, while no saint, had values which guided his work as a baseball owner. Although he was frequently labeled a cheapskate, players, fans and countless charities benefited from Ebbets' largesse. Charles Ebbets never forgot he was not merely a baseball club owner, but also a steward of a truly national game, a role with responsibilities beyond the bottom line.

Ebbets' understanding of his stewardship responsibilities extended to league affairs, where he worked constantly to improve the game for the fans, his fellow owners (who were both his competitors and partners) and the players themselves. By 1925, many of Ebbets' innovations had been in place so long, they were probably taken for granted. The Pittsburgh— Brooklyn game was part of a schedule, once the subject of bitter debate among owners, but now thanks to Ebbets, accepted with minimal objections. Had the game been rained out, fans and club officials would have benefited from a user-friendly rain check designed by the Brooklyn club president. And even if rain only delayed the contest, the visiting players could retreat to a comfortable locker room, something Ebbets pushed for, even though it cost him money. Above all, for Ebbets, improving the game meant working for competitive balance, and he regularly tried to convince the other owners to help the lower-level clubs even when it was of little benefit to his own team. By far the most important of these initiatives was his proposal to structure the draft so the teams with the worst record got first choice of new talent, a concept now the norm in every professional sport. None of this happened because Charles Ebbets was a genius or a saint, but the Brooklyn club president, in spite of his weaknesses and shortcomings, left baseball both in Brooklyn and throughout the major leagues in better condition than he found it.

Towards the end of the Brooklyn's 1920 pennant-winning season, Charles Ebbets sat on the porch of "his snug little [Flatbush] home" and discussed his long baseball career with Frederick Boyd Stevenson of the *Brooklyn Daily Eagle*. Eventually the conversation turned to the Brooklyn club owner's decision to build his new (and expensive) state-of-the-art ballpark. Considering Ebbets' limited financial resources, the project was fraught with risk, and success was by no means certain. In analyzing Ebbets' decision to give Brooklyn a new ballpark, Stevenson claimed the baseball magnate's "American spirit" overcame his inherited English "conservatism" and Dutch caution. If, however, Stevenson knew more of Ebbets' family history, he might well have drawn different conclusions about the influence of the Brooklyn magnate's English (Ebbets) and Dutch (Quick) ancestors, who took no shortage of risks when they came to the United States.[2]

Leaving one's native country for good is never without risk, but, typically, the further back in the past, the greater the obstacles and potential problems. While the Ebbets and Quick families didn't come over on the Mayflower, both sides of Ebbets' family arrived in this country before there even was a country. Ted Steele's comprehensive history of the Ebbets family begins with Daniel Ebbets, an English bricklayer who arrived in old New York at the turn of the century—the 18th century. Not only was Daniel a risk taker, he was also considered responsible by his new neighbors, who made him a free man (citizen and voter) of New York in 1700 and a constable in 1711. Although the Ebbets family's early arrival on these shores is impressive, they came after the Quicks, Charles' mother's family, who crossed the Atlantic sometime before 1664, when New York was still the Dutch colony of New Amsterdam.[3]

If risk taking was in Ebbets' genes, it came with a sense of civic responsibility and a penchant for entrepreneurship. The generations between Daniel Ebbets, the English immigrant, and Charles Ebbets, the baseball magnate, included a sea captain, grocers and a liquor merchant, men who also served their community as tax collectors, street inspectors and turnpike commissioners. The Quick side of the family was no different, since James Quick, Ebbets' maternal grandfather, operated a china and glass business while serving as a leader in the city's volunteer fire department. Another ancestor on the maternal side, Thomas Snell, was a sea captain when American commercial ships were in constant danger from the warring British and French navies. Sadly, but not surprisingly, the Quick and

Snell families were slave owners before New York began the emancipation process in 1799.[4]

Even if, however, Ebbets thought of himself as following in his ancestors' footsteps, his immediate family, the urban environment he grew up in, his education and early work experiences had far more influence on the future baseball executive. Born on October 29, 1859, at 31 Clark Street in New York City, Ebbets was the third son and fourth child of John B. Ebbets (1824–1888) and Ann Maria Quick (1824–1871). Almost a decade earlier in 1850, John and Ann shared a house at 469 Greenwich Street in the city's Fifth Ward with two of Ann's siblings and their families. It was a temporary arrangement, if for no other reason than because John and Ann's family kept growing with the births of sons, John B (1852) and James Tunis (1855), preceding Charles' arrival in 1859. By the time the future baseball executive came into the world, the family had moved to the Eighth Ward, where they lived for the first 12 years of his life.[5]

Whenever young Charles ventured outside, first with a protective escort and later on his own, he experienced the full range of life in Civil War-era New York. Ebbets spent his early years in a part of Manhattan now known as SoHo (South of Houston Street). Bounded by the aforementioned Houston Street in the north, Canal Street to the south, Broadway to the east and West Street (or the Hudson River) to the west, the Eighth Ward was home to both the good and bad of the great city. Among the good were Niblo's Garden, a famous 19th-century theater, and the luxurious Metropolitan Hotel, both located on Broadway, in the Ebbets' neighborhood geographically but not financially. Far less attractive was Laurens Street (now West Broadway), noted for its brothels and the "pestiferous stench" derived from 250 families living in eight houses. Labeled "Rotten Row," Laurens Street was only three blocks from the Ebbets family's 1860 Clark Street home, but their own street didn't lack for problems. One newspaper account described "rowdies," who hung around women (definitely not ladies), living only a few doors away at 25 Clark Street. The address was apparently just one of the 101 brothels identified by sanitary inspectors in an 1865 study of the area, houses of ill repute complemented by 261 "liquor shops." It's no wonder the inspectors ranked Clark Street as one of four in the "most filthy condition" in the entire district, with disease a major threat to the residents.[6]

Simply surviving in those conditions was an accomplishment, and while the Ebbets family stayed in the Eighth Ward, over the next decade, John and Ann moved at least three times, understandably looking for a better environment for their young family. By 1870, the Ebbetses were at

143 West Houston, and a comparison with Clark Street in 1860 suggests some success in their search. In addition to the unsavory types mentioned earlier, many of the Ebbetses' Clark Street neighbors were immigrants working as laborers and washerwomen. Only three families had servants (the Ebbetses were one), and only a handful claimed more assets than John and Ann, who reported $5,000 in real estate (Ann) and $2,000 in other assets (John). On West Houston Street, the residents worked at white collar jobs, including clerks, an engineer and three doctors. Even the brothels were a step up, with the same 1865 sanitary inspection finding those around West Houston "generally in a cleanly condition," supposedly because of their proximity to the "great hotels" on Broadway. John and Ann may have partially financed better accommodations by taking in boarders, one of whom, George Bissell, a partially disabled Civil War veteran, would eventually marry Ebbets' older sister Charlotte. Beyond any rental income, John Ebbets supported his wife, six children and 74-year-old mother-in-law by various jobs in the liquor business.[7]

It was not the easiest of times to earn a living, let alone provide for a household of nine, since the Civil War caused "rampant inflation," driving up the cost of essentials like food, rent, and coal faster than any increases in income. Regardless of the popularity of drinking, there was less money for discretionary items like liquor, which couldn't have been good for John Ebbets' primary source of income. Beginning in 1862, incomes over $600 were taxed, but there is no evidence that Ebbets' father's income ever reached that level, suggesting the family got by, but with little margin for error. Considering Ebbets' loquaciousness, if he had grown up in real poverty, he would have talked about it sooner or later, probably at some length. Even more visible than the hard economic times was the human cost of the war, and young Charles doubtless saw disabled veterans even before he lived with one. Growing up in the Eighth Ward offered an education just through observation, and it's likely Charles knew what poverty and vice looked like, understood that life was not always fair or easy, and realized that his future held a lifetime of work.[8]

In addition to what he learned on the streets of the Eighth Ward, Ebbets received, by today's standards, a limited formal education. While he said little, if anything, about his time at School 39 on Clark Street, Ebbets' school days seem to have ended no later than the eighth grade. At the time, it was considered important for everyone to be able to read, write and understand basic arithmetic, but few people reached high school, much less college. In fact, only the so-called "learned professions"—medicine, the law and the ordained ministry—required a college education, opening business management positions to those with what today would be considered a shocking lack of educational credentials. While no details about Ebbets' own education have survived, it's possible to get a sense of the content of his education from the work of journalist/historian Mark Sullivan. A longtime newspaper columnist in the Progressive Era, Sullivan wrote a six-volume history of the period, entitled *Our Times: The United States 1900–1925*. Almost 200 pages of the second volume are devoted to an analysis of how a common educational experience shaped the beliefs and outlook of Ebbets' generation, especially business and political leaders.[9]

The premise that Ebbets and his contemporaries shared a common educational experience is based on the extensive use of the McGuffey Reader, or more typically Readers, which became the "backbone of education" especially for "standards of individual and social conduct." Compiled by the Reverend William Holmes McGuffey and his brother, Alexander, the first six books "became practically universal," except in New England, giving the publisher an almost monopolistic hold on the text book market for about 30 years, beginning in the 1860s. According to Sullivan, the content selected by the McGuffeys for their books emphasized "formation of character" while providing "ethical guidance." An experience highly relevant to Ebbets was that of Clem Shaver, a leader of the Democratic Party in the 1920s who never forgot the story of a boy whose bow string broke at a crucial time. Due, however, to the hero's "economical trait," he had another piece of string in his pocket which saved the day. The story had such a lasting impact on Shaver that even as a man of "comparative wealth," in his mid–50s, he was unable to pass by a piece of string lying on the ground. It's not hard to imagine similar stories having considerable impact on a young Ebbets, whose home life also reinforced the need for thrift.[10]

If Ebbets was to make his way in the world, he had to be frugal, but there is a thin line between frugality and cheapness and, like many baseball owners, Ebbets was frequently tarred with the cheapskate brush. In April of 1925, shortly after Ebbets' death, Tom Rice of the *Brooklyn Daily Eagle*, who knew him well, made the seemingly ludicrous claim that Ebbets was similar to John D. Rockefeller, one of the richest men in the world. The comparison appears more than a little inappropriate, since just one of Rockefeller's oil wells probably generated more revenue in one year than Ebbets' baseball club did in his entire 27 years as club president. Yet Rice insisted that like all those who "become rich by their own efforts," each was "a big man in big things and a little man in little things," especially when it came to money.[11] Rockefeller was also accused of being cheap, but there was more to it than stinginess, a value perhaps best illustrated by a situation where he insisted that a railroad which overcharged him $117 return the money because he needed it for charitable work.[12] Simply put, both men learned early in life that even small amounts of money could and should be put to good use. Even virtuous principles, however, taken to an extreme can degenerate into the unappealing behavior of a cheapskate, a characterization of Ebbets which will be explored throughout this book.

Another highly valued contemporary behavior, especially in business, was taciturnity. Indeed, the talkative were considered "probably not of the highest dependability for the weightier affairs of life." Whether taciturn people are born or made isn't clear, but either way, it wasn't part of Ebbets' makeup. His failure, perhaps beyond his control, to meet this standard may partially explain the frequency with which Ebbets' verbosity not only became the butt of jokes, but also hurt his chances to win support from his fellow owners. After Ebbets' death, Tom Rice claimed it was "fashion" among the National League owners initially to oppose anything recommended by the Brooklyn owner, before, in most cases, eventually accepting his proposal. In analyzing Abraham Lincoln's speaking style, Ronald White argues that the opposite of verbosity is not brevity but precision, which helps speakers make their case. Ebbets' inability or unwillingness to follow this standard may partially explain his difficulties in this regard. In any event, although Ebbets and his peers received a far shorter education than would be acceptable today, the content and the authority behind it established "ideals of conduct" that "to some extent [were] lived up to by several American generations."[13]

Although the Ebbets family wasn't part of the upper crust of New York society, young Charles had every right to be proud of the family's long history in Manhattan, including their part in the early days of what would become his chosen profession. Although baseball has no one creation moment, organized baseball had its earliest roots in amateur clubs formed in the 1830s and 1840s in New York City. The best known of these pioneering teams was the Knickerbocker Club of New York, made up primarily of middle class young men, many working as clerks and other occupations favored by the Ebbets family. So it's no surprise that two Ebbets, Edward (born 1821) and Arthur (born 1830), were members of the Knickerbocker Club in the 1840s. The two men were brothers, the sons of Daniel Ebbets, Jr. (1785–1855), a prominent New York City banker who worked at the same bank which employed another early ball player, one Alexander Cartwright. Daniel Ebbets, Jr.'s, and Charles Ebbets' grandfathers were brothers, so Charles and the two Knickerbockers were first cousins, once removed. Both Edward and Arthur went to San Francisco during the 1849 gold rush, but Edward came back, and although he seems to have given up baseball, his son, George A. Ebbets, played for the Active Club of New York. Charles Ebbets doesn't seem to have mentioned his baseball playing relatives, but it's hard to believe he didn't have some awareness of his family's connections to the early game. Although the career baseball executive apparently wasn't much of a player, not long before his death, Ebbets reminisced about learning "the first rudiments of baseball by playing house ball and one old cat," so baseball must have become part of his life at an early age.[14]

While each of the Ebbets family's moves during the 1860s must have required adjustments, remaining with the boundaries of the intensely urban Eighth Ward maintained some level of continuity. The new decade, however, brought big changes when the family moved to Astoria, Queens, in 1871. While no explanation of the move survives, it may have been related to the death of Charles' mother, Ann, on July 8, 1871. According to what Ebbets told a Brooklyn newspaper more than 40 years later,

he was supposed to finish his education in the new locale, but the precocious 12-year-old had other ideas. Supposedly Ebbets sneaked away and worked for two days on a schooner, which earned him the princely sum of 50 cents and clothing covered in "lamp black." Payment was made in old "ship plasters," some of which Ebbets kept as a remembrance of his first earned income. As pleased as Ebbets may have been with himself, however, the family didn't need those modest earnings, and the future magnate reportedly finished his education at an unnamed private school.[15]

Very little is known about the dozen years between Ebbets' sojourn in Queens and the beginning of his baseball career in

Charles Ebbets in the 1890s (National Baseball Hall of Fame and Museum, Cooperstown, New York).

1883. Much of what does survive comes from Ebbets' own reminiscences many years later and is, therefore, subject to memory loss as well as conscious or unconscious enhancement. A New York City directory lists a Charles Ebbets living at 321 West 18th Street in Manhattan in 1876, employed as a clerk. Another entry a year later has a man of the same name working in the wine business, something Ebbets never mentioned, but he may have been following in his father's footsteps. One unassailable fact is that on April 10, 1878, at the tender age of 18, the future baseball executive started a family in more ways than one. On that day, Ebbets married Minnie Frances Amelia Broadbent, almost two years his senior, the daughter of English immigrants, James Broadbent and Amelia Preston. In 1870, the Broadbent family also lived in the Eighth Ward, but no details survive as to how the two met. Since, however, their first child, Charles H. Ebbets, Jr., was born only five and a half months later, Minnie was pregnant on her wedding day. That fact, along with Ebbets' future decision to leave his wife for another woman, raises the question of whether this was a marriage of choice or convenience. The details of Charles' and Minnie's decision to run the risks of pre-marital sex are, of course, unknown, but what is beyond question is that Charles Ebbets made a decision which could, and did, have serious long-term consequences. While it may have been the first time Ebbets made a short-term decision without thinking or caring about the long-term risks, it definitely wasn't the last, some of which would hurt the Brooklyn baseball club.[16]

In the 1920 interview mentioned earlier, Ebbets listed his pre-baseball employers as William T. Beer, Dick and Fitzgerald, and Frank Leslie's Publishing Company, in that order. Finding employment at William T. Beer's architectural firm was probably facilitated by family connections, since Mr. Beer was Ebbets' uncle. In the same interview, Ebbets claimed he "drew up the working plans" for two prestigious Manhattan buildings, Niblo's Garden, a famous theater, and the Metropolitan Hotel, an upscale hotel. According to Ebbets, the experience was a great help when he planned Ebbets Field. Unfortunately, the last major renovations of both properties took place in the early 1870s, when Ebbets was 12–13 years old. Even if he was as talented as he was connected, Ebbets was far more likely to have been filling ink wells and emptying waste paper baskets than working on architectural drawings for two New York City landmarks. Most likely Ebbets exaggerated his role, but that's not to say he didn't learn about building design at his uncle's firm. The Brooklyn baseball executive was deeply involved in planning Washington Park and Ebbets Field, demonstrating knowledge he could very well have acquired at W. T. Beer.[17]

After leaving the Beer offices at 896 Broadway for the last time, Ebbets headed downtown to 18 Ann Street, in the heart of the printing district, to work at Dick and Fitzgerald, a book publisher. Founded in 1858, the company specialized in books about "entertainment and self-improvement aimed at the family, the home and the parlor." Ebbets never said what he did at the firm, but the most likely possibilities include clerical work or a sales position, since books were frequently sold door-to-door. Ebbets wasn't so reticent about his last non-baseball job, telling the *Eagle* he was a subscription clerk at Frank Leslie's publications. Leslie was a British immigrant and a master illustrator who developed multiple publications. Leslie died in 1880, deeply in debt, and his widow, Miriam, took over and turned the company around, even legally changing her name to Frank Leslie. If Ebbets worked for the firm during the turnaround, which given the chronology is certainly possible, he witnessed hard times, followed by the painful, but necessary steps to revitalize a company—invaluable experience for his baseball career.[18]

As 1882 drew to a close, Charles Ebbets had observed his 23rd birthday, followed about a month later by the birth of his third child, and second daughter, Lydia. Sadly, however, there were only two children living in the Ebbets household since Florence Gertrude, the couple's first daughter, died in September of 1880 at the age of nine months.[19] It was a hard lesson, if any was needed, about just how difficult and uncertain life could be. Ebbets was most likely still employed at the Frank Leslie organization, but probably unknown to him, events were unfolding which would ultimately lead him to his true calling. Ebbets would bring to his new profession a family history replete with entrepreneurs who preferred the risks of self-employment to the less intense, but also potentially less rewarding work of an employee. Relatively uneducated by modern standards, the future baseball executive had still learned values that could guide him throughout a business career. First, however, young Mr. Ebbets had to earn his spurs in the baseball business.

CHAPTER II

"The greatest mistake of our life"

If, as Shakespeare wrote, there is a "tide in the affairs of men, which, taken at the flood, leads on to fortune," that decisive moment came for Charles Ebbets in 1883.[1] The opportunity, supposedly thanks to his older brother Jack, was to work for a new baseball club started by a newspaper man (George Taylor), a lawyer (Charles Byrne), and two gambling house operators with Tammany Hall connections (Ferdinand Abell and Joseph Doyle).[2] Although the four men had no prior experience in professional baseball, they intended to start a franchise in Brooklyn, then an independent city with an 1880 population of over 566,000, third-largest in the United States.[3] Not only were the four men inexperienced, they also lacked players, a ball park and a league to play in, but they did have money (thanks to Abell and Doyle) to remedy those shortcomings. Perhaps more importantly, the economy's recovery from the depression of the 1870s and the creation of a second major league (the American Association) in 1882 suggested that there was a ticket-buying public which would support a new team in Brooklyn. Fueled by optimism and money, the new magnates built a ballpark on land leased in south Brooklyn, signed players, and joined the Inter-State Association for the 1883 season, "preparatory" to finding a "higher position" elsewhere.[4]

Midway through his 24th year, in May of 1883, Ebbets was living at 154 Alexander Avenue in the Bronx with Minnie, their son Charles Jr., and daughter Lydia, both under the age of five. Standing 5'9" with blue eyes, an oval face and square chin, Ebbets may have already sported the moustache depicted in later pictures.[5] Although the young husband and father never discussed why he joined the fledgling baseball club as a self-proclaimed "assistant secretary and handyman," the new venture most likely appealed to his entrepreneurial instincts and love for baseball.[6] Where else Ebbets worked at the time is unknown, but the seasonal, part-time nature of professional baseball allowed him to labor in other vine-

17

yards simultaneously. Baseball clubs in 1883 and throughout Ebbets' 40-plus-year career were small businesses, not just compared to today, but also relative to the contemporary economy. Some 14 years before the formation of the Brooklyn club, railroad tycoon Cornelius Vanderbilt referred to the Harlem Railroad as "a small thing," having "a little capital of only about $6,000,000."[7] Capitalized at $20,000 in March of 1883, the Brooklyn club was little more than a drop of water on the vast ocean of 19th-century commerce.[8]

Such small businesses needed very few employees except on game days when, for example, Chicago, which reportedly had the "model park of the 1880s," typically hired about 40 employees, including ushers, policemen and ticket takers, not to mention musicians.[9] According to Ebbets, his early duties included managing game day personnel as well as supervising ticket sales. Successful oversight of smaller things led to increased responsibility, and Ebbets was promoted to club secretary as early as October of 1886, primarily working at home games.[10] No information survives about Ebbets' salary, but since the average player made less than $1,500 in the early 1880s, it's unlikely that Ebbets was making more than $300–500, which he must have supplemented from other jobs.[11]

There was no career path for aspiring baseball executives, and the first generation learned by trial and error while Ebbets and his peers effectively served unstructured apprenticeships, learning by a combination of watching and doing. Ebbets' most important on-the-job training came from 15 years of working directly for club president Charles Byrne, especially when Brooklyn joined the American Association in 1884 and became a major league team. Described as "short, but very strongly built" with brown hair, Byrne more than made up for any shortcomings in stature by his "unusual strength and energy" as well as a "striking presence."[12] Not only was the Brooklyn club president a hands-on executive, he also took an active part in league affairs.

Ebbets' own career as a baseball club executive was shaped by values, practices and priorities, which if he didn't learn them from Byrne, his own inclinations were reinforced by watching his boss and mentor. Among the most important lessons was how Byrne made "the best interests of the national game" one of his highest priorities. Although he never neglected his own club and its bottom line, Byrne had a broader concern for everyone involved in major league baseball.[13] If this was more than cheap rhetoric, it meant players and fans were treated as more than dispensable employees and anonymous customers. Byrne set the tone for the club's attitude towards its fans in the inaugural 1883 season by encouraging free

National League owners whom Ebbets observed during his long apprenticeship. Of special note is Charles Byrne, Brooklyn club president (first row, last on the right) from the team's 1883 founding till his death in early January 1898 (*Spalding Official 1898 Baseball Guide*).

attendance by ladies and refunding fans' money when the St. Louis Browns failed to appear for an exhibition game.[14] Equally important was the example Byrne set in dealing with his players. While doubtless a tough negotiator, the Brooklyn president's interest in his players went far beyond their performance on the field, with his care of Dave Foutz's family after the latter's untimely death just one example.[15] Ebbets would frequently follow Byrne's example in this regard, going far beyond token or symbolic gestures to provide substantive help to former players and other baseball people.

Unlike most businesses, a major league baseball owner's chief competitors were also his partners. Every team, even the most successful, needed other clubs to compete against, and the better the competition, the higher the gate receipts. It was difficult to balance the competitor/partner roles, and here again, Ebbets benefited from Byrne's example. Never a passive participant, Byrne was considered a "vigorous fighter in baseball politics," but also a diplomat and "a generous enemy."[16] Ebbets watched his boss work aggressively for his own interests without alienating opponents whose vote he might need on the next issue. Equally important was Byrne's "capacity for and love for hard work," especially the "detail work" which in league affairs meant he often ended up with the "knotty problems."[17] As we shall see in future chapters, Ebbets would, in a similar fashion, frequently take on issues other owners were either unwilling or unable to address.

Working for the greater good of the game was certainly admirable, but the ultimate test of a baseball owner was his success or failure in putting together a competitive team. Throughout the early years of major league baseball, there was little, if any, formalized process owners could use to upgrade their rosters. Farm systems and the general manager's position were decades in the future, and while there were minor leagues in the 1880s, there was no structured draft or other system to acquire promising minor league players. The only possible means were trades or purchases, but for a startup club like Brooklyn, the only real option was buying talent. Fortunately, Byrne knew how to act quickly and aggressively and he had sufficient money, primarily from Abell, to do so. In both 1883 (Camden) and 1885 (Cleveland), Byrne beat other owners to the punch by signing players from teams on the brink of dissolution.[18]

When these moves proved inadequate, Byrne became even more aggressive, buying the entire New York American Association franchise for its few quality players and then purchasing three top players from the Association's best club, the St. Louis Browns.[19] Perhaps not surprisingly given the unpredictability of baseball, even with the former Browns stars, Brooklyn still finished behind St. Louis in 1888, earning Byrne no small amount of derision from the media.[20] Not in the least discouraged, the Brooklyn magnate kept buying talent, finally bringing a pennant to Brooklyn in 1889.[21] Watching all of this more or less at Byrne's elbow, Ebbets must have learned both the importance of constantly upgrading the roster and the need for a ready source of money. On the negative side, Ebbets may also have picked up from Byrne the temptation to play fast and loose with player transaction rules. Byrne did just that in early 1885, hiding the Cleveland players from other potential suitors during the ten-day waiting period when they were effectively free agents.[22]

Working for a small organization was an advantage for Ebbets because in addition to observing Byrne, he had plenty of responsibility early in his career, enabling him both to prove himself and learn on the job. Ebbets also benefited from Charles Byrne's active role in league affairs, which forced him to delegate to his small staff, especially the energetic and ambitious Mr. Ebbets. After the club finished its first season in the American Association, Byrne was appointed to the league's schedule committee and quickly assigned the "details" to his young assistant.[23] It was not a task for the faint of heart, since one sports writer claimed that chess masters became "raving maniacs" after just one attempt at schedule making.[24] The issues were not only complicated but contentious, because having the most attractive home dates was crucial to every club's bottom line. Unlike modern baseball, with multiple sources of revenue, especially television and radio, gate receipts were almost the sole source of revenue. In addition, the lack of night baseball and, in many places, Sunday games (the only day most people were off from work) meant holiday or Saturday home games (called "plums") were every magnate's highest priority. Just one example of how difficult and acrimonious the scheduling issues could become was the 1888 National League meeting, where the debate took 12 hours and didn't end until 3:00 a.m.[25]

Such rancor wasn't the norm during American Association schedule discussions, or at least not after Byrne and Ebbets got involved. Both men knew or quickly learned that fairness and attention to detail were the keys to successful schedule making. Fairness was the solution to the problem of allocating the best dates by simply rotating the "plums" on an annual basis. Many years later, Ebbets claimed he originated the idea, but regardless of who thought of it first, it was an almost irrefutable solution. Once that source of contention was eliminated, Ebbets began working on the details, typically in January at his small office at Washington Park. On his desk, the enterprising schedule maker had written requests from owners, the prior year's schedule, a calendar and, especially important, a railroad timetable. The geographic reach of late-19th century baseball would have been impossible without the railroad, but travel was time-consuming and expensive. Two key issues were equalizing, as much as possible, the miles traveled and knowing what was feasible in terms of "jumps" from one city to another. For example, even traveling overnight (which was the norm), it was impossible to close out a series in St. Louis one day and begin another the next day in Boston.[26] So pleased were the owners with Ebbets' work, they also assigned him the responsibility of preparing the umpires' schedule.[27]

Byrne's and Ebbets' schedule making reputation clearly preceded them when Brooklyn joined the National League in 1890, and the highly sensitive task was quickly handed to the two men by making Byrne chair of the schedule committee.[28] Once again, Ebbets delivered a quality product since the 1891 schedule was approved in less than 20 minutes with the details "not much more than looked over." Knowing a good thing when they saw it, the owners also directed that Ebbets' system be used in future years.[29] Unfortunately for Ebbets, schedule making became even more complicated when the National League and American Association con-solidation left him stuck with the nightmare of preparing a 12-team schedule for 1892. Wasting no time, Ebbets got to work two days after Christmas, too busy even to speak with the media.[30] Not only were there more teams and more mileage, but Sunday baseball was a problem because some clubs wanted to play on the Sabbath, while others wanted no part of it.[31] Ebbets' handling of the volatile issue was just one more example of his gift for schedule making. Rather than get bogged down trying to honor each club's wishes, he solved the problem by simply not scheduling any Sunday games, but allowing interested clubs to play on the Sabbath by mutual agreement.[32] Perhaps not entirely convinced of Byrne's and Ebbets' objectivity, two other clubs submitted draft schedules, but as the *Eagle* predicted, the proposed schedule was approved unanimously with "a vote of thanks to Mr. Ebbets."[33]

Even when using Ebbets' system, not everyone was adept at schedule making, something National League president Nick Young proved by somehow preparing an 1893 schedule without a single Brooklyn-New York Saturday game, the most profitable day of the week in the Sabbath-observing East.[34] Even worse was the 1894 schedule, where the ineffectual Mr. Young scheduled Washington to play in Cincinnati when the team couldn't get there until that night. Even Ebbets couldn't untangle the mess, forcing the league to move an entire series from Washington to Pittsburgh, which understandably didn't sit well with the revenue-challenged Washington club.[35] Not surprisingly, Ebbets ended up helping Young with the schedule, adding further enhancements such as a more systematic rotation of the Western clubs' visits to the East, saving time and money in the process.[36] Working on schedules gave Ebbets invaluable experience in finding solutions to complex problems while also earning him a baseball-wide reputation for competence. According to the *Brooklyn Daily Eagle*, Ebbets' proficiency at schedule making showed "an aptness for detail and symmetry that would prove valuable in any other profession," but fortunately for baseball, Charles Ebbets had found his calling.[37]

Another major responsibility of baseball club owners was offering their fans an accessible and attractive venue. Since the most challenging parts of building the first incarnation of Washington Park were probably over when Ebbets joined the club, he most likely didn't get any practical experience in building a ballpark from the ground up. Fortunately for Ebbets, but not for Byrne and his partners, the Brooklyn club secretary did gain valuable experience in ballpark construction under extremely adverse circumstances. On the night of May 18–19, 1889, two of the wooden grandstands at Washington Park caught fire, leaving nothing but "a dismal, charred and blackened ruin," reportedly with $18,000 worth of damage.[38] Fortunately no one was hurt, and since the Brooklyn club was on a Western trip, there was no immediate revenue loss. That was the extent of the good news, however, since the club was due back in just ten days for a Decoration Day doubleheader with the archrival Browns, probably the biggest revenue date of the season.

Crises provide opportunities, and this was Charles Ebbets' chance to show he could work under pressure. With the approval of the owners, Ebbets got started and in just one day not only settled with the insurance company but also obtained the building permits and signed the construction contracts. Work was to begin on Tuesday, May 21, with the removal of the debris, which was to be left on nearby vacant lots as free firewood for the poor. Regardless of who made that decision, it showed that the club's ownership, even in a crisis, thought about the community.[39] The contract was awarded to D. E. Harris, the original builder, who promised to complete the work in a little over a week, working, if necessary, at night by electric light. Since the work meant building new wooden grandstands, similar "in form" to the old ones, with no site preparation, the short time frame, while challenging, wasn't as insurmountable as it might have seemed.[40] That didn't, however, take into account the weather, which failed to cooperate, but the contractor was still committed to finishing on time.[41]

Although he wasn't wielding a hammer and saw, Ebbets was said to be "one of the busiest men in Brooklyn." After a reporter was warned he could only find Ebbets by keeping a "sharp lookout," the writer watched the Brooklyn club secretary "pop up here and there" and doubted Brooklyn's best fielder "could have displayed more astonishing activity."[42] In the end, everyone's hard work paid off and the new stands were indeed ready for the Decoration Day, separate admission twin bill, with some 30,000 fans putting down their quarters to enter the rebuilt park.[43] Credit was clearly due to the contractor and his men, but Ebbets had demonstrated that he could produce in a crisis. His efforts didn't go unnoticed as the *Eagle* commented that "Mr. Ebbetts [sic] has shown himself to be a valuable man ... in this critical emergency."[44] Although he didn't know at the time, Ebbets gained experience which would serve him well when the time came to build not one, but two ballparks of his own.

While a split was the best Brooklyn could manage in the Decoration Day doubleheader, 1889 was the year Charles Byrne's team finally beat out the hated Browns for the American Association pennant. Even after a loss to the Giants in the first subway, or perhaps horse car series, Brooklyn ownership had good reason to be satisfied with the season, but had little time to enjoy their success. Massive change was about to engulf major league baseball in general and Brooklyn in particular, teaching Charles Ebbets no end of lessons in the process. The primary mover of these events was John Montgomery Ward, star player, future lawyer and organizer of the Brotherhood of Professional Baseball Players. Formed in 1885, the Brotherhood was the players' first major collective attempt to fight for higher salaries and better working conditions. Their initial efforts yielded no real success, and when the National League owners tried to impose the so-called Brush Plan, a salary scale with strict limits, Ward and his members sought a more radical solution.[45] Ward's plan, which was to be implemented in 1890, was to form a new league controlled by the players and friendly investors, with better rights for the players guaranteed through the new league's governing documents.[46] Not surprisingly, considering Brooklyn's population, the Players' League, as it came to be known, planned to put one of its eight clubs in Brooklyn.

As with crises, challenges to the status quo provide opportunities as well as threats, especially for those willing to take aggressive action like Charles Byrne. In a series of moves which taught Charles Ebbets how to fight a baseball war, Byrne quickly re-signed his players, preventing large-scale player defections.[47] Byrne then turned his attention to American Association affairs, and when the St. Louis owner, the controversial Chris von der Ahe, continued his war against the Brooklyn club, Byrne wasted no time in accepting an invitation to join the more established National League.[48] Moving to the National League brought both long- and short-term advantages, coupling the long-term benefit of a more stable circuit with the short-term advantage of weak 1890 competition due to player defections to the new league. Having protected his own roster and found a new home for his team, Byrne next faced head-to-head competition with the Players' League Brooklyn club, a far more difficult proposition.

The local threat became real in December of 1889 with the incorporation of the Brooklyn Players' League franchise, led on the field by Ward himself and off the field by some well-known Brooklyn names—George M. Chauncey, Wendell Goodwin and Edward Linton.[49] Like Byrne and his partners in 1883, the Players' League owners had no prior experience running a baseball club. Unlike the Dodgers owners, however, the new magnates' primary motivation was enhancing investments in real estate (Linton and Chauncey) and transportation (Goodwin), not baseball success.[50] The mixed motives raised questions about their level of commitment, questions underscored by a relatively small cash investment and the decision to play home games in East New York (a section of Brooklyn), inconvenient for fans but important to the group's non-baseball investments.[51] Byrne publicly dismissed any possible danger to the Dodgers from the Players' League club, comments made perhaps before he fully grasped the National League's wartime strategy and its potential to harm his team.[52]

Relying on the same strategy they used to defeat the Union Association in 1884, the National League owners intentionally scheduled as many head-to-head matchups as possible against the new league. In Brooklyn, this meant the two clubs would play on the same day over 80 percent of the time.[53] Instead of giving Brooklyn fans continuous baseball (one club at home, while the other was on the road, today's norm in two-team cities), the discerning fan had to choose between the two leagues on an almost daily basis. There was actually even a third alternative, a new Brooklyn club in the American Association, but it was so weak on the field and at the box office, it didn't even complete the season.[54] Being the clear favorite to win the National League might have worked in the Dodgers' favor, but the same discerning fan knew full well that the National League retained only 38 players from 1889, significantly diluting the quality of play.[55] Too much baseball quickly led to apathy, as the *Eagle* commented in late April that "the public is already growing indifferent" and predicted "a lapse of interest" in Brooklyn baseball.[56]

The Brooklyn newspaper was more than a little prophetic, since 1890 was a financial disaster for both the fledgling Players' League and the more established National League. Hardest hit were the National League's New York Giants, which had to be bailed out by investments from multiple owners, including Brooklyn's Ferdinand Abell, creating a questionable situation where magnates owned stock in more than one team.[57] In Brooklyn, Byrne and his partners could take some satisfaction from the Dodgers winning the National League pennant, but even that achievement was marred by the World Series with Louisville, which was stopped tied at three games apiece due to bad weather and a lack of interest.[58] The accounting ledgers of both Brooklyn clubs were awash in red ink, with Byrne's team reportedly losing $25,000 and the Players' League team not far behind at $19,000, plus another $41,000 expended on "equipment."[59] Neither league could afford to continue the conflict, which led to negotiations on a club to club basis. Perhaps the most drawn-out of these negotiations was in Brooklyn, discussions which had far-reaching implications for the Dodgers, the owners and even Charles Ebbets.[60]

The delay in Brooklyn was not due to the number of options since, as Ferdinand Abell pointed out, the only choices were for one side to buy the other out or for the two sides to form a consolidated club.[61] Based on the 1890 financial bloodbath and their limited interest in baseball, it's unlikely Goodwin, Linton and Chauncey had any interest in buying out Byrne, Abell, et al, and no record survives of Byrne and his partners trying to acquire the Players' League club. Most likely, neither side had enough cash and/or the inclination to see the potential seller realize a profit from the situation. The result was a reluctant marriage in the form of a new corporation, capitalized at $250,000, controlled by Byrne and his partners. The major sticking point was where the new club would play its home games. Despite Abell's and Byrne's public protestations that Washington Park was the better location, they unaccountably gave in, subject to receiving $40,000, $30,000 from their new partners and $10,000 out of the next year's profits.[62] One positive from the drawn-out negotiations was the buyout of the obstructive Edward Linton, who at one point obtained a court order to temporarily block the proposed deal.[63]

To this day, it's not clear why Byrne and Abell agreed to move to East New York, since Washington Park was clearly the superior venue. Although the club had enough money to purchase talented players during the 1880s and enjoyed a very profitable season in 1889, the promised $40,000 in new funds were apparently so important that the two men made a very bad long-term decision in an exchange for an immediate cash infusion. Almost a decade later, sports writer William Rankin claimed that he and other writers had warned Abell that moving to Eastern Park was a bad decision, but the Brooklyn magnate went ahead, as Rankin put it, "with his eyes open."[64] Regardless of how much or little Ebbets had to do with the negotiations, he must have learned a lot even if it was only in hindsight. Certainly he saw and would soon see even more directly the problems caused by marginally committed owners. Ebbets also learned the importance of moving quickly to sign players during baseball wars, but if he didn't real-

Ferdinand Abell, majority Brooklyn Dodgers owner from 1883 until he was bought out by Ebbets in 1907. Abell frequently lamented the amount of money he invested (lost) in baseball (*Brooklyn Daily Eagle*, December 10, 1899).

ize it then, he would learn that doing so depended upon having ready money or at least access to it. The Brooklyn magnate left no doubt that the experience taught him the importance of ballpark location, telling his fellow owners a decade later that the move to "a God-forsaken place and staying there like martyrs for eight years" was "the greatest mistake of our life."[65]

Although the 1890 World Series was stopped by mutual agreement, the Dodgers played a final match on November 1 for the financial benefit of the club's "efficient secretary, Charley Ebbetts [*sic*]," an indication that he wasn't highly paid.[66] Considering the difficult negotiations with the Players' League owners, which were far from resolved at that point, Byrne's and Abell's decision to host a special game for Ebbets' benefit speaks volumes for their regard for him, as does the players' willingness to participate. Ebbets' skillful schedule making and his oversight of the 1889 post-fire construction were major accomplishments, but he also contributed in smaller, but no less important ways. Score cards, for example, had been part of major league baseball for many years, but through 1888, Brooklyn offered the fans little more than the scorekeeping form itself.[67] That changed in 1889, when Ebbets created a 32-page booklet which included the complete home schedule, ticket prices and brief biographies of the players. Ads, which likely paid for most, if not all, of the cost, kept the score card affordable at five cents, with almost all of the additional revenue going directly to the bottom line. While it's not clear if Ebbets should be credited with both the idea and the implementation or solely the latter, the new score card was very popular, since the *Eagle* reported that "the sale was great."[68]

As hard as Charles Ebbets worked at his baseball responsibilities, the seasonal nature of late-19th century major league baseball allowed him ample time for other activities for both business and pleasure. An example of the former was a football score card designed and copyrighted by Ebbets and Walter Eschwege of the *World*, supposedly the first of its kind, designed to help fans follow another sport without numbers on uniforms.[69] Another money-making proposition was a bowling scorebook, but in the case of bowling, his second-favorite sport, Ebbets also volunteered his time and talent, especially for schedule making.[70] Bowling has a long history stretching back at least to medieval England, possibly even into early Egypt, and outdoor bowling was so popular in the Manhattan of Ebbets' ancestors that a small area in today's downtown financial district is still called Bowling Green.[71] Although Ebbets' adopted hometown apparently didn't take to the game quite so quickly or at least in an organized fashion, by 1894 the *Eagle* proudly claimed that Brooklyn was home to more large tournaments (leagues) and bowlers than any other city.[72]

The extensive coverage of bowling in contemporary newspapers and the participation by prominent people like Bernard York, Democratic political leader and Ebbets' future lawyer, illustrates the sport's popularity with middle- and upper-class men. Well before television and radio, there was far less to do during the long winter months, especially any kind of physical exercise. Bowling helped fill this gap by offering both exercise and fellowship for reasonable investments of time and money. Ebbets bowled for a number of different teams and also served as president/captain of the Prospect and Carleton Club teams.[73] As he did in baseball, Ebbets made multiple contributions to bowling organizations in Brooklyn and beyond, but unlike baseball, he was also proficient at the game itself. In November of 1894, he made five straight strikes on the way to a "record game of 225," bowling so effectively that "as each ball swept the pins off the alley, the spectators applauded with vigor."[74] Barely a month later, Ebbets "solved" the 4–7–9 split and went on to an even greater accomplishment in January of 1896, when he somehow made a 7–10 split, an accomplishment anyone who has ever rolled a bowling ball can appreciate.[75]

Considering Ebbets' national reputation as a baseball schedule maker, it's no surprise he was frequently asked to apply his magic to bowling schedules, but Ebbets also took on other leadership roles. One of the more popular bowling leagues in Brooklyn was the Shaughnessy tournament, and the *Eagle* claimed that Ebbets "deserves all praise for his indefatigable efforts and to him most of the credit is due for the success of the competition."[76] By the end of 1897, Ebbets was held in high regard throughout Brooklyn's bowling community, something that augured well for possible future success on a more national stage. In the meantime, the Brooklyn bowler and baseball man was gaining additional leadership experience while establishing a wide range of contacts within the still independent city of Brooklyn. Another activity that gave Ebbets similar opportunities was the short-lived Nassau Athletic Club. Founded in 1885 to provide exercise for young men, the club had financial problems which were rectified by Ebbets so when the club disbanded in 1889 all its bills had been paid.[77]

Ebbets' extensive involvement in Brooklyn sporting activities also gave him opportunities for social networking, and he took advantage by joining the Carleton Club, a men's social club in Brooklyn. Founded in 1881, the membership was described as the "usual cadre of local businessmen, attorneys, sons of prominent clergy and doctors," none of which

described Ebbets by background or profession.[78] Nor was Ebbets' participation in social organizations limited to the upwardly mobile world of
the Carleton Club. By the end of the 1897 baseball season, Ebbets was a
member of a Masonic Lodge, the Brooklyn Elks, and fraternal benefit
organizations including the Royal Arcanum.[79] The latter offered financial
protection against sickness, accidents and deaths when such assistance
wasn't readily available to working men. Ebbets believed enough in the
concept that earlier in 1897, he proposed a similar program for baseball
players.[80] Nothing seems to have come of the idea, but helping baseball
players in need would remain a priority for Charles Ebbets almost literally
until his dying day.

While there is no reason to doubt Ebbets' commitment to these
organizations, the connections could only benefit a future baseball magnate. However, even before he became president of the Dodgers, Ebbets
used his community involvement to his advantage in the contentious field
of politics. Although Ebbets was still living in Manhattan in 1883, by 1885
he had moved his family to 5th Street in Brooklyn, and they lived at multiple addresses in the same area for more than 20 years.[81] In the fall of
1895, Ebbets sought election as a Democratic candidate for the New York
State Assembly in the 12th district, a portion of Brooklyn's 22nd Ward.[82]
Washington Park, then the former home of the Dodgers, was located in
the district, which at least one letter writer to the *Eagle* claimed was pre-
dominantly Republican.[83] Perhaps playing off this assumption, the Republicans nominated Charles Lawrence Lincoln, who the *Eagle* claimed
"springs from the same stock as the late President Lincoln."[84] To no one's
surprise, Ebbets gave his all to the campaign, to the point that the *Eagle*
claimed it was unlikely any "candidate for the legislature in this county
has made a more spirited canvass than Charles H. Ebbets."[85] The hard
work paid off when Ebbets garnered 4,101 votes to Lincoln's 3,852.[86] For
better or for worse, Charles Ebbets was on his way to Albany.

During the late 1890s, members of the New York State Assembly
served one-year terms and with one lone exception, Ebbets' 1896 experience seems to have been uneventful. The exception, however, could hardly
have been more important for Brooklyn's future: the proposed consolidation of Brooklyn, Manhattan, Queens, the Bronx, and Staten Island into
an urban powerhouse reminiscent of the great corporate giants of the day.
The proposal had been debated for two decades with strong feelings on
both sides. From the pro-consolidation point of view, there were sound
practical reasons why being part of Greater New York was not just a good
idea, but essential for the then-independent city of Brooklyn. The City of

Churches had grown so much it was close to exceeding the capacity of its water supply, with horrific potential risks of fire and disease looming if something wasn't done. Not as lethal, but also very serious was Brooklyn's limited debt capacity, which jeopardized funding for badly needed municipal construction projects. Consolidation into Greater New York had the potential to solve these problems, but political independence dies hard, and in spite of all the logical arguments for consolidation, many in Brooklyn were opposed, including the *Eagle* and its editor, St. Clair McKelway.[87]

The issue came before the New York State legislature twice during Ebbets' term, and the first time, he was one of only three Brooklyn Democrats to support the measure, which passed by an overwhelming 91–56 margin. Ebbets chose the issue for his maiden address, saying that regardless of whether it cost him re-election, "it will be the happiest day of my life when I vote for the consolidation of Brooklyn and New York."[88] The legislation next went to the Mayors of Brooklyn and New York, who both vetoed it, bringing it back to Albany for another vote. Although those supporting consolidation claimed to have 85 to 90 votes when they only needed 76, in the end, the bill received just 78 votes, passing thanks to seven Democrats' votes, including that of Charles Ebbets.[89] The consolidation took effect on January 1, 1898, simultaneous, as we shall see, with another major change in Charles Ebbets' life. Ebbets' support of consolidation isn't surprising, since his involvement in business and civic life in Brooklyn was probably more than sufficient to convince him of the practical rationales. The Brooklyn Democrat does, however, deserve credit for twice going against the wishes of his own party and a number of his fellow Brooklynites to support what he believed to be in the community's best interest. Ironically, consolidation would eventually play a part in the Dodgers' departure from Brooklyn, since the consequent shift of political power to Manhattan made it difficult for Brooklyn politicians to help Walter O'Malley build a new ballpark in the 1950s.[90]

His fellow Democrats couldn't have been that upset with Ebbets' support for consolidation, since he was nominated for a second term, although there may have been a lack of candidates because the *Eagle* predicted that the Democratic prospects in 1896 were "poor."[91] The 1896 election was, of course, the famous Bryan-McKinley presidential campaign, and the overwhelming preference of Brooklyn voters for McKinley cost the Democrats dearly, including Ebbets, although he ran ahead of his party.[92] Ebbets' failure to win re-election didn't stop him from trying again in 1897, when he garnered the Democratic nomination for a seat on the Greater New York City Council. Once again an uphill battle was predicted, with the *Eagle* claiming "none of the [Democratic] candidates has a chance of election."[93] No matter what the prognosticators thought, however, no one expected Ebbets and Henry Nostrand, another Democrat, to run so closely that only a few votes separated them in the race for one position. Not surprisingly, given the microscopic margin, intense debate including protracted legal action ensued until a judge finally declared Ebbets the winner by a mere 127 votes out of over 46,000 cast.[94] Even that didn't settle the matter, and further legal action spilled over into early 1899, but in the end, Ebbets retained the seat.[95]

Ebbets' decision to diversify his activities may have been at least partially due to skepticism about the future of the Brooklyn franchise, where little went well after the move to Eastern Park. Although there was some reason for optimism after a strong finish in both halves of the 1892 split season, the club's performance deteriorated to regular fifth- or sixth-place finishes, once falling as low as ninth. Chronic second-division finishes did nothing to improve the relationships in the ownership group, especially with equally disappointing results at the box office. Financial information for 19th century clubs is notoriously vague, but it appears that a break-even result in 1891 was followed by a $15,000 loss the following year, although Abell put the number at almost $40,000.[96] The club then reportedly made some money the next three years, but suffered losses in both 1896 and 1897, the final years of the expanded ownership group.[97] Nor was the poor return at the box office the only financial problem. The sole incentive for the questionable move to Eastern Park was the $30,000 in new money from the Players' League owners plus an additional $10,000 from operating profits. Not only did the poor operating results make the latter payment highly unlikely, Chauncey, Goodwin and the others paid only $22,000 of the promised $30,000, and their stock was held as collateral against the balance due.[98] The situation also wasn't helped by dissension between Abell and Joseph Doyle from the original Dodgers ownership group. The exact nature of the disagreement was never disclosed, with the *Eagle* attributing it to a financial issue outside of "baseball policy" while the *Herald* simply called it a "misunderstanding."[99] Whatever it was, the split was so great that "reconciliation becomes an impossibility," and Abell bought out Doyle in early 1892.[100]

Abell must have wanted Doyle out pretty badly to invest/sink more of his own money in the club, but if he thought it was the solution to the Dodgers' problems, he was quickly disabused of that notion. Early in 1894, the former gambling house operator began complaining publicly that the "other owners do not take a proper interest in the club."[101] Apparently the consolidation agreement had no requirement for additional investments by the owners, so the club was at the mercy of their sense of responsibility, something sorely lacking among the Players' League group.[102] Probably annoying Abell even more was that as part owners of the land at Eastern Park and the transportation company that carried the fans, Chauncey, Goodwin and their partners benefited financially at no additional cost. The minority owners never did step up to the financial plate, leaving Abell more and more frustrated, but with few options. He was more than willing to sell his stock, but given the circumstances there were few potential buyers. Although Abell tried to convince transportation magnate Albert Johnson to buy out the minority shareholders, nothing came of it.[103] Finally in early January of 1897, Abell threatened to place the club in receivership, but the minority shareholders didn't so much as blink, with Chauncey dismissing the threat by saying Abell talked too much.[104]

With little success on the field or at the box office, amid ownership dissension that threatened to wreck the franchise, things looked bleak for the Brooklyn club at the end of 1897. Clearly the years at Eastern Park had gone badly, but not for Charles Ebbets. He not only had learned a great deal about running a baseball team, but had also built and expanded his network of friends and contacts, won one political election and hoped for another success that fall. Even with all the problems facing the owners, they appreciated Ebbets' work so much that they sponsored another special benefit game for him, this time to honor his 15 years of service.[105] After it was announced, the Father of Baseball himself, Henry Chadwick, chimed in, wholeheartedly endorsing the honor for his "old friend," whom he had known since 1883.[106] The game took place on October 9 before a big crowd in "perfect October weather." As Ebbets sat there in the autumn sunshine surrounded by friends and admirers, he could hardly have foreseen he would never again be quite so universally popular as he was on that beautiful afternoon.[107]

CHAPTER III

"I have put every dollar
I own into the club"

Bleak was probably a generous description of the outlook for the Brooklyn baseball club at the end of 1897. Seven years in the metaphorical wilderness of East New York must have seemed like the prophesized years of biblical famine, with little or no prospect of an equal number of years of plenty. The team's 61–71 1897 record earned them a tie for sixth place, barely in the first division of the 12-team National League and 32 games out of first. Much more worrisome, however, was the even worse performance at the box office, where an 1897 loss in the $10,000–14,000 range followed on the heels of an $11,000 deficit a year earlier.[1] Most likely, Ferdinand Abell, who was understandably fed up with underwriting deficits, once again reluctantly put up the cash to pay the unpaid bills. But even after any less than enthusiastic largesse on Abell's part, the club was still supposedly $56,000 in debt, with no profits on the horizon to repay those obligations.[2] All told, it wasn't a pretty picture.

Although it may have seemed like things couldn't get any worse, a diligent reader of the *Eagle* would have noticed another dark cloud on the horizon—the problematic health of Charles Byrne, the driving force behind the Brooklyn club since its inception. An early May 1987 report that Byrne was recovering from an attack of the grippe (flu) was no great concern, but some eyebrows should have been raised when he missed a Western trip, instead taking an extended, health-related visit to Hot Springs, Virginia.[3] By the end of the month, however, the Brooklyn magnate was back home, claiming to be fully recovered, so it may have seemed like business as usual, especially when Byrne went to New England in early June, looking for badly needed talent.[4] Any sense of normality, however, was short-lived when Byrne took to the road again in early August, not on baseball business, but for his health.[5]

The August trip clearly wasn't sufficiently restorative since season's end saw Byrne again on the way to Hot Springs for a month's visit before going to Philadelphia for the National League owners meeting.[6] Byrne typically took an active part at league meetings, but even after the extended respite in Virginia, he could only play a very limited role, further confirmation of his declining health.[7] Neither Abell nor Ebbets could have been surprised, therefore, when the situation continued to degenerate, and on December 11, the *Eagle* proclaimed Byrne "dangerously ill" and "not expected to recover."[8] In spite of this dire prognosis, it is a testament to Byrne's constitution that he rallied and held on until January 4, dying at his home in Manhattan.[9] If any evidence was needed of Bryne's total commitment to the Dodgers, it was found in his estate, which consisted almost entirely of his investments in the Brooklyn club.[10]

Losing a leader of this magnitude was devastating, and it was hard to argue with the *Eagle's* contention that the club's affairs were in a "chaotic state," but new leadership was already on the way.[11] At some point during the Byrne death watch, Charles Ebbets approached Abell with the surprising, but positive news that he was no longer just Abell's employee, but also his new partner.[12] What was not only surprising, but impressive was that Ebbets had accomplished something Byrne and Abell hadn't been able to do, buy out the old Players' League stockholders.[13] Somehow, during this bleak holiday season, Ebbets persuaded George Chauncey, the trustee for the group, to sell him their entire holdings, reportedly for $25,000, or about 33 cents on the dollar.[14] Although the latter claim is difficult to evaluate, as seen in Chapter II, the original consolidation agreement called for the Players' League group to invest $30,000, but they only put up $22,000. If so, the recalcitrant magnates redeemed their investment in the Dodgers, but weren't so fortunate with their original Players' League investment.

Why was Ebbets able to buy out the minority owners? In addition to Chauncey, the other remaining large investor from the Players' League group, Wendell Goodwin, was suffering from ill health and financial problems, so he and/or his family had incentive to sell.[15] Indeed, considering the extremely fragile state of the Brooklyn club, getting out with what they could was the prudent move for all the minority investors. Also entering into the equation was Chauncey's personal relationship with Ebbets. In his 1945, "informal history" of the Dodgers, Frank Graham recounted a supposed conversation between the Brooklyn realtor and the Dodgers employee in which Chauncey offered to sell Ebbets some of his stock as an incentive to work even harder.[16] Since Graham was, at most, a small child at the time, he wasn't an eyewitness, and it's hard to know how much

credence to give his account. Regardless of the accuracy of the story, however, the two men became close friends, and helping Ebbets while ridding
himself of an increasingly problematic investment was a win-win for
Chauncey.[17] The friendship between the two men lasted beyond the grave
when Ebbets, in his will, appointed Chauncey to organize an annual dinner
on the anniversary of the Brooklyn's magnate's birth.[18]

Far more interesting and important is how Ebbets managed to come
up with the estimated $25,000 purchase price. Many years later, Chauncey
said that Ebbets funded the purchase with a combination of cash and notes
(commitments to pay at a future date), but the breakdown was never disclosed.[19] Ebbets appears to have had three basic sources of money: his
Dodgers salary (which wasn't that high if he was still being given benefit
games), money earned from his scorecard and schedule creations (another
small amount), plus his share of a bequest from his great-grandfather,
William Quick. The bequest consisted of two properties in lower Manhattan which had been held for years as investments, with the rental
income divided among the many heirs. The properties became the subject
of a lawsuit instituted by Ebbets' older brother, James, and were sold in
1886, with the proceeds divided among the beneficiaries. It is estimated
that Ebbets received about $4,700, which could have funded part of the
stock purchase price.[20] Prior to that transaction, however, Ebbets bought
a house at 328 1st Street in Brooklyn, which according to the 1900 census
was owned free and clear of any mortgage. The safest conclusion is that
Ebbets bought the stock primarily with notes, and to the new magnate's
credit, Chauncey later praised him for always paying on time.[21]

If Chauncey and his partners saw Ebbets as a financial life raft, the
news was no less welcome to Ferdinand Abell, ecstatic to no longer be the
only one putting his money at risk. Supposedly Ebbets' purchase gave him
37 percent of the club's stock, with Abell the majority owner at 51 percent
and the remaining 12 percent held by the Byrne estate.[22] Understandably
willing, not to mention anxious, to see how far Ebbets might go, Abell
gave his new partner until February 1 to buy him out as well. Regardless
of whether Ebbets exercised the option or not, he was to become club
president, which, although delayed due to Byrne's death, was formalized
on January 12.[23] Prior to that, however, Ebbets held a dinner for the media
at Brooklyn's Clarendon Hotel to discuss his plans, which he amplified a
few days later in an interview with the *Sun*. Making his own commitment
clear, Ebbets claimed he had "put every dollar I own into the club, and I
propose to run it in a way to popularize the sport in Brooklyn." To no
one's surprise, Ebbets had little enthusiasm for continuing at Eastern Park,

but had neither plans, nor, more importantly, "money to build a new grounds." Somewhat surprisingly given his club's desperate need for revenue, Ebbets was cautious on the question of Sunday baseball, saying he would favor it, if the "people of Brooklyn desire it."[24]

Over the next few days, Ebbets confirmed that veteran manager Billy Barnie, with whom he was reportedly "warm friends," would return as manager and claimed the club had money to upgrade its roster.[25] Ebbets also stressed that any chance for a new park was dependent on the transportation companies doing "the proper thing," that is, pay for it.[26] Thankfully, the public didn't hold Ebbets responsible for the club's current woes, so he enjoyed a honeymoon period with both the *Sun* and the *Eagle* noting the fans' positive reaction to his new role.[27] More than a little carried away, the latter paper gushed that there was "probably no man in baseball today who is more popular with magnates, managers and players."[28] With the almost euphoric atmosphere, it may have seemed like only a bump in the road when Ebbets wasn't able to exercise the option on Abell's stock. The significance of Ebbets' failure to do so was downplayed with the claim that Abell now wanted to stay involved, and Ebbets would supposedly buy enough of Abell's shares to have a majority interest.[29] However, that purchase also didn't happen, and it wouldn't be long before Abell would again become uncomfortable with the club's financial situation.

Having worked for the Brooklyn team for 15 years, Ebbets was well acquainted with the club's operations, but taking over as president meant far more responsibility. With all of the challenges facing him, the last thing Ebbets needed was more work, but that's exactly what happened when he was called to Washington to help league president Nicholas Young with the 1898 schedule.[30] Attending to league business when he needed every available minute for his new responsibilities confirmed that Ebbets already understood his dual responsibilities at the club and league level. Unfortunately, the larger organization also had more than its share of problems. After absorbing four American Association teams in 1892, the 12-team National League was so top-heavy that only two teams, Baltimore and Boston, had won pennants. To make matters worse, winning was no guarantee of financial success, since Baltimore did no better than break even when it won the 1896 pennant and actually lost money in a close second-place finish the following year.[31]

A top-heavy, uncompetitive league was ripe for division and acrimony which, not surprisingly, permeated the National League in the 1890s. By early 1898, the owners were divided into two camps, large-market clubs led by John Rogers of Philadelphia and small-market teams under the leadership of John T. Brush of Cincinnati. Among, but not always with, the large-market owners was the difficult, prickly and easily offended Andrew Freedman, majority owner of the New York Giants. Due to disputes with fellow owners and general indifference, Freedman refused to spend money to improve his team which, considering the Giants' potential drawing power, hurt other clubs dependent on big paydays in New York City.[32] Ebbets' entry into this select, but divided club also marked the beginning of his long relationship with Barney Dreyfuss. The two men would serve together for over 25 years in a relationship that would see both good days and bad.

As disagreeable as Freedman was, he wasn't, as some have suggested, a "brutish lout or buffoon," but rather possessed "formidable abilities" including "an absolute genius for making money."[33] As we shall see in future chapters, Freedman's abilities were on full display in his dealings with his fellow owners, who usually gave into his demands, no matter how unreasonable, primarily because of the importance of the New York market. Freedman's most capable opponent was John T. Brush of the Cincinnati club, who suffered from locomotor ataxia, a syphilis-driven condition which gradually deprived him of the use of his arms and legs.[34] Brush used his "indomitable will" to dominate the magnates (other than Freedman), who both admired and feared a man who feared no one.[35] Owner of two small-market clubs, first Indianapolis and then Cincinnati, Brush was "deeply involved in every aspect of the league" and only a few years away from becoming the most powerful owner in baseball.[36]

Fortuitously, the primary agenda item at Ebbets' first owners meeting as Brooklyn club president was player rowdiness, a rare issue where there was agreement, allowing the new magnate to adjust to his role without getting embroiled in controversial issues. With the league meetings behind him, Ebbets returned to his most pressing problem, the site of the club's 1898 home games. Building a new ballpark required both time and money, but the one thing which favored quick action was the literal absence of bricks and mortar, since perhaps the only advantage of 19th-century wooden ballparks was the short construction period. Even so, if something was to be done in 1898, quick action was needed. Ebbets hadn't even been formally elected club president when the *Eagle* ratcheted up the pressure, claiming the issue "requires more hurry than any other feature."[37] The paper also had no doubts about what the fans wanted, claiming that "According to the cranks, any place is preferable to Eastern Park," but consensus, though helpful, didn't make the job any easier.[38]

Once a site was selected, no small matter by itself, the two major issues were the rent (there was no money to purchase land) and financing construction. Multiple accounts claimed that Byrne had tried to move the club to the Litchfield estate in south Brooklyn (near the first Washington Park) in 1897, but problems with the rent and construction financing killed the deal.[39] Ebbets sought funding from the local subway and elevated railroad companies which would benefit from increased traffic going to and from games, but supposedly Albert Johnson of the Nassau Electric Railroad didn't like the idea. Johnson, a wealthy Cleveland street car magnate and early financial backer of the Players' League, was a principal in the Nassau Electric Railroad, a transportation company operating in Brooklyn. As noted in Chapter II, Johnson had been wooed by Abell as a potential investor in the Brooklyn club, and his prior experiences may have made him wary of the financially fragile baseball business.[40]

Faced with a difficult problem and little time to solve it, Ebbets prudently tried to give the impression that he wasn't desperate. Rather than focusing solely on the Litchfield Estate, Ebbets let it be known he was looking at other options near Prospect Park, less than two miles from the club's former south Brooklyn home, but more convenient than East New York.[41] The new magnate was also smart enough to apply pressure on the subway and trolley companies by stressing that without help, i.e., someone else's money, he would "be compelled much against my will to play at Eastern Park."[42] Since the transportation companies and the ball club had similar customer bases, it wasn't in the former's interest to be seen as a stumbling block to better days for the borough's baseball club.

Another strength of Ebbets' approach was appealing simultaneously to three different companies, the Brooklyn Heights Railroad, the Nassau Electric Railroad and the Brooklyn Elevated Railroad.[43] If nothing else, this facilitated a divide and conquer approach, which is exactly what happened when the Brooklyn Heights Road agreed to provide half of the funding so long as the Nassau Electric company provided the difference. Still on the fence, Johnson agreed to consider it, but insisted he would not be rushed.[44] Not helping the situation was Frederick Uhlman, the receiver for the Brooklyn Elevated, who delayed a decision for several weeks (time Ebbets didn't have to spare) before declining because as a receiver (someone administering the company for the benefit of its creditors), he didn't believe he had the necessary authority.[45]

With time running out, Ebbets said there were three options left: the Litchfield Estate, a site near Prospect Park, or the highly undesirable last resort of another year at Eastern Park.[46] In the end, the Nassau Company agreed to provide the balance of the funding, so on March 15, just 45 days before the club's home opener, Ebbets summoned the press to another gathering at the Clarendon Hotel featuring a "nice collation." No matter how good the food, Ebbets offered far more important sustenance for Dodgers fans when he proclaimed, "Gentlemen of the press, we go back to south Brooklyn again, and near to our old home." According to Henry Chadwick, "hearty congratulations followed from one and all."[47] Clearly no fan of Eastern Park, John Foster of *Sporting Life* waxed eloquent, proclaiming the club was about to "leave the land of lost hopes, absolute impossibilities and graveyard contingencies and return to God's country." Foster claimed to be especially happy for the fans who had taken their "last whiff of Barren Island perfume," which emanated from garbage dumped on an island in Jamaica Bay, and could now attend a game "without starting out before luncheon and getting home after dinner."[48] Needless to say, Foster, who was at the ballpark more often than most fans, was speaking just as much for himself. While Foster may have been exaggerating for effect, the *Eagle* reported that the news was "heralded with great delight," and Ebbets, who was already "unusually popular in South Brooklyn," took "a veritable triumphant march to his home on 1st Street within a stone's throw of the new grounds."[49]

Newspaper accounts of the Dodgers' return to "civilized" Brooklyn were followed by a brief sketch of the deal's terms. Rent was reported to be about $5,000 a year, for ten years, a far cry from the $13,500 supposedly demanded by the Litchfield Estate a year earlier and also an improvement on the $7,500 paid at Eastern Park.[50] Much more important, of course, were the loans for the projected $25,000 cost of building the ballpark. No further details were forthcoming other than a *New York Times* report that the loans were to be repaid by the "traffic to and from the grounds."[51] It sounds as if the construction costs were paid directly by the transportation companies, with repayment to come from the additional baseball-related passenger traffic. The other alternative would have been for the two companies to loan the money to the Brooklyn club, with repayment over a multi-year period. Even over ten years, this would have been an additional $2,500 a year in expense for a team struggling just to break even. Had the financing taken that form, it's highly likely the club would have struggled to make the payments, which would have been reported by the newspapers. Since nothing of the sort was ever reported, most likely the club was never directly liable for the loan. Given the fragile state of the club's finances, getting someone else to pay for his new park was no small accomplishment for the new club president.

Unlike the financial details, there was no shortage of information about the new ballpark itself which, like the club's earlier south Brooklyn home, would be called Washington Park. Bounded by 3rd and 4th Avenues and 1st and 3rd Streets, there would be three separate stands, each with a different admission price. At 75 cents, the most expensive seats were to be located in an "L"-shaped grandstand built with a greater pitch to provide a better view than at the late, unlamented Eastern Park. To further improve the fan experience, there would be more seats in the third base side of the grandstand, where there was less exposure to the sun. The higher priced grandstand was designed to seat 5,000, while the pavilion located further down the third base line could handle 3,000 more fans at a 50-cent admission price. Although National League parks were supposed to have a limited number of 25-cent seats, Ebbets planned to accommodate another 3,200 fans at that price in the right field bleachers, the furthest seats from the action, for a total capacity of 11,200. Prudently, Ebbets remembered his transit partners by placing the main entrance equidistant from their local stations and also took care of the media with a box directly behind home plate.[52]

Although building a new park from the ground up in just 45 days probably gave Ebbets nightmares, it was child's play compared to his experience at Ebbets Field some 15 years later. Site preparation was minimal since the ground was "almost perfectly level," with only two "obstructions to be removed." Ebbets also had his architect prepare the plans during the loan negotiations so work could begin almost immediately, and he vowed the park would be ready by the April 30 opener even if it meant working at night under electric lighting.[53] Not taking any chances with the extremely short time frame, Ebbets opened a temporary office near the site so he could supervise the work himself.[54] Ground was broken by Ebbets' 16-year-old daughter, Maie, on March 23, and construction quickly got underway.[55] However, it quickly became clear that adjustments were necessary for the park to open on time, especially scaling back the size of the grandstand, a loss of 2,000 of the highest priced seats.[56] Further problems were caused by a carpenters' strike, but Ebbets' decision to use union labor paid off when the other trades continued working, and the park was finished in time for its grand opening.[57]

While the new ballpark was taking shape, Ebbets and manager William Barnie worked on the roster. Since they didn't have enough time to make large-scale changes, the two men were left with the 1897 team plus Byrne's acquisitions, rookie pitchers Joe Yeager and Ralph Miller, and veteran second baseman Bill Hallman. Trying to get the most out of the talent he had, Ebbets wrote to each player in January, calling for a fresh start regardless of the past. The players were told that their salaries would remain the same as the prior year, which Ebbets tried to make more palatable by reminding them that the club lost money in 1897. According to the *Eagle*, the letter, which the paper claimed was a unique approach, was well received by "several" of the players.[58] Unique or not, the letter and its release was a creative way to build relationships with players and fans. Ebbets also had to decide whether to make a pre-season Southern trip which, although not new in 1898, hadn't yet won universal approval. Back in February, Ebbets claimed such ventures were "a waste of money" and considering the club's finances, it's not surprising they opted to stay closer to home.[59] Interestingly, Brooklyn was joined by the Giants as well as the Phillies in training in New Jersey, with Brooklyn at Allaire, the Giants not far away in Lakewood, and the Phillies in Cape May.[60] Poor weather doomed the experiment, and all three clubs headed to more hospitable climes the following year.

Fortunately for Ebbets, Brooklyn began the 1898 season on the road, gaining additional time to finish construction prior to the opening of the new grounds on April 30 before an "immense crowd" estimated at 15,000. Perhaps it was more design than luck, since Ebbets helped National League president Nick Young prepare the schedule.[61] The *Eagle* called the large gathering a real "baseball crowd," consisting primarily of true fans. The bleacher crowd, eager to put down their quarters, began arriving about noon, while "Brooklyn's best citizens" occupied the grandstand. As they entered, fans expressed first "surprise" and then "complete satisfaction" with the new venue, critical only of the short right field fence. Maie Ebbets once again did the honors, raising the flag while "looking charming in a dress of military blue." Appropriately, it was a well-deserved "happy day for President Ebbets," who shared his box with Minnie and their four children.[62] While the loss to visiting Philadelphia was disappointing, it couldn't diminish Ebbets' achievement in meeting one of an owner's primary responsibilities in his first four months as club president. To his dismay, Ebbets also learned that he had some unanticipated competition from the residents of the building beyond right field, who charged admission to allow fans to watch the game from their apartments. Ebbets quickly remedied the situation with a canvas screen limiting both the view and the number of balls lost over the fence.[63]

While the new ballpark was a success, the beginning of the season brought on-the-field problems. Although the Dodgers won their next five games, they quickly went in the other direction, dropping six straight, prompting manager Barnie to vow that the club would win or "I shall know

Outside of Washington Park, Ebbets opened his first ballpark in 1898, just four months after becoming club president. The picture captures the wooden fence, the entrance to the 25-cent bleacher seats, and the apartment building behind the right field fence. As soon as the park opened, tenants began charging fans to watch games from their apartments, which led Ebbets to erect a canvas screen or "spite fence" (Library of Congress, Prints and Photographs Division, Bain Collection [LC-USZ62-23415]).

the reason why."[64] Neither results nor explanations were apparently forthcoming as the losing streak reached ten before a win which led the optimistic Brooklyn manager to proclaim, "we will [now] look for nothing but victory."[65] Ebbets made it clear that Barnie had full control of the team, so "the responsibility for victory or defeat rested with the manager."[66] While he could have been setting up Barnie for a fall, Ebbets was more likely trying to prevent accusations of interfering, a charge which would be lodged against him more than once.

Ebbets may have also stayed out of on-the-field issues because he was preoccupied with another problem, the seeming endless demand for free season passes. Although some 400 had been issued to politicians and municipal officials, the club's generosity in no way met the demand, to the point that the *Eagle* wryly noted that even Ebbets' former milkman, who voted against him in the recent election, felt that "sufficient arguments" for a pass.[67] Especially galling were those who allowed others to use their pass, an abuse Ebbets said he would "not stand for." Nor was it solely a local club concern, since the visiting team expected its share of the admission price regardless of whether Ebbets collected it or not.[68] While at first glance Ebbets' concern may seem to be an example of his cheapness, the problem would bedevil all of the magnates for years to come.

Unfortunately, the team's performance didn't improve, and by early June the *Eagle* claimed there was something "radically wrong with the Brooklyn team," including a clique and an unpopular manager. While Ebbets hadn't interfered to date, the paper believed "action, and that quickly, is necessary."[69] Not surprisingly, Barnie denied there was a clique, but claimed that if one did exist, he would put an end to it. In the manager's eyes, the problem was poor performance on the field, and he also claimed the club had been looking for new players for five weeks without success.[70] In spite of the losing record, the clique rumors and the *Eagle's* call for action, both Ebbets and Abell were reportedly reluctant to remove Barnie, but they couldn't have unlimited patience. Finally Ebbets held an informal board meeting on Sunday, June 5; after another 24 hours of further consideration, he recommended that Barnie be fired, and the board agreed. Barnie insisted he hadn't had enough time, but it was probably more the alleged dissension than the 15–20 record that sealed his fate. Publicly, Ebbets claimed the decision was based on the lack of on-the-field success and the resulting losses at the box office, something a club with fragile finances couldn't afford. It was, Ebbets said, simply "a business proposition" since "we are not in baseball for our health."[71]

With little time to find a replacement, Ebbets took the path of least resistance, giving team captain Mike Griffin the added responsibility of manager. Griffin, however, had one of the shortest managerial tenures in baseball history, lasting only four games before resigning, supposedly because he didn't want the burden of personnel decisions in addition to his responsibilities as captain and player. Ebbets had few, if any, options and, while it seems strange by modern standards, his decision to take on the manager's job himself was probably the best, if not the only alternative.[72] The team captain handled most of the in-game decisions, so during the regular season, the manager's on-the-field responsibilities were limited. Ebbets also had the prior example of Charles Byrne, who served as manager during the 1880s. Filling the position himself also gave Ebbets experience in player evaluation, something he would need as club president. Finally, it couldn't have been lost on Ebbets that there was a potential cost savings by not having to pay a new manager's salary.

As appropriate as the decision may have been, there was little reason to believe that the won-lost record would improve, and it actually deteriorated over the remainder of the season. In Ebbets' sole year as a major league manager, his record was a pathetic 38–68, and Brooklyn finished the 1898 season with a 54–91 record, 46 games out of first place, bad enough for a tenth-place finish in a 12-team league. According to the *Sun*, the players "imposed on their good natured president," and the clique, reported as led by Griffin himself and veteran third baseman Bill Shindle, actually ran the team.[73] While all of that may have been true, the real issue was the talent or lack thereof. Ebbets himself acknowledged that the Brooklyn roster was made up primarily of "dead wood" and/or "old talent" at a time when the club didn't have the means to upgrade its roster.[74]

A tenth-place finish doubtless also meant the club lost money for the third straight year, but events far outside Brooklyn made the financial situation even worse. The destruction of the battleship *Maine* in Havana Harbor on February 15 led to war with Spain on April 25, shortly before the Washington Park opening. Although the war, which ended on August 12, didn't even last the full season, the nation was too distracted to pay much attention to baseball. Ebbets told sportswriter John B. Foster he had foreseen the war's dire impact on baseball after only two weeks of the conflict, which meant "there was not going to be a penny in the game during the season."[75] Since there were even fewer pennies, not to mention quarters, for a losing club, the only question in Brooklyn was the depth of the financial bloodbath. In late September, the *Eagle* claimed the club would be lucky to lose less than $15,000, but by November, the paper reported that "to the satisfaction of the directors," the deficit was closer to $7,000, although it's hard to visualize the long-suffering Abell taking satisfaction from any loss.[76] Foster, on the other hand, put the deficit at $15,000, but also suggested it might be as high as $25,000 and speculated that the club was covering losses with loans, the interest on which endangered potential future profits.[77]

Total home attendance of 122,514 was almost 100,000 less than the last year at the perhaps now more fondly remembered Eastern Park.[78] An article in *The Sporting News* estimated it took revenue of $100,000 or more to break even, so if Brooklyn's expenses were in that neighborhood, home attendance of 122,000 generated a large loss, perhaps even greater than Foster's worst-case $25,000.[79] Amid the financial wreckage, Ebbets refused to compromise his principles. A common practice in the late 19th century was for teams which drew poorly at home to transfer home games to the parks of other clubs which did better at the gate. One such 1898 possibility was a Labor Day matchup with the Giants which could have been shifted to the Polo Grounds for better financial returns while still offering Brooklyn fans the opportunity, albeit less conveniently, to see the game. Ebbets would have none of it, proclaiming that not "even if the New

York Club gave him the entire receipts and he did not receive a dollar at Washington Park would he agree to any arrangement whereby the Brooklyn schedule will be broken."[80] It was a principle that Ebbets, to his credit, lived by throughout his long career.

It is hard to imagine a worse first year for a new club president, and it appeared that like Griffin, Ebbets might have one of the shortest tenures ever, but not by his own choice. By the end of August, other magnates speculated that radical change was needed in Brooklyn, and a strong possibility was consolidation with the Cleveland franchise. Cleveland owners Stanley and Frank Robison had had their fill of Cleveland, and there was talk of the Robisons bringing their "fine ball team" to Brooklyn. The biggest obstacle, according to the *Sun*, was that the Robisons wanted a financial inducement which Abell, who had already invested (and effectively lost) $100,000 over the past eight years, had no interest in providing. Under one possible scenario, Albert Johnson, the Nassau Electric Railroad principal who had helped finance Washington Park, would invest $20,000, which would go to the Robisons. The result would be an ownership triumvirate of Abell (50 percent), the Robisons (30 percent) and Johnson (20 percent). Totally left out of the equation was Charles Ebbets, who would revert to being the club's business manager, a position for which one paper, in a somewhat backhanded compliment, said "he is eminently fitted."[81]

The whole idea was downplayed by the *Eagle*, which argued that the *Sun* underestimated Ebbets' ownership position in the club and claimed that the Brooklyn president knew nothing of the proposed deal.[82] Foster, writing in *Sporting Life*, thought the Brooklyn fans "to a man" would support the consolidation, but he also believed that the Robisons preferred to consolidate with the ailing St. Louis franchise, which is what ultimately happened.[83] That preference may explain their final decision, but Ebbets' supposed refusal to any deal that gave the Robisons a controlling financial interest in Brooklyn was also reported to be a major factor.[84] Ebbets' obstinacy could only go so far, however, as Abell was understandably losing interest after so many years and so much money when all he had to show for it were "bound volumes of check stubs."[85] Once again, time was not on Ebbets' side as Baltimore owner Harry von der Horst predicted there had to be a winning team in Brooklyn in 1899 or the "club would have to go by the board."[86] If so, Ebbets' career as a club president would go with it.

CHAPTER IV

"It is the fair name of the Brooklyn club at stake"

By almost any measure, the 1898 season was a disappointment, but in spite of the abysmal tenth-place finish and the equally pathetic attendance, it wasn't a total loss. Faced with a seemingly insurmountable lack of time and money, Ebbets built a new and more accessible ballpark which would help attendance if he could improve the on-the-field product. Although it wasn't reflected in the record, the roster had also been upgraded with the addition of Jimmy Sheckard to an outfield already featuring .300 hitters Mike Griffin and Fielder Jones. Nor did season's end slow down Ebbets' effort to acquire new talent, as that fall he found and signed future Hall of Fame pitcher Joe McGinnity.[1]

Even with these acquisitions, however, Brooklyn still faced a major talent gap, a problem with few potential solutions. Minor league farm systems were years in the future, as was the amateur draft, while the minor league draft wasn't structured to help lower-level clubs improve their rosters. Major league owners first had to identify talented, young players and then purchase them, an added problem for clubs like Brooklyn with limited funds. A lack of money also limited the Dodgers' ability to buy proven major league players, while upgrading through trades was also difficult since Brooklyn couldn't afford to lose the few good players it did have. Building a competitive team was a long-term, uncertain process, so it's little wonder that the potential quick fix of buying the Cleveland club and bringing its players to Brooklyn looked attractive. Such a move would, however, probably have ended Ebbets' career as a magnate, although one paper thought the change would allow him to sleep better.[2] Regardless of the number of sleepless nights, however, giving up without a fight wasn't in Charles Ebbets' nature. After a long, 15-year apprenticeship, the 39-year-old club president had no interest in going back to managing ticket sellers and ushers.

While it probably offered them little or no satisfaction, Ebbets and Abell at least knew their situation was far from unique. The 1898 season was yet another reminder that the 12-team National League had far too few winners on the field and far too many losers at the box office. Even when the Brooklyn/Cleveland combination fell through, the sheer number of clubs in trouble meant other possibilities would arise, including the unsavory option of syndication. Syndicate ball, where the same people own multiple teams, is both unthinkable and impermissible today, and even in the late–19th century it wasn't without controversy. Coming off another uncompetitive season, however, marred by even greater financial losses, the harried magnates understandably preferred bad publicity to the ignominy of bankruptcy. So strong was the incentive that six different clubs became involved in some form of syndicate ownership before the first pitch of the 1899 season was even thrown.

Somewhat different because there was no real desire to continue both franchises, was the Louisville—Pittsburgh situation, where Louisville owner Barney Dreyfuss got control of the Pittsburgh franchise, became club president and took Louisville's best players with him.[3] A German immigrant who, unlike Ebbets, had access to family money, Dreyfuss was also not about to be forced out of baseball without a fight. Small in stature, Dreyfuss, like Ebbets, was a hardworking, baseball lifer.[4] Meanwhile the Robison family, having decided not to come to Brooklyn, instead bought out the controversial, but no longer powerful, Chris von der Ahe and moved Cleveland's best players to St. Louis. If the Robisons were looking for revenge on the Cleveland baseball fans, they got it and then some when the remnant produced the worst record in major league history, winning only 20 games.

From Brooklyn's perspective, the best potential syndicate partner was the talented, but financially weak Baltimore franchise, and Abell claimed the possibility had actually been discussed two years earlier.[5] Although nothing came of those conversations, further financial losses for both clubs, with little basis for optimism about the future, pushed Ebbets and Abell into a serious courtship of the Baltimore owners, Harry von der Horst and Ned Hanlon. It would have been hard to find a potential partner with more talent, since over the last five years Baltimore had won three pennants and finished second twice. It was a record Ebbets and Abell could only dream about, but surprisingly the club's performance hadn't generated anything resembling financial success. After breaking even in 1896, its last pennant-winning season, the Orioles lost money in each of the next two years, including a $20,600 deficit in 1898, similar to some estimates for tenth-place Brooklyn's operating loss. The Baltimore club drew so poorly that by June of 1898, attendance at home games was measured in hundreds, producing receipts that "just about paid for the lost baseballs."[6] All told, Baltimore's second-place team attracted just 123,416 fans, only slightly more than those who saw Brooklyn's woeful club, albeit at a new ballpark.[7]

Being president of a baseball team where Abell controlled both the stock and the bank account had its challenges for Ebbets, but under a syndicate with Baltimore, the situation would be complicated even further by the introduction of two new partners, men with very different personalities. Baltimore majority owner Harry von der Horst had purchased the Orioles with money from the sizeable fortune his father earned in the brewery business. Although the younger von der Horst was described as "smart and energetic enough when he tried," the Baltimore magnate was also "too fond of living to keep his mind on unpleasant things," of which there was no shortage in late-19th century baseball. Although his motivation was supposedly the prestige of a winning team and not making money, von der Horst was also reportedly "beside himself" after a third consecutive year without a profit.[8]

Although any deal required von der Horst's approval, Baltimore manager Ned Hanlon brought far more to the proposed consolidation. Described as a "shrewd, quiet man" with the look of "a slightly bored bank clerk," Hanlon had an "understated air of assurance," seemingly not caring "what anyone thought of him." Reportedly a "man of precision and logic," the future Hall of Fame manager built Baltimore into one of the top teams in the National League by putting together a talented roster and then training them in ground-breaking strategy such as the hit-and-run play. Von der Horst needed Hanlon badly, something the latter used to get complete control of the baseball operations as well as a minority ownership position. Perhaps predictably, Hanlon and von der Horst weren't on the best of terms, with their personal differences exacerbated by the team's financial woes and concerns that the club wasn't playing up to its potential.[9]

With both ownership groups dissatisfied with the status quo, the December 1898 meeting of the National League owners at Manhattan's Fifth Avenue Hotel was the ideal venue to begin negotiations. Unfortunately, or perhaps fortunately, both Ebbets and von der Horst were absent due to illness, allowing for straightforward discussions between Abell and Hanlon, neither of whom lacked incentive to make a deal.[10] For Hanlon, the proposed syndicate was an opportunity to get free of von der Horst, while Abell had the even more tangible motivation of recovering some of the $100,000 he claimed to have lost on baseball in Brooklyn.[11] After discussions on December 15, Abell told the *Eagle* that while the talks were very preliminary and no deal was close, he also believed the environment was more favorable because of the new park in Brooklyn and continued financial losses in Baltimore.[12] The environment must indeed have been favorable since discussions progressed so rapidly that two days later, the *Eagle* claimed a deal was "a certainty."[13] According to the paper, Abell was the "prime mover" in the proposed arrangement, which to the surprise of no one would give Hanlon complete control of the team itself, since "Foxy Ned" wasn't about to "consent to play second fiddle to anyone."[14]

Ebbets, although still recovering from his illness, assured an *Eagle* reporter that the deal had his full support, even claiming he "made the proposition" himself as the best way to give Brooklyn a championship team. The Brooklyn club president acknowledged that he and Abell would have to give up "a considerable portion" of their stock and conceded that Hanlon would have complete control of the baseball side, but claimed the "financial end will remain in my hands," whatever that meant. Although Ebbets was well aware of the concerns about syndicate ownership, he felt any issues could be worked out to the public's satisfaction.[15]

With the outlook for consolidation of the two clubs apparently so positive, the lack of further news in December might have been explained by the distractions of the holiday season. When no word was forthcoming by the middle of January, however, rumors surfaced that something or, more likely someone was holding up the negotiations. It wasn't at all surprising that Ebbets was cast in the obstructionist's role, since the deal offered obvious benefits to the other three men, but not to him. Not only would the consolidation put Ebbets below two people, instead of one, in the ownership hierarchy, it wasn't clear what work would be left for Ebbets, especially with Hanlon's insistence on complete control of baseball operations. Some in the media questioned whether Ebbets could hold on to the title of president even if he accepted a reduced role.[16] Abell tried to help Ebbets by saying he favored him as club president because of all his good work. However, Abell also worried that if Ebbets were "deposed" from his position, he would "naturally be painfully sensitive" to the public's logical conclusion he was "thrown down."[17] It was at best a weak vote of confidence which could hardly have reassured Ebbets. Interestingly, another media report claimed that local fans sympathized with Ebbets because he was a Brooklyn man and supposedly didn't take any salary in 1898.[18]

No matter how much sympathy they accorded Ebbets, however, Brooklyn fans were also concerned that the deal might be derailed, implicitly recognizing that without radical change, major league baseball might be doomed in Brooklyn, especially amid talk of circuit reduction. Both hopes and fears had reached the point where no news was definitely not good news.[19] As January progressed without word of an agreement, rumors began circulating that Hanlon and von der Horst were becoming impatient and might impose a deadline.[20] Hanlon told the media that he and von der Horst were "disgusted" by the inaction on the Brooklyn side, since closing documents had been ready for a week. Without naming names, the disgruntled Baltimore manager also claimed "certain individuals are not acting with fairness" and "seem anxious to kill the Brooklyn club."[21] Since there weren't many possible suspects, most observers doubtless thought Hanlon was talking about Ebbets.

Finally, in early February, it was revealed that while the problem was indeed a Brooklyn owner, it wasn't either Ebbets or Abell. Most people had likely forgotten there even was a third owner, the estate of deceased club president Charles Byrne, which owned about ten percent of the stock. William Bryne, the deceased's brother and executor, could and would stop the deal unless the estate's interests were bought out for $10,000. The issue was not, however, the price, but the means of payment, since Abell had offered $7,500 in cash with the balance in notes. William Byrne, however, probably understood full well the uncertainty of the baseball business, especially in Brooklyn, and had no interest in relying on the club's long-term financial prospects. Abell's reluctance to a cash buyout was probably because he was the one who had to come up with the money. Reportedly, Ebbets met with Byrne some 10–12 times as Abell's representative and, not surprisingly, even inquired about buying the stock himself. What is, however, more than a little surprising is Byrne's claim that he told Ebbets to tell the public and the media, that he, Byrne, was the obstacle, but the Brooklyn president instead "swallowed all the abuse."[22] Over 100 years later, it's impossible to know why Ebbets acted as he did, but revealing the notes/cash dispute could have put pressure on Abell, and Ebbets was not in a position to risk offending Abell.

The stalemate was finally broken on February 4, when Hanlon and von der Horst met with Abell and Ebbets at the Hoffman House on Broadway in Manhattan. About 3:00 p.m., all but Abell headed downtown for one more meeting with William Byrne and then returned for further discussion. Finally, just before heading back to Baltimore, Hanlon told the assembled writers, "the deal is now practically a certainty" since the four men had finally surrendered to Byrne's demand for a cash settlement.[23] Hanlon planned to return on the following Tuesday for the closing, but in the kind of comic relief one expects of Brooklyn baseball, William Byrne couldn't find one of the stock certificates, further delaying the transaction until that issue was resolved.[24]

Although the media, Dodgers fans and even the parties themselves might have thought the day would never come, syndicate baseball arrived in Brooklyn on February 27, 1899. As might have been expected, considering the convoluted nature of the process, the closing

Harry von der Horst, owner of the Baltimore Orioles and co-owner of the Dodgers from 1899 to 1905. (*Brooklyn Daily Eagle,* December 10, 1899).

transactions took place in two different locations, New York City and across the Hudson River in Jersey City, because the Brooklyn club was a New Jersey corporation. As had been reported all along, Abell and von der Horst would each own 40 percent of the stock in the Brooklyn club, with Ebbets holding ten percent. Hanlon would reportedly get "at least 10%" with the qualification that the level of Hanlon's holdings was "between himself and von der Horst." Similarly, Abell and Ebbets would own 40 percent and ten percent respectively of the Baltimore club. Ebbets remained club president with a $4,000 salary, an increase of $500, doubtless intended to lessen, probably in vain, the fact that Hanlon would be paid $10,000, more than twice Ebbets' salary, leaving no doubt about the new pecking order in Brooklyn.[25]

In entering into the syndicate, the new partners were operating on the logical assumption that a vastly improved team playing in a larger market would attract more fans, and they would reap significant financial returns. The *Eagle* certainly thought so, estimating that average attendance of 4,000, or over 300,000 for the season, "would mean a clear profit to the club of $70,000."[26] More wins on the field should have increased the number of quarters paid in at the box office, but the paper's projection of almost tripling the 1898 attendance in a top-heavy, uncompetitive league was more than a little optimistic. Still, with the potential for increased attendance, the last thing the new ownership group wanted was a lack of seating capacity, so attention now turned to expanding Washington Park.

Early in March, Ebbets and von der Horst toured the grounds and agreed to increase the seating capacity to about 15,000. Hoping an improved team would attract customers with more discretionary income, about 1,000 of the new seats in the extended third base grandstand would be at the top 75-cent price. With the high end of the market provided for, the new ownership group also decided to build a new 50-cent pavilion and a 25-cent stand on the first base side. The center field bleachers were to remain to handle the excess crowds that Ebbets and von der Horst hoped would be a regular feature.[27] Since the original ballpark was built in about 45 days, it's no surprise the additions were finished by Opening Day.

Beyond increasing Washington Park's capacity, the new construction featured an improvement designed by Ebbets himself. While his claim to have worked on plans for Niblo's Garden and other important projects during his brief architectural career is doubtful, Ebbets must have learned some things along the way. Drawing perhaps on that experience as well as his work on the two incarnations of Washington Park, Ebbets designed the new stands with a stairway from beneath the stand to a landing about seven to eight rows up, which allowed fans to reach the higher rows without disturbing those seated lower in the section. Although Ebbets may not have originated the idea, he somewhat immodestly predicted that it "will probably revolutionize the building of such structures in the future," and Barney Dreyfuss for one considered using it a year later in Pittsburgh.[28]

While Ebbets and von der Horst labored on the ballpark, Ned Hanlon had the enviable task of picking one major league team from two major league rosters. After the disagreeable results of training locally in 1898, the Brooklyn and Baltimore clubs headed south, where Hanlon confirmed the criticisms of syndicate ball by loading the Brooklyn roster with the top talent. Position players Hugh Jennings, Dan McGann, Bill Dahlen, Joe Kelley and Willie Keeler, along with pitchers Doc McJames and Jim Hughes, joined Hanlon in Brooklyn.[29] Of the everyday players, all but Dahlen (.290) hit over .300 in 1898, while both pitchers won more than 20 games. With those additions, optimism in Brooklyn soared, and over 20,000 people passed through the gates for the April 15 opener at renovated Washington Park, where "the tide [of fans] was apparently endless." Showing that fans sometimes do applaud owners, Harry von der Horst was greeted with an ovation which the new Brooklyn magnate didn't realize was for him. Perhaps recognizing the newly bought strength of the Brooklyn club, the schedule makers assigned the defending champion Boston Beaneaters as the opposition, and the men from New England provided the only blot on the day, winning 1–0 in 11 innings.[30] Hanlon's men won the next two from Boston, but otherwise got out of the gate slowly, finishing April just a game over .500. From that point on, however, it was all Brooklyn, as beginning on May 1, the Dodgers went on a 37–6 tear. By the end of June, they led second-place Boston by five games.

With the ballpark expansion finished and the season underway, Ebbets' baseball responsibilities were more limited, so he had more time to be attentive or, perhaps more accurately, inattentive to his political responsibilities. Through the bulk of the 1899 season, Ebbets' name was in the newspaper more frequently as city councilman than as baseball executive, and not in a good way. The notoriety was due to Ebbets' role as one of a small number of obstructive councilmen opposing a series of bond issues for a new Hall of Records, street repaving and construction of a Long Island water supply plant.[31] Each bond issue required the affirmative votes of 75 percent of the council members, and Ebbets and his associates either voted no or were absent when votes were taken.[32]

In the end, it took court orders to force passage of the Hall of Records and water plant bills, and even then Ebbets and his group avoided voting until they had no alternative.[33] Grudgingly acquiescing on the Hall of Records bond issue, Ebbets claimed, "Prison bars will not deter me from doing my duty, but I cannot see that any other course is left to us."[34] Similarly with the water plant bond issue, Ebbets and five of his associates "did not surrender gracefully," voting yes only to avoid incarceration while proclaiming their "unalterable belief" that "the city was the victim of a great swindle."[35] The contentious councilmen felt the same way about the Hall of Records project, reportedly awarded to a contractor at a cost $350,000 above the lowest bid, and the road paving bonds, where allegedly the contractor would realize an $800,000 profit on a $2 million job.[36]

Others implied that the obstructionists' motives weren't quite so pure, suggesting they were looking for bribes in exchange for their votes. Naturally the naysayers vehemently denied the claim, offering a $500 reward for proof of their bad intentions.[37] While it would be nice to think of Ebbets as a fiscal watchdog, a more likely explanation is that he was carrying out the wishes of Brooklyn political leader Hugh McLaughlin, who was trying to block "Tammany graft and Manhattan centered expenditures."[38] When Brooklyn's own interests were involved, Ebbets wasn't reluctant to spend public money, as a year later he "called up" a $300,000 resolution for a new wing to Brooklyn's Museum of Arts and Sciences.[39]

While Ebbets waged political guerrilla warfare, his ball club played out the 1899 pennant race, which had far less drama than whether or not Ebbets and his cronies ended up in jail. No team could have maintained Brooklyn's sizzling May and June winning percentage, so it was no great shock when they lost eight straight after the hot streak ended. The pennant-bound ship righted itself fairly quickly, however, and the Dodgers finished eight games ahead of defending champion Boston, Brooklyn's first pennant in almost a decade. The team's achievements were recognized at a testimonial event at the Brooklyn Academy of Music which included the more tangible reward of $2,500 to be divided among the players.[40]

Syndication had obviously paid off on the field, but what about at the box office? The pre-season projection of $70,000 in profits was based upon average attendance of 4,000, but the actual figure was somewhat lower, at about 3,400.[41] When the club held its annual meeting in early December, no financial information was released beyond the vague statement the club "cleared" about $15,000, far lower than the earlier projection.[42] However, sportswriter John Foster's report in *Sporting Life* that the team also paid off $50,000 in debt suggests that the $15,000 profit figure was considerably understated. Since Ferdinand Abell was likely the largest bondholder, he apparently got back some of the money he had reluctantly advanced to cover prior operating losses.[43]

Although the season was a success, the atmosphere didn't seem quite as joyous as it might have been, leading John Foster to evaluate the lower than anticipated attendance in a November issue of *Sporting Life*. Part of the problem, he believed, was that while Brooklyn had a large population, the residents were nowhere near as affluent as neighboring Manhattan, so the cost of a good seat (at least 50 cents) was beyond the reach of many Brooklynites. And while there was ongoing talk of attracting fans from lower Manhattan to Washington Park, which was closer than the Polo Grounds, the lack of direct rapid transit between Manhattan and the Brooklyn ballpark was a major problem. Another negative factor was the poor performance of the Giants, which prevented the development of a local, mutually beneficial rivalry.[44]

More importantly, however, Foster thought syndicate ball might be the real problem, beginning with objections to the "foreign ownership," that is, von der Horst and Hanlon. The *Sporting Life* columnist also claimed that the wholesale transfer of Baltimore's best players was "objectionable to the cranks." Clearly not a fan of the whole idea, Foster thought the Baltimore—Brooklyn syndicate was little more than a "poorly concealed plan to "hornswoggle" the Brooklyn baseball patrons out of their cash."[45] Even with two months for further reflection, Foster's views hadn't changed. In January, he argued that it would have been far better, and more widely accepted by the fans, if Abell and Ebbets (which really meant Abell) had acquired the Baltimore franchise and players, but kept von der Horst and Hanlon out of Brooklyn. Conveniently forgotten in Foster's analysis was whether or not the Baltimore magnates were willing to sell, not to mention Abell's publicly stated unwillingness to put more money into baseball. While Foster believed the two Brooklyn men had the best of intentions, in his opinion, they failed to "read the temper of the people aright," which produced a "divided championship" and a less than satisfied fan base.[46]

From a modern perspective, syndicate ball seems even more inappropriate, perhaps supporting Harold Seymour's contention that the Brooklyn-Baltimore consolidation "made a travesty of genuine competition."[47] At the time, however, joint ownership of multiple clubs was not prohibited, and the Baltimore—Brooklyn syndicate wasn't unique. The Cleveland side of the Cleveland-St. Louis combination was a far more competitive disgrace, winning only 20 games before so few fans that many of their home games were transferred to the opposing team's city. Although it was most likely unintentional, the Brooklyn-Baltimore owners left enough talent in Baltimore, including John McGraw and Wilbert Robinson, that the weaker club not only finished in fourth place, 24 games over .500, but earned a small profit. Furthermore, Barney Dreyfuss' Pittsburgh club was put together in a similar, if less blatant fashion, and the forthcoming resurrection of the Giants would in some ways make the syndicate deals look like normal business arrangements. While acknowledging the problems of syndicate ball, the *Eagle*, just prior to the December 1899 owners meeting, claimed that the arrangement saved the professional game in Greater New York from the dangers of Andrew Freedman's destructiveness and a poorly performing team in Brooklyn.[48]

How Ebbets felt about Foster's criticism is unknown, but it likely bothered him more than the other three Brooklyn owners because of his community involvement. Even so, it's hard to believe he had any regrets, since criticism of a profitable, pennant-winning team was preferable to another abysmal season that might have doomed the Dodgers during circuit reduction talks. If both Ebbets and Abell felt a little self-satisfied during the celebratory evening at the Brooklyn Academy of Music, it's more than understandable. There was, however, at that very moment, a cloud on the horizon, more important for what it foreshadowed than its specific significance. Known as the Wrigley case, the incident, which is almost totally forgotten today, absorbed a great deal of the National League owners' time and energy at their December 1899 meeting.

Perhaps surprisingly for something which caused so much debate, there was little or no dispute about the facts of what happened with George Wrigley during the last month of the 1899 season. After playing shortstop for the 11th-place Washington club in 1898, Wrigley spent 1899 in the minors, beginning with the Richmond club until it went bankrupt. Wrigley and a number of his teammates were then signed by Syracuse of the Eastern League. When the Eastern League season ended on September 9, Wrigley was placed on the club's reserve list, which meant, at least theoretically, he was off-limits to other clubs unless he was appropriately purchased by another major or minor league team.

Supposedly the Syracuse team offered to sell Wrigley to the Giants, but the New York club refused to negotiate a purchase price.[49] Instead the Giants, after getting the go-ahead from National League president Nick Young, simply signed Wrigley without permission from or payment to the Syracuse club.[50] Wrigley played in four games for the Giants when he was approached by the Dodgers, who needed a shortstop due to Bill Dahlen's illness. Unlike the Giants, Brooklyn went through the Syracuse club or its agent, purchased Wrigley's release and signed him in spite of Young's position that they could not do so. Wrigley then played in 12 late-season games for Brooklyn.[51]

Since Andrew Freedman was the Giants' lead owner, it was no surprise when the New York club protested Brooklyn's action, but Hanlon appeared unconcerned, confidently saying, "I don't see how we can lose the case." Since, however, a finding against Brooklyn might mean that any games Wrigley played in would be thrown out, the Brooklyn skipper prudently made sure that Wrigley played in as many losses as wins, so a decision against Brooklyn wouldn't hurt the club's pennant chances.[52] In spite of Hanlon's over-confident and somewhat foolish predictions, however, the league's Board of Arbitration ruled in favor of the Giants by a mail vote before further consideration at the December league meetings.[53] Still, with Hanlon's precautions and Brooklyn's big lead, there wasn't any significant risk to Brooklyn's pennant hopes and, in most cases, the issue would have been little more than a minor player dispute. Unfortunately for Ebbets and the Brooklyn club, however, this was only the opening salvo of an unexpected alliance between two powerful and dangerous men, the aforementioned Andrew Freedman and John T. Brush of Cincinnati.

Only 39 as the 19th century drew to a close, Andrew Freedman had already made fortunes in real estate and insurance while establishing himself as a political intimate and personal friend of Richard Croker, the head of the Tammany Hall political machine. Freedman's rapid rise to power and fortune were due to his "talent for administration and manipulation" and his connections at the highest level of New York City politics. Had it not been for Tammany Hall's 1894 election defeat, Freedman might never have taken more than passing interest in major league baseball, but with Croker not only out of office but out of the country, Freedman had time, not to mention plenty of money, on his hands. Unfortunately for major league baseball, Freedman filled the vacuum by purchasing a controlling interest in the New York Giants in late January of 1895.[54] As

Edward "Ned" Hanlon, manager of three National League championship teams in Baltimore, "Foxy Ned" became Brooklyn Dodgers manager and minority owner in 1899 as part of the Baltimore-Brooklyn syndicate. Like Ebbets, Hanlon wanted the lead role in the franchise, and the two men eventually struggled for control of the team (Library of Congress, Prints and Photographs Division, Bain Collection [LC-DIG-ggbain-06473]).

noted earlier, ever since the club's near-death experience in the 1890 Brotherhood War, a number of other National League magnates, including Brooklyn's Ferdinand Abell, owned stock in the New York Club. By 1899 Abell, John T. Brush of Cincinnati, Arthur Soden of Boston, and Albert Reach of Philadelphia all still held minority ownership positions in the club.[55]

Freedman was fortunate that he was talented and well-connected, since his success certainly wasn't due to his personality. Described as "sullen" and "combative," not to mention "naturally arrogant" with a "bad temper" and a "short fuse," it's no wonder Freedman's "capacity for resentment was enormous."[56] His difficult personality might have been offset to some degree by a winning team, but the Giants owner proved it wasn't just nice guys who finish last. Under Freedman, the team played poorly before small crowds, which didn't bother the wealthy magnate very much, but was bad news for visiting clubs who needed the big paydays large crowds at the Polo Grounds could produce. To make matters worse, Freedman became engaged in two bitter disputes, one with pitcher Amos Rusie and another with his fellow owners over the suspension of "Ducky" Holmes, dragging the magnates into treacherous waters. Fearing possible damage beyond New York's poor play, which was bad enough, the owners intervened at their own expense to resolve both issues, which won them no thanks from Freedman.[57] Instead the embittered magnate let his team fall apart, reaching a low point in 1899 with a 60–90 record and attendance of just over 121,000, down from a league-leading 390,000 only two years earlier, an almost unimaginable drop of almost 70 percent.[58] The poor financial returns mattered little to Freedman, whose fortune may have been greater than all other 11 owners combined.[59] The most unpopular owner in baseball by a wide margin, Freedman had "the league by the throat" and flaunted his disdain by not even bothering to attend owners meetings.[60]

Usually leading the opposition to Freedman at owners meetings was John T. Brush, one of the league's senior magnates and also a New York shareholder. After making a fortune, although smaller than Freedman's, in retailing, Brush acquired the Indianapolis franchise, lost it in 1890, and acquired the Cincinnati team in 1891. Given his experience in Indianapolis, Brush was understandably unhappy owning another small-market team with marginal finances. Brush reportedly had been interested in purchasing the Giants but was beaten out by Freedman, who rejected subsequent offers from Brush to buy him out. The Cincinnati magnate led the opposition to Freedman on the Rusie and Holmes issues, which didn't endear him to Freedman. Not surprisingly, the two became "bitter antagonists," supposedly once actually coming to blows.[61]

Although it would have been hard to find a more disagreeable personality than Freedman's, Brush was also unlikely to win any popularity contests. Described as a "dour man" with "a gaunt afflicted frame," due to his previously mentioned deteriorating health, Brush's physical limitations masked a "resilient nature" and an "iron will" which he used behind the scenes in "backroom cajolery and relentless scheming."[62] While the Reds owner sounds like more than a match for Freedman in any non-physical altercation, Brush felt vulnerable because Freedman was an outspoken advocate for reducing the league to eight clubs, and Brush feared his club was marked for elimination.[63] Furthermore, unlike Brush, who cared deeply about baseball, Freedman didn't, making him more dangerous because he had no sense of stewardship for the game.[64] Most likely recognizing the weakness of his position and the need for a more indirect approach with Freedman, Brush asked Boston owner Arthur Soden (another minority Giants owner) to arrange a peace conference. An October 1899 meeting produced the desired result, and without Brush's leadership, the "anti–Freedman forces crumbled."[65] The impact of the Brush-Freedman reconciliation would be seen at the December owners meetings, and there was scarcely anything worse for Charles Ebbets and the Brooklyn club than a league dominated by Andrew Freedman and John Brush.

When the National League magnates gathered at New York City's luxurious Fifth Avenue Hotel during the second week of December, it was common knowledge that Freedman and Brush wanted an eight-team league, with Freedman at least committed to dropping Brooklyn.[66] It must have come as a big surprise, therefore, when far more time was spent on the peripatetic Mr. Wrigley than on the far more important consolidation issue.[67] The Wrigley situation was confused because although the facts were clear, the applicable rules and regulations were not, leading to a five-hour discussion by the league's Board of Arbitration on December 12. Basically a committee of owners, the board was empowered to resolve certain kinds of disputes, especially disagreements between teams over the rights to players, including minor league clubs protected by the National Agreement. In the Wrigley case, both the Brooklyn club and Syracuse of the Eastern League appealed the board's decision that Wrigley belonged to the Giants.[68]

In arguing Brooklyn's side of the case, Ebbets claimed that the only relevant governing document was the National Agreement. Section 17 of that document clearly said no club could negotiate with a player "at any time," much less sign him, if the player was under contract or reserve to another team, unless that team gave prior permission.[69] While that seemed clear, Brush, speaking for the board, but also effectively for the Giants, made the counter-argument that the Syracuse club's contractual rights to Wrigley expired at the end of the Eastern League season on September 9, and reserve rights didn't apply until the beginning of the next season. Therefore, according to Brush, in between seasons, Wrigley or any other player "is as free to do what he chooses as the bird that flies," which put Brush and Freedman in the unlikely position of supporting player's rights.[70] The same arguments were repeated for hours without changing any minds, and the board denied the appeal, which was no surprise since they made the original decision.

What seems clear more than 100 years later, and should have been clear to at least some at the time, is that both positions had merit, so the statesmanlike approach would have been to clarify the rules for the future and not punish the Brooklyn club. In arguing his position, Brush himself admitted there were no precedents because the issue had never arisen before.[71] However, more was involved than a relatively unimportant dispute over a marginal player. With Brooklyn's appeal denied, the scene shifted the next day to the National League Board of Directors meeting, effectively another committee of owners empowered to adjudicate other types of disputes between clubs. Having successfully defended their position at the arbitration board, the Freedman forces went on the attack, demanding that every game Wrigley played in be thrown out and the Brooklyn club pay $2,500 in damages, not to the league, but to the Giants. Freedman, of course, didn't lower himself to present his team's case, relying instead upon club secretary Fred Knowles. The board, after deliberating for six hours, agreed to throw out the Wrigley games, but was unable to reach a decision on damages, primarily because the Giants presented no basis for the $2,500 figure.[72]

Ebbets had engaged John Montgomery Ward to represent Brooklyn before the directors, but he was no more successful than Ebbets a day earlier. Understandably, the spirits of the Brooklyn side were downcast, with Ebbets grousing, "the case is prejudiced" and Ward telling *The World*, "a stone wall would be more susceptible to argument." Thinking the handwriting was on the wall, the paper proclaimed "Again Mr. Freedman downs Brooklyn," and labeled the Freedman-Brush combination the "most powerful ever formed in the National League."[73] Defeat in the Wrigley case was hardly a death blow to Ebbets and his partners, but it didn't augur well for the club's chances in the upcoming consolidation debate. On the following day, however, it turned out that the arrogance of the Brush-Freedman forces had gone too far. Given overnight to justify the $2,500 figure, Knowles admitted he couldn't do so, but still claimed $2,500 was the correct amount. This was too much for some of the magnates, and repeated motions for a Brooklyn to New York payment failed, though at the last minute a $500 fine payable to the league was approved.[74]

Amazingly, after so much time and rhetoric devoted to a relatively minor issue, the debate resumed the next day when the full owners meeting finally got underway. Since the Board of Directors report required the approval of the owners, Ebbets seized the opportunity to appeal the fine. The embattled Brooklyn owner insisted that the issue was not the money, but "the fair name of the Brooklyn club," and argued that the Dodgers had acted in good faith with no intent to harm the Giants. Having had more than enough of fighting an unseen, but powerful foe, Ebbets lashed out at Freedman, wishing the Giants owner was present to hear his words. Pulling no punches, Ebbets claimed "for several years he [Freedman] has endeavored to kill baseball," while the Brooklyn owners tried to build up the game, including spending $30,000 on a new ground. The Brooklyn magnate's words had some effect, as Robison of St. Louis and Hart of Chicago moved to substitute a reprimand for the fine, but ultimately the board report including the $500 fine was approved by a narrow 7–5 vote.[75] Wisely making sure Brooklyn's position reached the public, Ebbets gave the text of his speech to the *Eagle*, so Dodgers fans knew how hard he fought for their team.[76] Because of Hanlon's planning, the games which were thrown out had no impact on Brooklyn's pennant-winning season, and although Ebbets threatened not to pay the fine, in the end the club, however unwillingly, wisely did so.[77]

Having exhausted most of their meeting time on a skirmish before the big battle over circuit reduction even began, the magnates, somewhat surprisingly, took a rational approach to the controversial issue. It's impossible to know whether what happened was prearranged, but as soon as the discussion moved to the 1900 schedule, the ill-fated Harry Pulliam of the Louisville club intervened, saying he didn't want to vote on the schedule until he knew if his club would still be in the league. Having gotten the issue out in the open, Pulliam made things even easier for those favoring circuit reductions by announcing that Louisville would surrender its franchise "upon any equitable and fair agreement at the wisdom of the League." This opened the door for the Robisons, anxious to get out of Cleveland, to echo Pulliam's sentiments, followed by John Brush proposing the appointment of a committee to discuss the issues and report back to a future meeting. Not surprisingly, especially considering that no other franchises had been nominated for elimination, there was no opposition. In the end, the committee consisted of Brush, Arthur Soden of Boston, James Hart of Chicago and John Rogers of Philadelphia, which meant Brush would drive the process no matter who might be named chair.[78] Perhaps not surprisingly, with the exception of Hart, the other three members were in the Freedman camp, but the Brooklyn representatives raised no objection to the committee's makeup.[79]

Ebbets' and his partners' silence was most likely due to reassurances received outside of the meetings themselves. According to the *Eagle*, there was a marked difference in the treatment of the Brooklyn owners in the hotel lobby and corridors the night before. Ebbets was seen in a long conversation with Brush, where purportedly the Brooklyn magnate was assured that the Dodgers would not be dropped from the league.[80] While it's impossible to be sure why Freedman's demand to eliminate Brooklyn was denied, the vehemence with which Ebbets argued the Wrigley case made it crystal clear he was not going away quietly. Ebbets' physical presence was also a public reminder that while Freedman could draw on the resources of Tammany Hall, Ebbets had political connections of his own in New York City. Furthermore, unlike the gutted Louisville and Cleveland rosters, Brooklyn was talent-rich, which would make any buyout much more expensive, something the economy-minded magnates wanted to avoid. No matter the explanation, Ebbets fought for his team, and major league baseball in Brooklyn was safe.[81]

Some two and a half months later, the magnates returned to New York City to consider the circuit committee's recommendations. Not surprisingly, the lesser members of the two syndicates, Cleveland and Baltimore, were marked for elimination along with the perennially weak Louisville and Washington franchises. Those decisions were far easier than setting an "equitable and fair agreement," i.e., the fair price Pulliam laid down as a condition in December. Speaking for the committee, Brush explained that each club had three basic assets: players, grounds or the lease thereto and the franchise itself. The committee felt it was impossible (and probably too controversial) to value the first two, so it proposed letting the clubs themselves dispose of those assets and recommended each franchise be valued at $10,000. Louisville quickly accepted this, as, at first, did the Robisons for Cleveland, before the two brothers began a lengthy debate, finally getting a guarantee of another $15,000 for the grounds so they wouldn't be tempted to make the park available to an American League team. Neither the Baltimore nor Washington owners were willing to go so quietly, but negotiations outside of the meeting produced franchise values of $30,000 and $39,000 respectively, with the clubs authorized to sell their players and grounds and keep the proceeds. To pay for all of this, the committee proposed a five percent assessment on the gate receipts of the remaining eight clubs.[82]

With the most difficult and complex issues disposed of, the meeting turned into a support session for Andrew Freedman and the Giants, revealing the true cost of the Brush—Freedman reconciliation. First, the magnates discussed giving Freedman and the Giants priority on the players from the soon to be extinct franchises. Taking a balanced position, Ebbets admitted he, more than anyone else present, needed and wanted a strong local rival and was, therefore, willing to give New York "the first choice, and at reasonable figures," but doubted he would go "into the charitable business" of giving away players.[83] As the discussion continued, probably to everyone's surprise, the dark prince of baseball owners, Andrew Freedman himself, graced the meeting with his presence. The chorus of offers of help must have been music to his ears, if not his wallet. Even Ferdinand Abell, who complained frequently of how much money he had lost in baseball, got into the act, saying that "If there is anything else you want us to do Mr. Freedman, I wish you would speak out frankly."[84]

The last thing Freedman needed was encouragement, and he quickly took the offensive, claiming the primary issue wasn't players, but the lease on Manhattan Field adjoining the Polo Grounds, home field of the Giants. Even though they didn't use Manhattan Field, the New York club continued to lease the property for $15,000 a year so other leagues like the new American League couldn't place another major league franchise in New York City. Freedman claimed, with some justification, that keeping competing leagues out of Manhattan benefited the other owners at no cost. As a result, his club had been treated "in a very selfish way" by the other seven clubs, and unless the outrage was addressed, Freedman predicted with complete confidence, the club's stockholders wouldn't spend money to upgrade the Giants' roster. Given Freedman's dominant position and that on this occasion, at least, he had a point, it's no surprise the owners voted unanimously to reimburse the Giants $15,000 per year, net of any rentals, so long as the grounds were not leased to a club outside the National Agreement.

While Freedman didn't demand any specific players, he had previously told Boston owner William Conant he wanted Win Mercer of the soon to be extinct Washington club, and as a further peace offering, the owners awarded Mercer to New York at no cost, although Ebbets had the sense to vote no.[85] In the end, Freedman left the meeting not only with the reduced circuit he wanted (albeit with Brooklyn still in it), a free player and an annual payment of $15,000, but also with a refund with interest of the fine imposed in the "Ducky" Holmes affair. No one should have been surprised when Freedman's response to his fellow owners' generosity was a refusal to pay the Giants' share of the five percent assessment for circuit reduction costs or to spend money to improve his club, illustrating once again the downside of appeasement.[86]

Doubtless displeased by the abject surrender of the other magnates, Ebbets and his partners still left the meetings victorious, since they not only kept Brooklyn in the National League, but could further upgrade their roster with the best Baltimore players and make money disposing of the rest. In the end, Hanlon opted to bring Jimmy Sheckard and Harry Howell back to Brooklyn, both of whom had effectively had an additional year of major league seasoning in Baltimore, along with pitchers Frank Kitson and Joe McGinnity. Far more fascinating, however, is Ebbets' attitude about John McGraw, who had done so well with the crumbs left for him to manage in Baltimore. Understandably, Abell wanted McGraw in Brooklyn, but after a "discussion [that] waxed unusually warm," with both men "perspiring freely," Ebbets prevailed, and McGraw along with Wilbert Robinson ended up in St. Louis, although not for long.[87] Discussing this in more detail a few days later, Ebbets said McGraw's performance running the Orioles in 1899 had proven him to be more than a third baseman, and relegating him to that role in Brooklyn would hurt his performance. Incredibly, Ebbets went on to say that his real wish was for McGraw to go to the Giants, "because he is the man of all men who could assist in building up baseball across the river."[88] It was a prophecy that would come true beyond Ebbets' wildest imagination, and perhaps one of the best illustrations ever of being careful what you wish for.

Even without McGraw and Robinson, Brooklyn entered the 1900 season with an improved roster, but the other seven clubs were also strengthened by circuit reduction. As a result, it was a more competitive race, but a 17–5 record in June put Brooklyn on top. While they were threatened by rapidly improving Pittsburgh, Brooklyn won its second consecutive pennant by 4½ games. The two clubs then played a post-season series which Brooklyn also won, but more telling than the on-the-field results was that all the games were played in Pittsburgh. It was confirmation, if any was needed, of another disappointing year at the box office, as the *Eagle* claimed that the club actually lost money at home. Fortunately, the team continued to draw well on the road, otherwise the "losses would have been large."[89] Doubtless the estimated $15,000–19,000 received from the St. Louis club for McGraw and Robinson and one other player also helped the bottom line.[90] Ebbets blamed the club's poor home attendance on a one-sided pennant race, claiming "a championship club loses patronage almost as speedily as a tail end team."[91] Even so, Ebbets could be pleased that he had accomplished his main goals as club president by building a new park and putting together a profitable, championship team. It would be a very long time before he would enjoy that degree of satisfaction again.

CHAPTER V

"Sooner than give in to Freedman I would lose every dollar I have invested in the game."

Brooklyn has been called America's first suburb, and by 1900 there was no shortage of Brooklynites commuting to and from Manhattan. During the second week of December, there was one commuter who, even if he tried to keep a low profile, couldn't avoid attracting attention. Baseball fans among the passengers, perhaps glancing up from their newspapers, knew Charles Ebbets was headed to the National League owners meeting at the Manhattan's Fifth Avenue Hotel. Already noteworthy as a gathering place for politicians and financiers, it was an appropriate venue for baseball magnates to discuss the status of the national game.[1] As he thought about his own club, Ebbets had plenty of reasons to be pleased since the Dodgers were in markedly better condition than when he took over in early 1898. Not only did the Brooklyn club have a new and accessible ball park, Ebbets' team was two-time defending National League champions.

Yet no matter how satisfied Ebbets was with his own situation, the baseball horizon didn't lack for storm clouds. Of special concern, not just for Ebbets but the entire National League, was the threat of a new players' union and, even worse, a possible baseball war with a new league headed by a strong and visionary leader. Having already experienced two such conflicts, Ebbets knew full well the havoc that could be wreaked by the combination of dissatisfied players and would-be magnates bidding for their services. After checking his hat and coat, the Brooklyn president probably wasted little time seeking out his fellow owners to see just how bad the impending storms might be.

Leading off the list of potential threats was the Protective Association of Professional Baseball Players, the players' latest attempt to better their lot through collective action. Founded about six months earlier, the Association's secretary, veteran player Hughie Jennings, and attorney Harry Taylor, a former player himself, had requested a meeting with the owners.[2] Although the magnates probably wanted no part of it, the scars from the 1890 Brotherhood war were fresh enough that they knew simply ignoring the players was not an option. At the same time, however, the owners had no intention of making it easy for the fledgling union, so they delegated the task to a committee. By assigning the task to Arthur Soden, John Brush and John Rogers, the magnates sent a message of skepticism, if not outright opposition. Soden, the architect of the hated reserve clause, was extremely unpopular with the players, while Brush had led the effort to impose a salary cap, a major cause of the last baseball war.[3] Rogers, a lawyer in his own right, was prepared to match legal wits with Taylor should it prove necessary.

Although put somewhat on the defensive by Brush's attempt to pejoratively label the association a "secret organization," Taylor managed to get the players' three major demands before the owners, to no one's surprise, beginning with the reserve clause. Wisely, the players entertained no hope that the owners would abolish the hated restriction, so they instead asked for a limit on the number of years of the reserve and/or a limit on the number of reserved players. In addition, the new union wanted an end to farming (selling a player to a minor league club with the right of repurchase) and a provision that players couldn't be "bought, sold, assigned, claimed or selected" without their consent. Making no promises, the owners' committee asked for the requests in writing, which Taylor quickly provided in the form of a sample contract.[4] Whether it would have many any difference is questionable, but Taylor more than muddied the waters by submitting a proposed contract with further changes favorable to the players without disclosing them during the meeting. Leaving the owners to find those additional changes on their own opened the association to charges that they were trying to deceive the owners. In any event, the magnates completely rejected the players' demands.[5] Ebbets had little to say during the owners' discussion, but later described the proposals as "simply preposterous."[6]

Only at the end of their meeting did the owners devote any time to the threat posed by the American League. The debate, however, was limited to finding a way to prevent National League clubs from competing against each other for American League players (and bidding up the prices in the process), now considered free agents because the upstart league abandoned its minor league status under the National Agreement. Never missing an opportunity to rage about the league's poor treatment of his team, Andrew Freedman, once again got his way, winning first choice for his club with the remainder determined by lot. Even this wasn't considered a major issue since Brush claimed there were only a handful of American League players that could help National League clubs.[7]

If the limited time devoted to the American League meant the magnates didn't take the new circuit seriously, they made a major mistake. Unfortunately for the National League and especially the Brooklyn club, this wasn't a league based on a flawed concept like the Players' League or one headed by Henry Lucas (mastermind of 1884 the Union Association), whose vision exceeded his capacity. This time the National League was confronted by Ban Johnson, who was not only capable but "just as imperious and impressive as he looked."[8] Since taking over the Western League in 1894, the former sports writer had gradually upgraded his organization, changing the name to the American League for the 1900 season. More importantly, Johnson, after negotiating an agreement with Cubs owner James Hart, began head-to-head competition with the National League in Chicago, while avoiding, for the moment anyway, open warfare.[9]

Although the quality of American League baseball wasn't at National League levels, the lack of rowdiness, ownership infighting and syndicate baseball attracted sufficient fans to make the new venture a financial success. In 1901 Johnson planned to move teams into Baltimore, Washington and Philadelphia, while claiming major league status. Continuing to move cautiously, Johnson didn't pursue a franchise in Boston and expressed a willingness to negotiate further eastward expansion with the National League. While Ebbets and the other National League owners deliberated in Manhattan, Ban Johnson waited in vain in Philadelphia for an invitation that never came. Realizing direct competition was the only way he and his league would be taken seriously, Johnson stopped trying to negotiate, put a team in Boston, and began making plans to sign National League players.[10]

If Charles Ebbets was more worried than his fellow magnates about the American League threat, it wasn't evident in how he spent his time in early 1901. Media accounts about the Brooklyn magnate made little mention of baseball, focusing instead on Ebbets' increased involvement in bowling, his second-favorite sport. By 1900, bowling was popular enough throughout the country to spark the formation of a national organization, the American Bowling Congress. Apparently more of a loose confederation than a national governing body, the organization held its annual meeting on January 8, 1901, in Chicago.[11] Prior to the meeting, a group of Brooklyn bowlers decided to "push the candidacy" of one Charles Ebbets for A.B.C. president.[12] There was, however, no shortage of candidates, with Manhattan delegates favoring the incumbent (another New Yorker), who supposedly didn't want re-election, as well as a Chicago-sponsored nominee.[13] In the end, Ebbets lost to the Chicago candidate, with the result clouded by the convention's refusal to honor proxy voting, which supposedly cost Ebbets the election.[14]

Although the Brooklyn bowlers failed to get Ebbets elected in 1901, they weren't in the least discouraged and tried again a year later. Ebbets' chances were strengthened by the unanimous endorsement of Manhattan bowlers, which made him truly a Greater New York candidate.[15] Apparently bowlers were only slightly less fractious than National League owners, with the convention so badly divided there was talk of the Eastern bowlers splitting off to form their own organization with Ebbets at its head.[16] Cooler heads prevailed, however, with the Eastern delegates reportedly getting their way on the policy issues and accepting a compromise presidential candidate (not Ebbets) in return. Although supposedly his election could have been forced through, perhaps mindful of what he had experienced at baseball meetings, Ebbets wisely "did not care to rule over a divided house."[17] While remaining part of the national organization, the local bowlers formed the New York Bowling Association in September of 1902, and to no one's surprise, Ebbets was elected president, a position he "candidly acknowledged that he had sought."[18] Clearly bowling was still an important part of Ebbets' life, and just as clearly, he was quite popular in that world.

In addition to his two-sport career, Ebbets continued to represent Brooklyn on the New York City Council. However, 1901 was to be Ebbets' last year in that office, since a new city charter eliminated the council at the end of the year, leaving the Board of Alderman as the sole legislative branch of city government.[19] Ebbets' final year in office was no different, as he continued to use parliamentary maneuvers to oppose major capital projects.[20] Ebbets and a small number of his fellow Brooklyn councilmen's opposition was obviously effective, since their opponents took out newspaper ads denouncing them as "obstructionists" while calling on the electorate to "bombard them with telegrams, letters and post cards."[21] Slightly more generously, the *Eagle* said the baseball magnate and bowler was only a "partial obstructionist" with a favorite tactic of "absences for weeks at a time."[22] Not surprisingly, Ebbets denied being an obstructionist, partial or otherwise, claiming his opposition to Manhattan projects was retaliation against Manhattan councilmen who refused to support similar projects in Brooklyn. Political retaliation was not, Ebbets said, his preferred mode of operation, but it seemed "the only way for Brooklyn to get what it wanted."[23] Unsurprisingly, the Dodgers president didn't neglect his own self-interest, obtaining council approval for $50,000 for a new bridge over the Gowanus Canal, not far from Washington Park.[24] Even though his council service was going to end, Ebbets declined other nominations, not to devote more time to baseball and bowling, but supposedly because his eye was on a state senate nomination.[25]

Unfortunately for Ebbets, the impending baseball war wasn't about to wait for bowling elections, municipal politics or anything else. Skillfully taking advantage of the National League's clumsy handling of the new players' association, Ban Johnson not only recognized the union, but agreed to its demands.[26] After the National League magnates' December 1900 rejection of the proposed new players contract, union leader Charles "Chief" Zimmer had approached Arthur Soden, withdrawing everything except the initial demands on the reserve clause, farming and the selling/trading of players. Led by John Brush, and likely agreeing with Philadelphia owner John Rogers that they held an "impregnable position," the magnates refused to resume negotiations.[27] By February, however, with a bidding war for players staring them in the face, the magnates rethought their intransigent position and agreed to meet with Zimmer during their meeting in New York City.

Once again the magnates left the dirty work to a committee, with Brush and Soden reprising their roles and James Hart of Chicago replacing Rogers. Hart quickly went on the offensive, demanding that Zimmer tell them "every case in which a player is dissatisfied or has been dissatisfied within the past ten years."[28] Not intimidated by the impossible, not to mention unreasonable demand, Zimmer (the players wisely left Taylor behind) fenced verbally with Hart before the meeting got back on track.[29] Even though the players were in a stronger position, they retreated even further on the reserve clause, asking only that it be limited to one year. Back in December, even this would have been too much for the magnates to swallow, but now they saw the chance to get something more valuable in return—union support against National League players who jumped to the American League.[30] Although probably not without some misgivings, the owners accepted the players' demands in exchange for their commitment to expel "jumpers."[31]

Ebbets was pleased with the agreement, predicting that the Brooklyn players "will almost to a man sign National League contracts."[32] However, Ebbets and his peers were quickly disabused of any satisfaction they took from the union's supposed commitment on defecting players. Zimmer may not have been a lawyer, Philadelphia or otherwise, but he was too shrewd for the magnates. His agreement to the suspension of "jumpers" was given subject to "final action by the Protective Association as a body," which never happened.[33] In the end, the National League's concessions gained them nothing, and their players "transferred in droves to the American League."[34] Ebbets wasn't far off, however, in predicting that he would retain most of the club's players for the 1901 season, but what the American League didn't take in quantity, they made up for in quality. When the dust settled, Brooklyn lost star pitcher Joe McGinnity, outfielder Fielder Jones and third baseman Lave Cross. Conflicting stories came out about McGinnity and Jones, both of whom claimed Ebbets had treated them unfairly, which predictably the Brooklyn magnate denied.[35] In McGinnity's case, however, there is evidence that more than money was involved in his defection to the American League. The star pitcher's biographer claims McGinnity turned down $5,000 from Brooklyn to play for John McGraw and with Wilbert Robinson in Baltimore for the far lower figure of $2,800.[36] Years later, it was alleged that Brooklyn was decimated by American League defections because Ferdinand Abell was unwilling to put up the money.[37] While Ebbets and his partners may not have been willing to meet the players' demands, it seems unlikely that an inability or unwillingness to pay was the cause of the 1901 defections.

Unfortunately for Ebbets, his ball club and its fans, the loss of an ace pitcher, a starting outfielder and an infielder to the rival league was only the beginning, since a year later in 1902, two .300 hitters deserted to the new circuit. Especially damaging was the loss of future Hall of Famer Joe Kelley to the Baltimore club, but the defection could hardly have been surprising. Not only was Kelley from Baltimore, his father-in-law had purchased part of the team, and the move reunited him with his old cronies, John McGraw and Wilbert Robinson.[38] Also gone was long-time second baseman Tom Daly, who headed west to join the defending American League champion Chicago White Sox.[39]

Nor was that the end of American League raids on the Brooklyn roster. About ten days after the end of the 1902 season, Ebbets tried to sign pitchers Frank Kitson and Bill Donovan, but was rebuffed.[40] There was no reason to believe the reluctance was temporary, since the *Eagle* believed both men were lost to the American League.[41] As bad as this news was, things got even worse when Willie Keeler announced that not only had he jumped to the American League, but he would play for the circuit's New York franchise in 1903. Ban Johnson wanted Keeler so badly, the American League president personally signed the diminutive ball player to a two-year contract at $10,000 per year, reportedly the "most lucrative contract ever given to a player."[42] Keeler claimed he had every right to change teams, as his Brooklyn contract was only for one year, but Hanlon insisted that Keeler as well as Donovan had two-year contracts.[43] It's unclear how much, if any, negotiating took place with Kitson, Donovan and Keeler, so 1903 could have been the point at which Abell refused to put more money at Ebbets' and Hanlon's disposal. Regardless of how it happened, Brooklyn's roster had been decimated by the loss of four regulars (two future Hall of Famers) and three starting pitchers (one a future Hall of Famer).

The full impact of the American League war on the Dodgers' roster was, however, still in the future when the somewhat depleted Brooklyn club opened the 1901 season. Replacing players like McGinnity, Cross and Jones was no small matter, so it's no wonder Brooklyn got off to a slow start, playing just over .500 ball through the end of July. Over the last two months of the 1901 season, however, the new lineup came together, going 35–18, but the improved play was far too little, far too late, and Brooklyn actually lost ground to Pittsburgh, finally finishing third. While the player losses may not fully explain Brooklyn's failure to win their third straight pennant, the defections made it difficult for the Dodgers to compete with a Pittsburgh club almost untouched by American League raids. Supposedly the new league hoped to add Barney Dreyfuss' team to their ranks and intentionally decided not to pursue Pirates players.[44]

While Brooklyn failed to repeat as league champions, the third-place finish was certainly respectable, and attendance was actually higher than in 1900, suggesting the club at least broke

Andrew Freedman, a wealthy businessman with Tammany Hall connections, was the owner of the New York Giants from 1895 to 1902. Frequently labeled the most-hated owner in baseball, Freedman hoped to drive Brooklyn out of the National League (*Brooklyn Daily Eagle*, December 10, 1899).

even.[45] Although the Brooklyn club was in better shape than in the 1890s, Ebbets still had plenty to worry about, and American League player raids were by no means the primary threat. In fact, the greatest danger was from within the National League itself. The Brooklyn magnate would have been well advised to remember the biblical admonition "a man's enemies will be the members of his own household," a scriptural passage which for Ebbets became incarnate in the persons of Andrew Freedman and John Brush.[46] In late July of 1901, the *Eagle* reported, "Freedman has asserted that Brooklyn must go and his edicts have come to be looked upon as law," just the latest chapter in Freedman's long vendetta against the Brooklyn club.[47] While the average baseball fan may have found it hard to believe the New York owner had that much power, Ebbets knew all too well how frequently the other magnates caved in to Freedman. For that reason alone, the Brooklyn president had to be concerned in August when *The Sporting News* joined the chorus, predicting "One thing is certain. Brooklyn will not be in the National League circuit next season."[48]

Whether rumors of the Brooklyn club's demise were encouraged by Brush and Freedman as a smoke screen for their true intentions or were just idle media speculation isn't clear. In fact, the two men were actually willing to allow Brooklyn to remain in the National League, but on such a sharply reduced basis that the franchise would have had extremely limited value. In December, just as the National League owners gathered for the annual verbal fisticuffs in New York City, the *Sun* leaked Brush's plan for the creation of a baseball trust. Back in August, Brush and Freedman, along with Arthur Soden of Boston and Frank Robison of St. Louis, had met at Freedman's Red Bank, New Jersey, estate to discuss Brush's radical plan to re-organize the National League.[49] Under the proposal, the eight club owners would exchange their ownership interests for stock in a trust, run by a board of control which would appoint club managers and assign players to specific clubs, presumably seeking large crowds and competitive balance. Players would belong not to the individual clubs, but to the league itself, licensed in a similar way to jockeys at race tracks. Most important of all, the board of control would be in a far better position than individual owners to control or even reduce players' salaries.[50]

Parts of the trust proposal might even have appealed to the four club owners left out of the Red Bank meeting (Philadelphia, Pittsburgh, Chicago, and, of course, Brooklyn) because they were on Freedman's crowded enemies list.[51] For the uninvited, however, there was a major problem with the plan and, in this case, the devil wasn't in the details, but out in plain sight. Ownership of the proposed trust wasn't going to be shared equally (perhaps too much to expect) or even allocated on some kind of rational basis. Rather Freedman (30 percent), Brush, Robison and Soden (12 percent each) would control about two-thirds of the trust, with the other four clubs limited to one-third. Of that group, Philadelphia and Chicago were to have ten percent each, Pittsburgh eight percent and, to no one in Brooklyn's surprise, Ebbets and his partners would get a mere six percent.[52] No explanation was ever offered for the proposed percentages, leading to the almost inescapable conclusion that the proposal was a blatant power grab. Although the *Sun's* publication of the plan, especially the ownership percentages, didn't help Freedman's and Brush's cause, it's hard to understand how the two men thought any of the other four owners would accept the plan, especially after being left out of the Red Bank meeting. Perhaps it was simply self-destruction by arrogance.

Persuading at least one more owner to join them was no formality, since without an additional vote (which obviously wasn't coming from Brooklyn), the proposal was going nowhere. During the December owners meeting, Frank Robison claimed that the plan was to be presented to the other four clubs prior to the meeting, but it wasn't possible because of Brush's illness.[53] The Reds owner confirmed this, saying he had been able to meet only with Dreyfuss in Pittsburgh the week before and hoped his "explanation will be satisfactory to the Philadelphia people and the Brooklyn people."[54] While Brush's illness doubtless delayed things, the order of consultation suggests that the pro-trust party thought the Pittsburgh magnate would be the most amenable, but they were mistaken.[55] As a result, when the meeting began at the Fifth Avenue Hotel on December 10, the Brush/Freedman forces were still a vote short. First on the agenda was the election of officers, and there was significant sentiment for a stronger leader than long-term incumbent Nicholas Young. Dreyfuss, far from sold on Brush's plan, nominated Albert Spalding, which was quickly seconded by Ebbets.[56] The pro-trust party tried to delay the election, insisting the owners must first decide whether the 1892 National League—American Association consolidation had a ten-year life or was a perpetual organization. It was a key question because it would be far easier to push through the trust proposal if the old organization had lapsed than to amend the existing constitution, which would give the opponents numerous opportunities to thwart the plan.[57]

Nothing was resolved until the following day, when the anti-trust forces, confident they could prevail on the constitutional issue, moved a resolution that the National League was a perpetual organization. Under the leadership of Philadelphia owner Rogers, they won by a 5–1 vote (with two abstentions), Soden having broken ranks with the pro-trust side.[58] Little else was accomplished, although Ebbets took the opportunity to vent his dismay about being kept in the dark about the trust plan.[59] After a night's sleep, and doubtless some debate in smoke-filled rooms, the magnates tried to elect a president, but 25 consecutive ballots were evenly divided between Spalding and Young, leaving Spalding one vote short of winning the election. By this point, the owners were at such loggerheads they couldn't even agree on a motion to adjourn, at which point the Brush/Freedman forces left the room, taking with them, or so they thought, a quorum and the possibility of any action in their absence. Seizing the moment, however, and steamrolling the predictably weak Nick Young, Rogers insisted, "once a quorum, always a quorum," and rammed through Spalding's election by a unanimous, albeit 4–0 vote, just before 1:30 a.m.[60] To no one's surprise, however, the issue was far from resolved.

Charles Ebbets was far from naïve, so it's highly unlikely he believed a mere parliamentary ploy could defeat Freedman and Brush, especially with Freedman's Tammany Hall connections. Perhaps the sole surprise was that it took only "a matter of hours" for a court order to stop Spalding from functioning as National League president.[61] The result was a league without executive leadership which amazingly dragged on for months, another reflection of the seasonal nature of the baseball business in the early twentieth century. The one time-sensitive issue was the schedule, which while typically finalized later than in modern baseball, couldn't be indefinitely postponed. Ebbets couldn't have been pleased with the state of affairs in the National League at the end of 1901, but the Brooklyn owner at least had one thing to celebrate, the announcement that Charles Jr. was engaged to marry Martha J. Ronayne, also of Brooklyn. In his early 20s, young Charles was employed as the inspector of school supplies for the Borough of Brooklyn.[62]

The National League owners' failure to resolve their differences drew plenty of attention from the press, including the public airing of the acrimony between the Giants and Dodgers owners. The relationship was bad enough, but Freedman made things even worse by trying to hire Brooklyn's manager, Ned Hanlon, during the December meetings. It's difficult, if not, impossible to see the two men working together, but Hanlon confirmed the rumor. Supposedly it was only "Foxy Ned's" promise not to leave von der Horst as long as the latter was in baseball that kept Hanlon in Brooklyn.[63] Ebbets made no secret of his feelings, telling *Sporting Life* in early February 1902 that he would prefer to "lose every dollar I have invested in the game" before he would "give in to Freedman." The Brooklyn owner also had no doubts about the appropriate course of action, saying "Freedman should be removed from the League and baseball" because "he has done enough harm."[64]

When the National League leadership stalemate still wasn't resolved by March, something had to be done, so the magnates met in New York City on April 1, perhaps not fully cognizant of the irony of the date. Ostensibly the purpose of the meeting was to approve the schedule, something they had to do regardless of their feelings towards one another. League secretary Young, Ebbets and Robison all came prepared with draft schedules. First, however, apparently determined to avoid the late-night or early-morning antics of December, the magnates unanimously agreed to end all sessions no later than 11:00 pm.[65] Since the opening session didn't begin until 8:40, no real business was discussed that evening, and the meeting reconvened on April 2. In what seems like a pre-determined process (although he claimed otherwise), Soden told the assembled magnates they first needed to deal with the leadership issue, which gave Chicago's James Hart his cue to read a letter from Albert Spalding resigning his tenuous position as president. Hart then moved the owners' acceptance of the longtime baseball man's graceful exit. Amazingly, even though he had once again prevailed, it wasn't enough for Freedman, who gave a long and unnecessary speech brimming with criticism and threats, refusing to accept Spalding's resignation because his election wasn't legal.

After Brush echoed Freedman's sentiments, a long debate ensued in which Brush and Freedman argued that there wasn't time to find a president and, for at least 1902, the league should operate under a board of control (without the trust) of three owners. In the process, Freedman took a shot at Ebbets, suggesting that since the league office was in New York, Ebbets could easily serve on the board because he "is right here, with nothing else to do."[66] Considering the source, it's not surprising that Dreyfuss and Ebbets both opposed the idea of a league run by a committee.[67] In the end, the only person the owners could agree on as a potential president was William Temple, former Pittsburgh owner and donor of the 19th century post-season trophy which bore his name.[68] Foreshadowing future controversies over the president's position, Ebbets suggested John Montgomery Ward and got no response for his trouble.[69]

Having dispatched a telegram to the unsuspecting Mr. Temple, the magnates turned to the schedule with a lengthy debate, illustrating once again both its importance and complexity.[70] Speaking confidently and, in this case with a justifiable lack of modesty, Ebbets argued "my schedule is the best" and was appointed to a committee directed to report back the next day.[71] When the magnates assembled the following evening, they learned that William Temple had declined their offer. At this point it was clear even to the most recalcitrant that the board of control was the only option, so the debate focused on who and how many (three or four). Ebbets was nominated, but when the dust cleared Soden, Brush and Hart were chosen and, probably to no one's surprise, Brush became the chair.[72] That brought the schedule back before the owners with Ebbets reporting for the committee, and the Brooklyn magnate was either so convincing or the magnates were so exhausted that the schedule was adopted unanimously.[73]

With the schedule and temporary leadership finally in place, life in the National League finally shifted to the playing field. It's a tribute to Ned Hanlon's managerial ability that even after two years of defections to the American League, the Brooklyn club was more than competitive. After spending the first half of the 1902 season in third place, the club climbed to second in July, where it remained for the remainder of the season. Unfortunately, the Pirates, still virtually untouched by American League raids, kept increasing their lead, finishing 27½ games ahead of Brooklyn with an exceptional .741 winning percentage.

Although they had failed to win approval for their trust plan, Freedman and Brush were far from finished manipulating the National League to their advantage. Working in concert with Baltimore manager John McGraw, the less than holy trinity carried out a deceptive plan which put McGraw in New York as manager of the Giants along with some of the Orioles' best players, including former Dodger Joe McGinnity. If that alone wasn't enough to infuriate Ebbets, he also had to accept Brush's Reds team acquiring Joe Kelley, another Dodgers defector. Nor was this the final act in a drama that would change the National League landscape for more than 20 years. Brush sold the Reds to the Fleischmann group (including August "Garry" Herrmann) and shortly thereafter was appointed managing director of the Giants by Freedman, who sold the team to Brush in September of 1902.[74] While Ebbets (along with almost everyone else) must have been ecstatic to have Freedman finally out of baseball, the Brooklyn magnate now faced head-to-head competition with the equally difficult, but more effective Brush off the field and McGraw on the field. Ebbets had once wished John McGraw was in charge of the New York club, and he would have decades to repent of that wish.

Amid the re-shaping of the Giants, Brush called the National League owners to a meeting in New York on September 24 "to discuss the present condition and future of the Organization."[75] Very little reading between the lines was necessary to know that the issue was the ongoing war with

John T. Brush around 1911, about a year before his death. Owner of the Cincinnati Reds before buying out Andrew Freedman and taking over the Giants, Brush was a major force in National League affairs. After taking control of the New York team in 1902, Brush and his manager, John McGraw, quickly built an organization that dominated the National League for more than 20 years (Library of Congress, Prints and Photographs Division, Bain Collection [LC-DIG-ggbain-09870]).

the American League. Brush began by seeking the magnates' opinions, which were almost unanimous for continuing the fight, with Ebbets on the side of the hawks. As committed as the magnates claimed to be in September, by December peace had become a lot more attractive, and the magnates appointed a committee of James Hart, Frank Robison and August "Garry" Herrmann to negotiate with the American League.[76] Herrmann was a member of the new Reds ownership group and was destined to play a major role in league and inter-league affairs. While involving a new magnate in such sensitive negotiations may have seemed unusual, Herrmann's personal relationship with Ban Johnson, dating back to the latter's years as a sportswriter in Cincinnati, couldn't hurt the negotiating process. Two days later, in an extremely ill-fated decision, the owners unanimously elected Harry Pulliam from the Pittsburgh club as the league president, a position he had declined less than a year earlier because he was "too young and life is too short."[77] Seldom would words prove to be so bitterly prophetic.

In January of 1903, the two leagues met in Cincinnati with peace clearly everyone's priority and quickly hammered out an agreement. Describing the proposed deal to *Sporting Life*, Pulliam stressed that the key points were mutual recognition of the reserve clause, the inviolability of player contracts, and avoiding scheduling conflicts in cities with two teams. The provisions were crucial to club finances, since agreement on the reserve clause and contracts at least limited player salaries, while fewer scheduling conflicts helped the revenue side of the business. Understandably those issues were more important to the majority of the magnates than the Brooklyn and New York owners' concerns about an American League club in New York and the rights to specific players.[78] But the proposed pact almost ran aground on those issues, putting Ebbets and Brush, for once, on the same side. Uppermost in Ebbets' objections was the proposed allocation of Keeler, Kitson and Donovan to the American League.[79] In addition, Brooklyn supported Brush's concerns about the establishment of an American League team in New York.[80] Writing in *The Sporting News*, Abe Yager acknowledged that Brooklyn had not been treated fairly, but predicted Ebbets had little chance against 14 other magnates who wanted peace.[81]

When the National League magnates gathered in Cincinnati ten days later to review the proposed peace agreement, the paper's prediction proved accurate, since every vote went against Ebbets and Brush. On the issue of an American League club in New York, the owners qualified the National League acquiescence by defining New York as Manhattan, with no obligation to help an American League club find a site, a major challenge to any such venture.[82] With regard to players, Ebbets admitted, as he later told the *Eagle*, that the disputed players weren't worth sabotaging an agreement both the public and the press wanted, so he agreed to have Brooklyn's claims adjudicated by the league.[83] That effectively meant surrendering Keeler and Kitson for nothing, but Brooklyn was reimbursed for Donovan as part of resolving another conflict. Section five of the proposed agreement stated that there could be no circuit change (placing a club in a present one-team city) without a majority vote of both leagues. Reportedly the American League's price for awarding Donovan to Brooklyn was the elimination of that sentence. Since the provision protected Pittsburgh, Cincinnati and Brooklyn from American League incursions, the National League owners decided it was worth losing one player, but were willing to compensate Ebbets for his loss. Although it took almost a year, Brooklyn was paid $8,000, half coming from Pittsburgh and Cincinnati and the balance from the five remaining clubs.[84]

Unlike the owners meetings in Manhattan, once the Cincinnati meeting adjourned, Ebbets had the long train ride across Ohio and Pennsylvania to reflect on the proceedings. Most likely, Ebbets' mood was as bleak as the winter landscape outside his window. Although he understood the benefits of the peace agreement, two years of baseball war had gutted his championship team while his closest competitor was on the way to becoming a powerhouse. Ebbets was optimistic by nature, but he couldn't have had too much hope about a potential 1903 pennant in Brooklyn. Yet once again, Hanlon kept his club competitive at or above .500 throughout the year, but it was only good enough for fifth place. For some reason, however, although the results on the field weren't as good, almost 225,000 fans came out to Washington Park, 32 percent more than in the 1900 pennant-winning campaign.[85]

As per usual, the magnates returned to New York City in December of 1903, this time for a meeting mercifully free of crises and conflicts. One decision of note, favored by Ebbets, was to direct the schedule committee to plan for a 154-game season, a 14-game increase. The longer schedule generated more revenue, while additional expenses would be limited since the games would be played within the period of the players' existing contracts.[86] After the meetings adjourned, Ebbets entertained the magnates at his new venture, the Superba bowling alleys, a bowling alley and restaurant Ebbets and a partner had opened earlier that fall on Fulton Street in today's Bedford Stuyvesant section of Brooklyn.[87] The investment may have simply been a financial opportunity in another sport he loved, or possibly Ebbets wanted to diversify his interests due to concern about the financial future of the Brooklyn club. Considering what lay ahead, that would have been prudent thinking on Ebbets' part.

CHAPTER VI

"Sabbatarians who wanted to regulate the morals of everybody"

Although the January 1903 peace agreement required Ebbets and Giants owner John Brush to accept an American League franchise in New York City, they were officially relieved of any responsibility to help their new competitor find acceptable grounds. Restricting the new American League club even further, or so Ebbets and Brush thought, was another part of the agreement, limiting the junior circuit's team to Manhattan Island. In the end, the best location the new franchise could find was at the far northern end of Manhattan, so far from Brooklyn it's unlikely many of the over 200,000 people who passed through the Hilltop Park turnstiles in 1903 were Dodgers fans.[1] Considering Ebbets' other problems, he could be forgiven for putting direct American League competition towards the bottom of the list.

It must, therefore, have been an even greater shock to the Brooklyn owner when the Highlanders tried to offset their remote location by bringing some games to another part of Greater New York, a location much closer to Ebbets' fan base. Early in January of 1904, the New York Highlanders announced plans to play Sunday games at Ridgewood Park in Queens, just across the border from Brooklyn. Ebbets knew the site well because in the 1880s, the Dodgers played Sunday games there, drawing large crowds before Sabbitarians (those opposed to sport and other social activities on Sunday) forced them to cease and desist.[2] Ebbets wasted no time firing off a telegram to Garry Herrmann, calling on him to "take proper official action immediately."[3] Ebbets appealed to Herrmann, not as president of the Cincinnati Reds, but as head of the National Commission, major league baseball's new governing body. Recognizing that club disputes would never be completely eliminated, the new National Agreement between the two leagues established a three-person panel consisting of the two league presidents and a third party. Since Herrmann had a long-standing, mostly positive relationship with American League president Ban Johnson, he was acceptable to both sides and the logical choice for the third position.[4]

Ebbets got a second shock when he read in the *Eagle* that Herrmann supposedly supported the American League's position.[5] Outraged, the Brooklyn owner sent off a second telegram, later published in the *Eagle*, publicly telling Herrmann, in no uncertain terms, "you are wrong."[6] Sensing Ebbets' anger, Herrmann wired back that he had not expressed an opinion to the *Eagle*, nor had he authorized anyone to speak for him.[7] The issue, for the Brooklyn magnate, wasn't Sunday baseball, but the Highlanders' intent to play outside of Manhattan. Ebbets insisted, and his fellow National League owners agreed, that the peace agreement limited the American League franchise in New York City to Manhattan. Playing anywhere else was a circuit change, requiring the majority approval of both leagues, something that wasn't going to happen. Ebbets emphatically told the *Eagle* that Brooklyn would never have agreed to the peace agreement if it gave the Highlanders "a roving franchise."[8]

Unfortunately, but not unexpectedly, Ban Johnson disagreed just as emphatically, arguing that there was no written agreement restricting the American League to Manhattan.[9] Even more unfortunately for Ebbets, Johnson was literally correct; the agreement or understanding had never been reduced to writing. Herrmann himself admitted as much in a letter to National League president Harry Pulliam, explaining that since both sides wanted the peace agreement adopted without amendments, the National League owners, especially Ebbets, accepted in good faith Johnson's oral commitment that "our grounds will be located on Manhattan Island."[10] While the issue may seem relatively minor, any threat to a club's only real source of revenue was important. Ebbets reminded his fellow owners of their self-interest in the issue, claiming that if the Highlanders played at Ridgewood, Brooklyn's gate receipts would be cut in half, which, while probably an exaggeration, would also lower their income.[11] The Dodgers owner was also concerned that another major league team playing so close to Brooklyn might convert local people into American League fans, especially now that former Dodger and Brooklyn native Willie Keeler played for the Highlanders.[12]

With Johnson and Pulliam supporting their respective leagues' positions, Herrmann had no choice but to call a hearing before the National Commission in Chicago on February 13. Ebbets called it "the hardest discussion I have ever entered into," so "warm" that supposedly reporters could hear the magnates' voices out in the hall. Although a literal interpretation of the peace agreement would have found no limitation on where the American League club could play in New York City, Herrmann wisely and appropriately decided in favor of Brooklyn.[13] When the Brooklyn and Giants owners accepted another major league team into New York City, they paid a high price for peace, possibly higher than the other six clubs combined. Their willingness to do so was based on an understanding, even if it was an oral one. Permitting the American League to violate the spirit of the agreement would not only have hurt the Brooklyn club, but gotten the new relationship between the two leagues off to a bad start. Once again, Charles Ebbets had successfully stood up for his ball club and, in this case, the rest of the National League.

As upsetting the whole episode was, it may also have prompted Ebbets to re-open the Sunday baseball question, since on Sunday, April 17, 1904, the Dodgers, for the first time in their 20-year history, played a regular season game in Brooklyn on the previously sacred Sabbath. While New York law clearly prohibited "public sports" on Sunday, the regulations were applied inconsistently, with officials in rural areas more likely to look the other way. It was due to such laxness that Charles Byrne's Brooklyn club was able to play Sunday games in more sparsely settled Queens for four years in the late 1880s. The Sunday prohibition was enforced more strictly in New York City, although in Brooklyn judges were more concerned about games where admission was charged. Ebbets never explained his decision to take on the Sabbatarians in 1904, but the Ridgewood Park case must have at least reminded him of the potential return. Arrayed against Ebbets and anyone attempting to play on "the Lord's Day" were well-organized inter-denominational religious groups fully prepared to wage war against this blasphemy.[14]

It's surprising that Ebbets didn't attempt playing Sunday games sooner. He was well aware of the profitability of games at Ridgewood Park, where in 1886, for example, 14 Sunday games drew average attendance of 4,000 fans, twice the weekday average at Washington Park.[15] Yet when Ebbets took over the club in 1898, he was noncommittal, saying the Dodgers would play on Sundays "if the people of Brooklyn desire it."[16] No matter how strong the opposition, there was no shortage of Brooklynites on Ebbets' side as evidenced by some 12,000 fans who passed through the gates at Washington Park without buying a ticket. Free admission, however, wasn't due to any special largesse on Ebbets' part, rather he was using a subterfuge to get around the admission charge restriction. Instead of selling tickets, Ebbets borrowed an idea from some Brooklyn amateur teams, allowing fans to enter the grounds for free. Once inside, however, they had to buy a score card for 25, 50 or 75 cents, with the type of card corresponding, not coincidentally, to a seat location.[17] The large crowd, a Brooklyn victory and the lack of any police interference made the experiment such a smashing success that Ebbets quickly decided to schedule more Sunday games.

Not only didn't the police interfere, the captain in charge claimed he hadn't seen any "violations of the Sunday base ball law," suggesting he saw what he wanted to see.[18] The possibility of regular Sunday baseball looked even brighter when Police Commissioner William McAdoo said that in his opinion, there wasn't anything illegal taking place. Police commissioners, however, are appointed and not, therefore, subject to as much public pressure as elected officials, such as Mayor George B. McClellan, Jr., who had McAdoo arrest some participants for a test case. Even this obstacle seemed surmounted, however, when Justice William Gaynor, a future mayor of New York, ruled for Sunday baseball. The Sabbitarians were not, however, easily defeated, and when Brooklyn District attorney John Clarke brought a second test case before the court, the scorecard ploy was found to be just that. The court ruled that baseball on the Sabbath, by itself, was not illegal, but paid admissions were, effectively ending the experiment for 1904. At that point, the issue was less important to Ebbets because attendance at Sunday games had dropped off dramatically, almost in lockstep with the team's performance.[19]

Later that year, however, the players in the test case were acquitted on appeal, making the original anti–Sunday baseball ruling seem less definitive.[20] Naturally, Ebbets tried again in 1905, and a game was played on April 23 before a crowd of 11,642, without arrests although the police took evidence for possible litigation.[21] Ebbets was more than a little aggressive in his choice of dates, since the game was played on Easter Sunday, the holiest day of the Christian year.[22] Even more tangible evidence of Sunday baseball's appeal was provided a week later, when a mammoth crowd estimated at 30,000 attended a Brooklyn—New York contest. So large was the throng that they overwhelmed the woefully outnumbered scorecard sellers. Faced with the inevitable, Ebbets, with great reluctance, allowed an estimated 10,000 fans in for free.[23] Although attendance again fell off when the Dodgers' record plummeted, 5,000 fans attended what proved to be the final 1905 Sunday game on May 21. Once again, Sabbatarian forces prevailed when Police Commissioner McAdoo prohibited Sunday games where there was an admission charge (including the scorecard ploy), the game was advertised, or it created a neighborhood annoyance.[24]

Blocked, but far from defeated, Ebbets tried a new solution to an old problem early in the 1906 season. By now the financial benefits of Sunday baseball were so obvious that John Foster predicted regular Sunday games would enable the Brooklyn club "to declare a dividend one year after another."[25] The problem, however, was how to charge admission without seeming to do so, and the ever resourceful Ebbets came up with the idea of a "voluntary contribution box."[26] Once again, the first game was scheduled for Easter Sunday, with Deputy Police Commissioner Arthur J. O'Keeffe warning Ebbets that while the police wouldn't stop the game, they would take evidence for presentation to the magistrate.[27] When the time came, however, O'Keeffe claimed he didn't see any violations since the one in ten patrons who failed to drop coins "into the yawning mouth of the boxes," weren't denied admission. Ebbets, in spite of involuntarily granting an estimated ten percent of the crowd free admission, was "delighted" with the day's work.[28]

As a result, Sunday baseball at Washington Park continued into June without police interference, although there were problems with "donations" of counterfeit money and small boys who dropped in pennies and took the best seats.[29] Ebbets found ways to deal with those problems, but there was little he could do when new Police Commissioner Theodore Bingham ruled against the contribution box, claiming it really wasn't voluntary.[30] Ebbets and his attorney, Barney York, met in vain with the police officials, who were adamant about enforcing Bingham's directive. The Brooklyn magnate was understandably "clearly angry" with "Sabbatarians who wanted to regulate the morals of everybody."[31] Resolute to the end, Ebbets tried one last time on June 17, when before a crowd of about 12,000, he and some players were arrested. When the court affirmed the Police Commissioner's edict, Ebbets knew that manipulating the existing laws was a lost cause. New legislation was the only solution, something that would take more than a decade to accomplish.[32]

All of this was in the future when the National Commission blocked the American League's 1904 plan to invade Ebbets' market. Considering how much time Ebbets spent fighting the potential incursion, the Brooklyn magnate was fortunate Ned Hanlon was on hand to put together the 1904 roster. Since 1900 Brooklyn had lost future Hall of Famers Willie Keeler, Joe McGinnity and Joe Kelley, plus other less well-known, but solid players. Shortly after the December 1903 National League owners meetings, another big hole was torn in the Brooklyn lineup, but this time the wound was self-inflicted. To the surprise of most Dodgers fans, the team traded star shortstop Bill Dahlen to the rapidly rising Giants for shortstop Charlie

Babb and pitcher Jack Cronin. Since Cronin had a 31–35 record with five different teams and Babb was a rookie who hit only .248, Brooklyn fans, according to the *Eagle,* were left scratching their heads about the trade, not just once, but also on their "second and third estimate." The paper admitted that the deal seemed "on the surface to be the most asinine in the history of the game," but the writer then backed off, claiming Hanlon was "entitled to the benefit of the doubt," and gave two possible explanations for the seemingly lopsided exchange. While Dahlen was an excellent player, his contributions were somewhat offset by his unwillingness to follow the minimal rules Hanlon set for his players. In addition, the soon-to-be former Brooklyn shortstop refused to accept a cut in his $4,000 salary to a level more "commensurate with the times and the finances of the club."[33] Although no one could have known it at the time, the deal left a gaping hole at shortstop that wasn't adequately filled until the 1940 arrival of Pee Wee Reese.

Any moderately astute Brooklyn fan reading about ownership's efforts to cut Dahlen's salary had to wonder if the club could afford a competitive team, dooming the Dodgers and the fans to the second division. Hanlon quickly denied this, claiming talk of "a cheap team" was so much "hot air," and promised the 1904 club would by no means be "a cheap affair."[34] While the extent of the club's financial resources would be debated for years to come, the Dahlen trade marked the beginning of a total rebuilding of the team's roster. In 1898, Ebbets inherited a roster which wasn't even close to being competitive, but the problem was solved, albeit only temporarily, with the transfer of another team's best players to Brooklyn. With such quick fixes no longer available, the potential sources of new talent were once again limited to acquiring players from other major league clubs and/or the minor leagues, since modern alternatives such as free agency and the amateur draft didn't exist. Building another pennant-winning club under those conditions wasn't going to be quick or easy.

Through 1903, in spite of the gradual gutting of the Brooklyn roster, Ned Hanlon had somehow cobbled together a winning team, but in 1904 his magic either ran out or the cumulative effect of the defections was too much for even a Hall of Fame manager. After playing .500 ball for the first two weeks of the season, the situation deteriorated rapidly in May when a 9–18 record put the club firmly in sixth place. Things got no better in June, and by early July, Ebbets was in Troy, New York, looking over New York State League talent.[35] After a horrible 7–21 July record dropped the club to seventh place, Ebbets was back on the road in August, touring the Southern Association, where he signed three new prospects.[36] While none worked out, Ebbets had found a fruitful source of talent which would provide Brooklyn with future stars like Napoleon Rucker, Jake Daubert and Zack Wheat. In the end, the 1904 Dodgers finished in sixth place, 41 games below .500 and an even 50 games behind their resurgent neighbors from Manhattan.

Reviewing the team's performance in early August, Abe Yager, wrote in *The Sporting News* that with von der Horst ill and Abell "out of it," Ebbets and Hanlon were "practically alone in the management of the club." In Abell's case, being "out of it" meant not putting any more money into the team. Yager, however, claimed that this was less of a problem, since the club was profitable in spite of its poor performance and also had the Baltimore consolidation proceeds. Agreeing with John Foster, Yager argued that if Sunday baseball became legal in Brooklyn, the club would be "on Easy street."[37] Regardless of the state of the treasury, however, Hanlon claimed that the demands of other National League clubs were so outrageous that acquiring major league players was impossible, leaving developing young players as the sole source of new talent.[38] To that end, the club drafted 23 players from minor league clubs and submitted a 1905 reserve list of almost 60 players, which the National Commission accepted only reluctantly.[39] Responding to rumors that the club didn't have or wouldn't spend the money to improve the team, Yager claimed that the payroll was $39,000, an average salary of just over $2,000 per player and, according to another report, well in line with other National League clubs.[40] Whether or not, however, the club had money to acquire new players was less clear.

Little more was said about Brooklyn's 1904 finances, but another club, the Philadelphia Phillies, were in such dire shape, the magnates held a special meeting in October to address the crisis. By then, the Phillies were bankrupt with over $8,000 in debts and only $800 in cash. Included in the debts was about $3,500 in past-due player salaries which the magnates couldn't, and didn't ignore, voting to pay the players from league funds. Follow-up action came in December, when the existing owners were expelled and the franchise was awarded to a group of new investors. It was a reminder that like any other business, the long-term survival of a major league baseball club could not be taken for granted.[41]

By the time the 1904 season ended, Ebbets was trying to win a different kind of race In late September, the Democratic party chose the adopted son of Brooklyn as its State Senate candidate for the Sixth district, encompassing Brooklyn's Eleven and Twelfth Assembly districts.[42] Ebbets' candidacy was endorsed by the *Eagle*, which praised him as being "public spirited," "enterprising," "capable" and "straightforward." The paper also believed Ebbets would do well at the polls since the Democratic Presidential candidate, Judge Alton B. Parker, a member of New York's highest judicial tribunal, was expected to run well in Kings County.[43] Regardless of his other faults, Ebbets was never accused of making a less than wholehearted effort, so it's no surprise that he ran an aggressive campaign to the point where his wife said he hadn't had a meal at home in weeks.[44]

In his more than 20 years in Brooklyn, Ebbets had developed extensive personal relationships which gave him both name recognition and, at election time, votes. In 1904, however, Ebbets wasn't supported by organized labor, or at least a local carpenters' union which complained that he broke his promise to use "a firm regarded as fair by the building trades" to build the Superba lanes.[45] As a final touch to his campaign, Ebbets umpired a baseball game in reportedly frigid conditions at Washington Park, between some Dodgers and a church team from his district. Afterwards he treated both teams to dinner at the restaurant at his bowling alley, assuming, *The Sporting News* said, that the way to get their votes was "through their stomachs."[46] As hard as Ebbets worked, however, it wasn't enough, as he lost by fewer than 1,000 votes. It appears that Ebbets' candidacy was swept away by Theodore Roosevelt's landslide victory, even though Parker ran better in Ebbets' districts than William Jennings Bryan had four years earlier. Ebbets himself ran slightly ahead of Parker, but still lost in what proved to be his final political campaign.[47]

Ebbets' defeat in the November 1904 election might have been for the best, since by the following winter, pressing baseball business awaited him in Brooklyn. On March 1, 1905, the *Eagle* reported a rumor that Ebbets had sold his stock and would retire from baseball, something Ebbets vehemently denied.[48] The rumors may have been caused by the less than stable ownership situation where the two active members, Ebbets and Hanlon, held only about 20 percent of the stock between them, with almost all of the balance owned by von der Horst and the retired Abell. Understandably, the *Eagle* believed change was needed, recommending "some local sporting man" buy out Abell's interest.[49] It was a difficult situation, especially with two strong personalities in Ebbets and Hanlon, both of whom wanted control.

Fearing someone else (read Hanlon) would get control of the club, Ebbets struck first.[50] Perhaps inspired by the *Eagle's* recommendation to buy out Abell, especially by someone of his choosing, Ebbets made the idea a reality, but with a twist. Instead of targeting Abell, who was apparently unwilling to sell, Ebbets arranged for a bowling buddy, Henry

Medicus, to buy a large block of von der Horst's stock, which combined with what Ebbets owned and/or controlled gave the two Brooklyn men 51 percent, just enough for control. An added benefit was that for the first time in the club's history, the majority interest was owned by Brooklyn men, something well received locally.[51] About six years younger than Ebbets, Henry Medicus was the son of Charles Medicus, a highly success-ful furniture manufacturer. Although born in Manhattan, Henry had lived most of his life in Brooklyn and had inherited the business from his father just two years earlier. Reportedly a regular at Washington Park as well as an avid bowler, Medicus was just the kind of "sporting man" referred to by the *Eagle*, who had money to invest but no desire or need for a big say in club affairs.[52] While the sale helped keep Hanlon in his place (not in charge), it probably didn't provide any new money since the funds Medicus invested went directly to von der Horst.

Known for his disciplined, always in-control approach, Hanlon was, for at least once in his life, taken by surprise when von der Horst sold to someone other than himself.[53] And the surprises weren't over for "Foxy Ned," since only a few days later, Ebbets lowered the boom a second time, informing Hanlon of a $6,500 cut in his $12,500 salary. According to Ebbets, the drastic reduction was part of some necessary cost-cutting, and team leadership needed to set the example. Ebbets also claimed he had taken a cut, although that turned out not to be the case.[54] To some extent, the magnitude of the cut was a negotiating ploy, but it sent a clear message that Ebbets intended to use his new power and considered Han-lon far from indispensable. Unfortunately for Hanlon, if he wanted to stay in the major leagues in 1905, he had little choice, since the timing meant no other positions were open. In the end, the two men negotiated on the

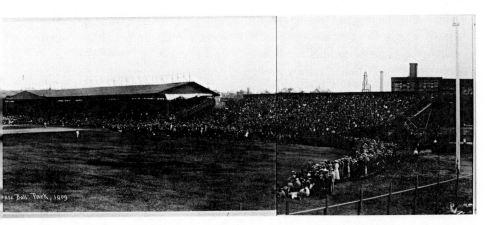

Washington Park, after several upgrades. This 1909 picture gives a sense of the size and scope of Ebbets' first ballpark (courtesy John Thorn).

train carrying the club south for spring training and agreed on something less than $12,500, but "considerably more than" $6,000 for one year.[55]

Even with the growing tension between Ebbets and Hanlon, the men worked together on roster moves, overhauling both the infield and the pitching staff in the process. Pitchers Jack Cronin (acquired for Dahlen), Ned Garvin and Ed Poole, none of whom would ever again grace a major league roster, were replaced by minor league acquisitions Harry McIntire, Elmer Stricklett and Mal Eason (a future major league umpire). But pitching wasn't Brooklyn's major 1904 problem, rather it was an offense with three regulars hitting below .200 on a team that scored only 497 runs, next to last in the league. Dutch Jordan and Mike McCormick, two of the three who hit below .200, weren't asked back, and like the pitchers they were replaced by minor leaguers. As a result, Brooklyn had a 1905 lineup dominated by unproven minor leaguers, hardly the best way to compete with the growing juggernaut in Manhattan, not to mention the improving Cubs and Pirates. About the only saving grace was a legitimate major league outfield, led by Jimmy Sheckard and Harry Lumley.

Since the lineup was at best untested, it's no surprise that Brooklyn was left at the starting gate, losing their first six games en route to a 15–28 mark at the end of May, which was followed by an even more dismal 3–20 performance in June. To no one's surprise, Hanlon had "become sour on his job," unhappy with the alleged unwillingness/inability of Abell and Ebbets "to put up the cash for first class players," complaining that he "has no voice in the club."[56] Whatever basis Hanlon had for his unhappiness, Ebbets insisted the team had "money to give and give it quick for good players."[57] At the same time, however, multiple media accounts reported players' complaints that they had been short-changed in their pay, charges Ebbets strongly denied.[58] Also about this time, reports of Ebbets' cheapness began appearing regularly in the media, a label he would carry beyond the grave. It was, Ebbets said, "the worst season in twenty-three years" (since inception), the first time the club had ever finished last, 56 1/2 games out of first and reportedly losing about $25,000.[59]

Elaborating on his "worst season in twenty-three years" comment a few days later for the *Eagle*, Ebbets tried to deflect the large amount of "unpleasant comment" directed at him as typical for a last-place club.[60] Far less understanding was sportswriter John Foster, who claimed, "at least one hundred of the better known base ball enthusiasts" in Brooklyn threatened to no longer attend Dodgers games "so freely" because management "is taking no initiative" to improve the club. The fans, Foster wrote, wanted "real base ball and not the promise of base ball," which meant Ebbets "can't expect to operate a $20 club to compete with a $100 club in New York."[61] The vast gap in financial resources between the two clubs wasn't about to go away, but whatever Ebbets was going to do to improve the situation, he would have to do it with another manager. Probably to no one's surprise, Hanlon opted to become the Cincinnati manager, blasting Ebbets and Medicus on his way out of town for not seriously trying to re-sign him.[62] Hanlon may no longer have been the Dodgers' manager, but his struggle with Ebbets for control of the Brooklyn club was far from over.

Prior to the creation of the general manager's position, hiring the field manager was one of the owner's most important responsibilities. Since Ned Hanlon came to Brooklyn as part of the Baltimore consolidation, Ebbets hadn't yet been required to make that decision, and it would frustrate him for almost a decade. The first problem was the lack of proven candidates, especially in the National League, where all the pennant-winning managers for the past ten years were either retired or under contract to other clubs. Player-managers were also popular, but Brooklyn didn't have any candidates on its roster, and acquiring someone from another club meant trading one of Brooklyn's few talented players. That left a small pool of candidates with experience, but little or no past success. In the end, Ebbets settled on Patsy Donovan, a good player who had managed three different clubs, but never finished higher than fourth. He was reportedly a good judge of talent, which was confirmed beyond any possible doubt when he later convinced the Red Sox to sign Babe Ruth. At least the hiring was well received, with *Sporting Life* reporting that Brooklyn was being "congratulated on all sides," especially since Donovan had experience in similar "adverse circumstances." Still, the paper noted, good hire or not, the club had to put up the money to improve its roster.[63]

Whether or not Ebbets was able to pay for new talent may have been debatable, but simultaneous with signing Donovan, the Brooklyn owner demonstrated he knew full well the need to upgrade the roster. The one bright spot in the Dodgers 1905 lineup was Jimmy Sheckard, who rebounded from a poor 1904 season to hit .292 in 1905. Even so, the Brooklyn out-fielder's performance couldn't keep the club out of last place, and a player of his caliber would command multiple players in return, just the thing for a team with a lot of holes in its lineup. Resisting the temptation of cash offers from John McGraw and the Giants, Ebbets made a far more productive deal with Chicago, trading Sheckard for two outfielders (Jack McCarthy and Billy Maloney), a third baseman (Doc Casey), and a pitcher ("Buttons" Briggs), plus $2,000 in cash. Although Briggs didn't work out, Ebbets replaced one-third of his lineup, a deal which would look even better when McCarthy actually outhit Sheckard (.304/.262) in 1906. Although the trade was negotiated prior to Donovan's hiring, it had the new skipper's endorsement.[64]

Hiring a manager and making the Sheckard trade were not the only major decisions on Ebbets' mind during this period. Throughout the early years of the decade, Ebbets had careers in baseball, bowling and politics. Ebbets' decision to leave the political arena was effectively made for him by the voters in late 1904. Decisions about his future in bowling were more drawn out. Ebbets continued to attend A.B.C. conventions through 1906, but one final and apparently galling defeat in the 1906 presidential election led to a vow never to attend another convention.[65] Nor was Ebbets finding a lot of satisfaction at the local level, especially with the Eastern Alley Owners Association, an ownership group he headed.[66] Perhaps the A.B.C. defeat was the last straw, since Ebbets resigned from the presidency of the alley owners association in April of 1906 and then sold his interest in the Superba bowling alleys later that year.[67] Although it was reportedly "one of the best paying ventures of its kind," Ebbets wisely decided that no magnate could serve two masters.[68] For better or worse, Ebbets had decided to make baseball his life's work.

CHAPTER VII

"I know we get robbed. I know it."

With his focus solely on baseball, Ebbets had more time for league affairs, and he began making regular recommendations on how to improve the game both on and off the field. Sometimes the proposal took the form of applying one of Ebbets' local innovations throughout the league. One such example was "a new style combination admission ticket and rain check" which Ebbets introduced at Washington Park towards the end of the 1905 season.[1] Previously, if a game was rained out, fans had to wait on line for a rain check, typically handed out by small boys, which was inconvenient with the risk of careless or even dishonest distribution. Ebbets' solution was a ticket to be torn in half upon admission, with the fan keeping the rain check portion just in case.[2] Pleased with his new creation, Ebbets raised the subject at the December 1905 owners meeting and was appointed to a committee to report back at a future meeting.[3]

After discussion of the proposed admission ticket/rain check, the committee felt Ebbets' proposal "perfect in every detail, but one," the possibility that the ticket-tearing process might cause extensive delays at the gate. When the magnates heard the committee's report in February, they understandably preferred to test the new format, which was agreeable to Ebbets, who pledged to give it a "thorough trial" at Washington Park during the 1906 season. The committee also recommended that the league adopt a uniform ticket to combat the problem of fake tickets, but no action was taken on the proposal.[4] Ebbets' handling of the project was consistent with the comprehensive, detailed approach he took on schedule making and other issues. The Brooklyn magnate was back at it in June, proposing that the owners mandate fully equipped dressing rooms for visiting teams and structured practice times before games. Both proposals passed unanimously.[5] It's no wonder Abe Yager predicted that Ebbets "promises to be as big a factor in baseball legislation" as was Charles Byrne.[6]

Working on business issues like the new ticket format didn't distract the Brooklyn owner from the ongoing need to upgrade his team's roster. In addition to the Sheckard trade, Ebbets and Donovan signed first base- man Tim Jordan from Baltimore of the Eastern League. Jordan was effec- tively Ned Hanlon's last gift to Brooklyn, since the former Dodgers skipper had his eye on the big first baseman a year earlier.[7] With Jordan and Lum- ley on the Brooklyn roster, the club had two power hitters, sparking spec- ulation throughout the season that one or both would be sold, rumors Ebbets just as consistently denied.[8] With the addition of Jordan, Ebbets and Donovan had replaced five of the club's eight regulars and added one new pitcher, Jim Pastorius. Even with their rebuilt roster, however, Brook- lyn again got off to a horrible start, losing ten of their first 11 games. After that, however, Donovan's squad improved, playing close to .500 ball the rest of the way, far from a championship pace but a big improvement over 1905. By June, John Foster praised the club's "git up and dust" and pro- claimed them "tail-enders no longer."[9]

The 1906 National League season was somewhat unusual since only three teams finished above .500, with one, the league champion Cubs, winning 116 games, a record which still stands, albeit tied by the 2001 Seattle Mariners in a 162-game schedule. Brush's and McGraw's Giants had the dubious distinction of finishing 40 games above .500, but 20 games out of first place. Although Brooklyn was 50 games off the pace, they came in fifth, edging out Hanlon's Reds, doubtless giving Ebbets a reason to smile. Just a year after what he claimed was his worst season in baseball, Ebbets considered 1906 the "most prosperous [season] in both major leagues" of his almost 25 years in baseball, with some estimates putting Brooklyn's profits at $30,000.[10]

Although the 1906 season gave Ebbets reason for optimism, he should have known better than to predict that one of the most successful eras in Brooklyn club history was about to begin and that the Dodgers would be "a large factor in the next [1907] race."[11] As it turned out, the team's 1907 on-the-field performance would be the least of Ebbets' problems. Back in January of 1906, Joe Vila wrote in *The Sporting News* that when Ned Han- lon grudgingly accepted a $4,000 salary cut in March of 1905, Ebbets actually increased his own salary by the same amount, even though at the time Ebbets claimed he had also taken a salary cut.[12] It appears that Ebbets never denied the story, but later offered the incredibly weak excuse that since he held two positions, president and manager, he was entitled to the higher figure under the club's constitution. This prompted the *Chicago Sunday Tribune* to wonder sarcastically if Patsy Donovan was the club's "bat boy or a water cooler."[13]

If Ebbets thought Hanlon's lack of public reaction to the story meant his former manager wouldn't cause any trouble, Ebbets was not only mistaken, but badly underestimated Hanlon, never a good idea. At the club's November 1906 annual meeting in Jersey City (the Dodgers were still a New Jersey corporation), majority shareholders Ebbets and Medicus, along with Charles Jr. and two other men were elected to the team's board of directors. Hanlon, however, now aligned with Ferdinand Abell, claimed that Medicus and the two Ebbets were not eligible to serve on the board because as the club's officers in 1905, they failed to notify the Secretary of State's office of the election results from that year's annual meeting.[14] Hanlon also had another trick up his sleeve, a lawsuit demanding that Ebbets and Medicus return $16,000 in salary Hanlon claimed had been paid to the two men in violation of the club's constitution. While the prospect of repaying that sum or even part of it was bad enough, the real problem was the allegedly illegal board election. If Ebbets and Medicus couldn't serve as directors, the way was open for Hanlon and Abell to take control of the Dodgers and conceivably move the team to Baltimore.[15] That possibility loomed even larger in December, when Hanlon purchased Orioles Park in Baltimore, supposedly "the first step toward getting that big league club" he and local fans wanted.[16] Ebbets was now faced with litigation which could take a long time to resolve, with the outcome uncertain at best.

Ebbets' new-found focus on baseball also meant a more hands-on role in club operations. Early in 1907, a time of year when Ebbets was usually preparing for the A.B.C. convention, the Brooklyn magnate took a baseball trip west to Ohio and then south to Florida. Included on the itinerary were stops in Harrisburg, Pittsburgh and Atlanta to sign players, attendance at a joint schedule committee meeting in Cincinnati, and evaluating Jacksonville, Florida, as a potential spring training site.[17] The Florida visit was so productive, Ebbets arranged the entire spring trip including hotels, exhibition games and railroad travel. Ebbets' gift for detailed planning would benefit the trip's participants, since only two of the 33 nights would require sleeping on the train.[18] Ebbets' lengthy agenda for his long trip illustrates, again, both the small size of baseball management structures and the club president's very much hands-on responsibilities during the Deadball Era. Ebbets also spent some of the off-season thinking about potential new sources of revenue such as offering fans the chance to pay for the opportunity to accompany the club on the spring trip.[19] Back in Brooklyn by early February, Ebbets didn't slow down, working on the 1907 league schedule and his ticket proposals in anticipation of the February owners meeting. The time was well spent, especially when the magnates accepted the proposal for a uniform ticket.[20] An estimated six to seven million tickets were involved, and the owners gave Ebbets the added responsibility of organizing the printing of the combination ticket/rain check.[21] To top off an incredibly busy off-season, even though at risk of losing control of the club, Ebbets planned to spend $5,000 on upgrades at Washington Park, including complying with his own, now league-mandated requirement for visiting team locker rooms.[22]

As busy as he was, Ebbets couldn't ignore the stockholder war, although at the moment there was little he could do about it. In December of 1906, not long after the contested annual meeting, Hanlon and Abell filed their lawsuits on both the allegedly flawed board elections and the supposed illegal salaries.[23] The two malcontents were far from done, filing a third lawsuit in February 1907 over the $40,000 received for shutting down the Baltimore National League franchise. According to the suit, the funds were lent to the Brooklyn club and never repaid, so Abell and Hanlon wanted full repayment plus a hefty $10,000 in interest. Not surprisingly, Ebbets claimed the action was "sour grapes" on Hanlon's part since both he and Abell were part of the ownership group that transferred the money to the Brooklyn club.[24] The Abell and Hanlon alliance was somewhat surprising and has never been explained; perhaps Abell saw Hanlon as his last chance to get some of his investment back. With all of the issues tied up in the courts, little happened other than Ebbets' claim that the minority owners would, if they could, move the club to Baltimore, something Hanlon denied.[25] Making the delay even more personally painful for Ebbets, a court-imposed injunction restricted his salary to $4,000.[26]

In addition to all of these concerns, Ebbets still had plenty of work to do on the club's roster. Unfortunately, he spent a lot of time negotiating with Tim Jordan, who thought his salary should be doubled to $5,000, but while the final figure was never disclosed, Ebbets refused to give in.[27] Early in 1907, sports writer John Foster identified pitching as a primary Brooklyn need, and Ebbets took a big step towards filling the gap when he signed Napoleon Rucker, reportedly the best left-hander in the Southern Association.[28] Ebbets drafted Rucker on Donovan's recommendation, and it proved to be sage advice since the left-hander would have a distinguished career in Brooklyn, although frequently pitching with little run support.[29] The signing was the first of a series of fruitful acquisitions from the Southern Association, where Ebbets and his scouts found the foundation of the 1916 pennant-winning club. Once Rucker arrived in Brooklyn in 1907, Ebbets, recognizing talent when he saw it, didn't hesitate to pay the left-hander the higher salary promised if he made good, even though

Rucker lost his first three starts.[30] In the end, however, Ebbets and Donovan made few roster changes for 1907, perhaps figuring more experience would lead to improvement on the 1906 record.

Ebbets' optimism was apparently contagious, since Foster noted "a real revival of baseball interest" in Brooklyn. Predictably, the critic of the Baltimore syndication attributed the positive outlook to building "a team which is able to come up, as it were, from the ground," compared to the one "bought at a fancy price and then stuck in the ground to be looked at." Some seven years later, Foster still believed the Baltimore syndicate "a mistaken policy," one the owners went ahead with even though they had supposedly been warned it wasn't a good idea.[31] All the optimism was short-lived, however, when Brooklyn's 1907 start was even worse than the prior year, losing 15 of their first 16. Once again, however, the Dodgers righted the ship and played at an almost .500 pace the rest of the season, coming in fifth for the second straight year. Attendance also stayed strong with close to 23,000 witnessing a July doubleheader with Chicago.[32] Although that crowd was an aberration, the *Sun* estimated that the club generated a second consecutive profit of around $30,000.[33]

While Ebbets was grateful for the profits, he also knew the financial success made the club even more attractive to Hanlon and Abell. Going ahead with the litigation was risky and expensive, so it would be far better to buy out the two men. Equally clear was that the best strategy was to isolate Hanlon by first reaching an agreement with Abell, who was far more likely to have at least some goodwill towards Ebbets. While few details were provided at the time, about five years later, Ebbets claimed Abell sold his interest for $20,000, accepting just $500 in cash and the rest in notes, a truly favorable arrangement for Ebbets.[34] With Abell out of the picture, Hanlon had little choice but to follow suit, reportedly for $10,000. All of the lawsuits were dismissed, freeing up the additional $6,000 in Ebbets' salary, which supposedly helped pay off Hanlon.[35] In a 1912 account of the settlement, Ebbets told the oft-repeated story of the Giants' supposed offer of $30,000 for Jordan and Lumley at about the same time the Brooklyn magnate desperately needed money to buy out Hanlon and Abell. According to Ebbets, he declined the offer against his lawyer's advice.[36] Contemporary newspaper accounts, however, put the proposed Jordan/Lumley transaction in December of 1906, almost a year earlier, suggesting that Ebbets conflated the two events, perhaps because it made a better story.[37] In any event, according to the *Eagle*, in November of 1907, almost a decade after becoming club president, Ebbets now owned 59 percent of the stock and was finally in control.[38]

Earlier in 1907, the *Eagle* published an article in which an unidentified writer asked Ebbets about his primary duties as club president. Speaking with his tongue almost cemented in his cheek, Ebbets claimed his three top responsibilities were limiting free passes, limiting free passes and limiting free passes. After that, the Brooklyn magnate said the rest of his duties were "merely perfunctory" and "give me no trouble whatever."[39] The story is part of the foundation of Ebbets' cheapskate image, but no matter how it sounds a century or so later, the free pass issue was of major importance, not just to Ebbets, but his fellow owners as well. Nor was this the first time the Brooklyn club magnate publicly stated his concerns. During the turmoil of his 1898 inaugural season as club president, Ebbets complained about unjustified demands for passes, pass holders who abused the privilege by giving their passes to others, and the requirement to pay visiting clubs their share of every admission, paid or not.[40]

Ebbets' public comments were probably at least partially a rhetorical shot across the bow of potential pass supplicants, but the Brooklyn owner also didn't hesitate to discuss the issue with his fellow magnates, beginning as early as 1901, when he was still a new club president.[41] By December of 1908, the Brooklyn club was giving out 500–600 passes annually, and

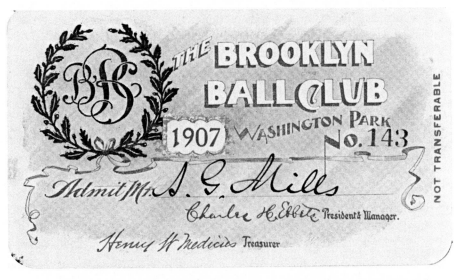

Season pass to Washington Park given to former National League President A. G. Mills for the 1907 season. While Ebbets gladly gave free admission to Mills, the abuse of passes would frustrate the Brooklyn magnate and his fellow owners for years (National Baseball Hall of Fame and Museum, Cooperstown, New York).

Ebbets frankly admitted to his fellow owners that he had lost control of the situation. Not only didn't the pass holders pay admission, Ebbets estimated that 40 percent of them allowed others, who would otherwise have bought tickets, to use their free pass. All told, Ebbets believed the passes cost each club about $5,000 per year between lost paid admissions at home and lower gate receipt sharing on the road. Since the other club owners had similar problems, Ebbets believed the best solution was a league policy which local magnates could use as an excuse for denying free passes.[42] Unfortunately for Ebbets, any possible league solution faced resistance from John Brush and the Giants, who believed it was a local club issue.[43]

Other proposed solutions attempted to limit unauthorized transfers by requiring pass holders to countersign the use of their pass as well the use of coupon books instead of a card, but dissatisfaction over the excessive number of free passes continued unabated.[44] By 1915 the owners' concern shifted to protecting the visiting clubs from undue financial harm.[45] The debate focused on setting a maximum number of free admissions, with the visitors to be paid for admissions above that limit. However, with almost every owner, including Ebbets, arguing that his situation was unique, it was hard to reach agreement even on how to calculate the maximum.[46] Finally in February of 1916, the magnates agreed on the methodology, but set a maximum payment of $500 per year, which would go to the league contingency fund, not the visiting clubs.[47] Although it's doubtful anyone was fully satisfied, the compromise was renewed annually throughout the rest of Ebbets' career.

The time and energy the magnates devoted to the issue demonstrates that it wasn't an example of Ebbets' cheapness, or, at the very least, he was no cheaper than his fellow owners.[48] Looking back so many years later, not just at the issue, but at admission prices of 25 and 50 cents, it seems like the owners spent undue time on a trivial issue. However, they had to look at it not just as losing 25 cents for one free admission, but in terms of multiple admissions which reduced their one major source of revenue. Looked at this way, along with the difficulty in finding a joint solution, it was a very real problem, one the magnates never completely solved. Most, however, would have agreed with Ebbets' 1908 judgment that "I know we get robbed. I know it."[49]

While the 1907 season marked Brooklyn's fifth straight second-division finish, the team's recovery from a poor start, combined with two consecutive years of financial success, gave Ebbets reason for hope. More importantly, Ebbets, for the first time, had control of the club, with only the compliant Henry Medicus as a partner. With the fight for control of the Dodgers behind him, Ebbets' to-do list for 1908 began with important issues related to Washington Park. As part of his whirlwind construction of the park a decade earlier, Ebbets signed a ten-year lease which expired in the spring of 1909. Not at all anxious to repeat the experience of building or finding a new park on short notice, Ebbets negotiated a five-year extension, supposedly accepting a significant rent increase in the process.[50]

Although Ebbets was probably far from overjoyed with the higher rent, he hoped to recapture some of the extra expense from 5,000 new seats at the more profitable 50-cent price, to be added by expanding the pavilion and moving the bleachers to the outfield. The visiting locker room also had to be upgraded to bring Ebbets' own park into full compliance with the higher standards he himself had convinced his fellow magnates to adopt some 18 months earlier.[51] Although initially the cost was estimated at $20,000, by the time the work was done, the total expense was reported to be $33,000.[52] The only negative aspect of the lease renewal was that supposedly "no option was available for 1913," although management claimed they had "no fear of being compelled to move."[53] Surprisingly, neither that statement nor a tantalizing, vague June comment by Ebbets that the club would have "a new home picked out for them ... long before" the 1913 expiration, doesn't seem to have attracted any media attention.[54]

While finalizing the Washington Park plans, Ebbets went to Cincinnati in January for a National League schedule committee meeting in preparation for the February owners meeting.[55] Prior planning was essential since there was plenty of debate about scheduling issues when the magnates gathered in New York City on February 26. The major concern was conflicting dates with the American League, a problem for six of the eight National League owners since only Dreyfuss (Pittsburgh) and Herrmann (Cincinnati) didn't share their market with an American League club. Through the committee's hard work, the number of conflicts had been reduced from 57 in 1903 to just 13 five years later. Ebbets also pushed a change which helped his own club, but was well within the basic principles of fairness he consistently advocated. Previously, the Giants, who no longer needed financial help, played at home on two of the three holidays, with Brooklyn limited to just one. Probably without too much difficulty, Ebbets convinced Herrmann and Dreyfuss, his fellow committee members, to begin rotating the dates on an annual basis. Perhaps not surprisingly, Giants owner John T. Brush objected, this time to no avail, to what appears to be an eminently reasonable proposal.[56] Once the schedule was adopted, Ebbets reported as chair of the uniform ticket committee.

Although a less contentious issue than the schedule, there was plenty of debate since, while the magnates liked the uniform ticket, there were, as usual, differing opinions on the specifics.[57] Another Ebbets idea which, although not discussed, would ultimately prevail was to offer cash rewards to teams finishing second through fourth (to be divided among the players), thereby offering additional financial incentives to teams, especially in one-sided pennant races.[58]

Not long after the owners adjourned, Ebbets told the Brooklyn players gathered for the trip south that manager Patsy Donovan was in charge and "there will be no interference from this office."[59] Since both the 1906 and 1907 Dodgers clubs got off to poor starts, Ebbets and Donovan may have believed the challenge was simply avoiding a bad beginning in 1908. Whether for that or other reasons, the two men made only minor roster changes, acquiring pitcher Irvin "Kaiser" Wilhelm and third baseman Tom Sheehan while giving a 1907 sub, John Hummel, a more prominent role. Standing relatively pat was a decision both men, especially Donovan, would have cause to regret. Although Brooklyn got off to a decent start, it didn't last as a combined May and June record of 16–31 sent the team plummeting to the basement while attendance quickly declined.[60]

Not surprisingly, the media started looking for scapegoats, and the *Eagle* claimed that in spite of Ebbets' promises, Donovan didn't have complete control, so he couldn't get rid of the "dead wood" and acquire new talent.[61] Ebbets, of course, denied this, pointing out that only seven players remained from the 1906 team and claiming that every effort was being made to upgrade the roster.[62] As the 1908 season began, there was a sad note for Ebbets in particular and baseball in general when Henry Chadwick died on April 20, marking the end of an era dating back to the early days of organized baseball. Ebbets had known Chadwick since the Brooklyn magnate's own entrance into the game in 1883 and served as a pall bearer at the legendary sports writer's funeral. Determined to preserve Chadwick's memory, Ebbets led efforts to raise money for a monument at Chadwick's grave in Green-Wood Cemetery and the Chadwick Memorial window at the Church of Our Father in Brooklyn.[63]

It's literally impossible to think of a worse season for fan apathy in Brooklyn, since 1908 was arguably the most epic pennant race in National League history with the Giants, Cubs and Pirates battling to the very end and beyond. Three contending teams meant that over 40 percent of Brooklyn's home games impacted the race, but that apparently wasn't of sufficient interest to entice Dodgers fans to Washington Park. As a member of the league's board of directors, Ebbets played a part in the resolution of the season's most controversial contest, the famous or infamous Merkle game of September 23. When league president Harry Pulliam upheld umpire Hank O'Day's decision that the game ended in a 1–1 tie, both clubs appealed to the league's Board of Directors. The Giants wanted the disputed run to count, giving them the victory and the pennant, while the Cubs wanted the game forfeited to them since the tie hadn't been played off the next day. Serving with Ebbets on the board were Garry Herrmann, new Boston owner George Dovey, outspoken Cubs owner Charlie Murphy, Barney Dreyfuss of Pittsburgh, and league president Pulliam, an ex-officio member.

There was no shortage of conflicts of interest among the board members, since both Murphy and Dreyfuss (Pittsburgh was the third contender) had a vested interest in the board's action. Naturally the two men were disqualified, with Dreyfuss storming out of the room, threatening that "You will be sorry; I am through with the National League." Murphy also wanted Ebbets and Herrmann disqualified because of supposed statements to the media. However, both men denied the charges and were allowed to continue, avoiding the absurdity of Dovey serving as a committee of one.[64] Probably because he was the longest serving of the three remaining owners, Ebbets chaired the hearing, which consisted of multiple player and eyewitness affidavits plus the interrogation of the two umpires, O'Day and Bob Emslie. The three magnates quickly dismissed Chicago's appeal, and after a little discussion decided to support, not so much Pulliam, but the two umpires who had no doubts about their decision. Ebbets claimed that the board's action was the most important taken by a "baseball tribunal" in his 26 years in the game, and their decision was clearly correct. Correct or not, the action earned Ebbets the enmity of Cubs manager Frank Chance, who felt the Brooklyn magnate wanted the Giants to win the pennant.[65]

Brooklyn, meanwhile, staggered to the finish line, finishing a dismal seventh with a pathetic .344 winning percentage. *Sporting Life* termed the Dodgers' performance "the greatest disappointment of the 1908 National League season," which the paper blamed on poor hitting and management's failure to upgrade their roster.[66] A sixth consecutive second-division finish with little basis for future optimism meant someone was going to pay the price, and to no one's surprise, the someone was Donovan, with John Foster speculating that Ebbets wanted a manager who was more of a disciplinarian.[67] Ebbets' sights were set on former Dodgers shortstop Bill Dahlen, now at the end of his playing days with Boston. The Brooklyn owner thought he had negotiated an inexpensive arrangement with Boston owner Dovey for the rights to Dahlen, but by the December 1908 league meetings, nothing had been finalized.[68]

If Ebbets didn't have enough baseball problems, a personal crisis, of his own making, erupted in November of 1908 when multiple newspaper accounts reported Ebbets had been named as the co-respondent in a divorce suit filed by Claude A. Nott against his wife, Grace. Nott, reportedly "one of the most famous hotel men in the country," had been good friends with Ebbets until about a year earlier. Supposedly Ebbets and Grace met at a card party at the Hotel Somerset, managed by Nott in 1903, and the two had been living together on G Street in Flatbush as Mr. and Mrs. Nott. Described as "a handsome woman," Grace was a "familiar figure" at Washington Park during the 1908 season. Not surprisingly, Ebbets offered no public comment, but the story obviously did nothing for his image.[69]

No matter how unhappy Ebbets was about his private problems becoming public, he had to prepare for the December owners meeting in New York City. Ebbets' first concern was the National League's relationship with Western Union. The communications company had equipment in major league parks which transmitted game information to subscribers, including newspapers, taverns and other places where baseball fans gathered. It was a complicated situation since the owners couldn't afford to offend the newspapers, which effectively gave them a lot of free advertising and needed the wire services to cover the sport. However, the magnates were also understandably unhappy about providing information which allowed potential ticket buyers to follow games at no cost. Ebbets believed the owners should collectively negotiate some level of payment from Western Union and, not surprisingly, the Brooklyn magnate was named chair of the previously inactive telegraph committee to do just that.[70]

Ebbets' appointment as chairman of the telegraph committee was in addition to his responsibilities as chair of the schedule and ticket committees, something league president Pulliam acknowledged by saying "I burden Mr. Ebbets with several assignments, but that is because of the good work he does."[71] Given the exchange the two men had earlier in the day, it's surprising they were still on speaking terms. Pulliam, who was breaking down under the strain of the Merkle incident, told the owners he had been informed of a potential scandal, but was unwilling to share the details with the owners. The troubled league president's comments incensed Ebbets, who correctly insisted that he and his fellow magnates had a right to know.[72] Pulliam finally gave in and disclosed an alleged attempt by Dr. Joseph Creamer, supposedly connected with the Giants, to

National League owners meeting, December 1908. Owners of note include Brooklyn minority owner Henry Medicus (back row, second from left), John Heydler, National League secretary and future president (back row, fourth from left), controversial Chicago owner Charles Murphy (front row, second from left), August "Garry" Herrmann, Cincinnati Reds president and head of the National Commission (third from left), Harry C. Pulliam, doomed president of the National league (number 11), Ebbets (second from right, front row) and Barney Dreyfuss, Pittsburgh owner (second row, right) (National Baseball Hall of Fame and Museum, Cooperstown, New York).

bribe the two umpires prior to the October 8 makeup of the Merkle game. Although Pulliam, as league president, typically chaired the owners meetings, he left the room for some reason and Ebbets took over the chair, providing an opportunity to observe how Ebbets handled an issue of even greater significance than the Merkle game appeals.[73]

Wisely, Ebbets first asked each owner to express his feelings about how to proceed and, to their credit, the magnates unanimously agreed that the issue had to be taken seriously. Barney Dreyfuss argued that the umpires' statements about the alleged bribery attempt should be turned over to the local district attorney, but the lack of any corroborating evidence made Ebbets reluctant to do so.[74] Once everyone had been heard, the Brooklyn magnate argued that it was pointless to try to "thrash out the details," so they should consider three issues—appointing a committee to investigate, going to the district attorney, and making a public statement immediately.[75] Ebbets was especially concerned about the need to say something to the press, who knew the owners were meeting in executive session, blanketing the situation in "such a veil of secrecy" that if the magnates didn't "dissolve the mystery," the media would attempt to do it for them.[76] Ebbets handled the discussion in a competent and honorable fashion, clearly concerned about the threat to the game's integrity and anxious to do what was in the best interest of baseball.

In the end, the owners appointed a committee to investigate while seeking legal advice about going to the district attorney. Addressing Ebbets' concerns, the magnates also made a statement to the press. To no one's surprise, probably least of all Ebbets, the Brooklyn magnate found himself a member of an investigatory committee to be chaired by Brush. Since Creamer was supposedly on the Giants' payroll and, if successful, the alleged bribes could have benefited New York, the appointment of the Giants owner as committee chair carried more than a suggestion of conflict of interest. However, the verbatim transcripts of the owners' discussions don't contain even a hint of a cover-up. In carrying out its investigation, the committee found no corroboration of the umpire's claims, so its only action was to ban Creamer from all major league ballparks for life.[77]

Meanwhile, none of Ebbets' other problems had been resolved, or at least not to his satisfaction. Early in January of 1909, Claude Nott was granted a divorce from Grace, with Ebbets identified as the other party and, therefore, a confirmed adulterer.[78] Dodgers fans, however, were likely more concerned about the team's new manager, who hadn't been named because Ebbets' supposed deal with the Boston club had fallen through. Ebbets was incensed with Dovey, who supposedly agreed in the presence of witnesses to accept cash for Bill Dahlen's release, but now insisted on players instead.[79] Although Ebbets was ready to up the ante, when Dovey demanded John Hummel, one of Brooklyn's best players, Ebbets rejected the idea. With few options left, Ebbets elevated 1908 team captain Harry Lumley to the manager's position, reportedly telling Lumley he had the "chance of his life." However, Ebbets also gave his new manager a less than rock-solid endorsement, since he also directed Lumley to make the seventh-place Dodgers "a winner" or he "would have to find someone else."[80] Of the four managers Ebbets hired during his career, only Lumley's selection was questioned at the time the appointment was made. According to the *Evening World*, Donovan was fired for being "too friendly" with the players, making Lumley's hiring odd since he was "far more friendly in the way that got Donovan in trouble." In what was probably one of the shortest honeymoons on record, the paper didn't think the new skipper would last the season.[81]

Although hiring his new manager was difficult and frustrating for Ebbets, it was at least part of his job description. The Brooklyn magnate couldn't have anticipated, however, the fire storm which erupted at a joint National League—American League schedule meeting in Cleveland on January 18–19, 1909. The complex task of schedule making, especially when dealing with Ban Johnson, was difficult enough, but Ebbets and Barney Dreyfuss were confronted with the increasingly bizarre behavior of National League president Harry Pulliam. According to Ebbets, Pulliam spent most of the meeting at the hotel bar, "in no condition" to understand the discussions, and made things worse at dinner that night by telling "Jew stories of a respected member [read Dreyfuss] of this league," something Ebbets understandably felt "a distasteful and discourteous proposition." To make things even more difficult, Pulliam refused to support the schedule approved by the joint meeting, forcing Ebbets and Dreyfuss to try to work things out with him at the league offices in New York. No progress was made in those discussions, with Pulliam eventually ordering the two men to leave what was effectively their office.[82]

Nothing had changed by the February 16 owners meeting in Chicago, which began with debate on the proposed schedule but quickly degenerated to more acrimony between Ebbets and Pulliam (Dreyfuss was absent). Pulliam failed to defend or explain his position, merely complaining that Dreyfuss and Ebbets had been "very insulting" to him. When Ebbets tried to respond, Pulliam beat a hasty retreat behind a column, where the increasingly frustrated Brooklyn magnate couldn't even see him. Order was restored, and the schedule debate resumed with lengthy complaints from St. Louis owner Stanley Robison, prompting Ebbets to say he was "heartily sick of being on the schedule committee" and wishing the complainers would try it for themselves. Notwithstanding Robison's grousing and Pulliam's antics, the schedule was approved unanimously, indicating that Ebbets and Dreyfuss still had the confidence of their peers.[83]

Approval of the schedule apparently got the magnates refocused for a long discussion on funding league expenses which wasn't resolved when they adjourned for the day. Unfortunately, when they reconvened the next day, Pulliam demanded that Ebbets "settle" or apologize for what happened the day before, but the Brooklyn owner responded in kind, threatening to move that Pulliam be fired. Fortunately, Pulliam left the room, enabling the owners to calm Ebbets down and, more importantly, Garry Herrmann to give a detailed and disturbing report on Pulliam's deteriorating mental state which the Reds magnate felt bordered on insanity. Both upset and repentant, Ebbets worried he was only "adding another nail to his [Pulliam's] coffin." Herrmann comforted the troubled Brooklyn owner, telling Ebbets that not only were his comments accurate, but he was glad Ebbets had spoken up, in the hope that it would "have some effect on him [Pulliam]." Ebbets, who only moments earlier refused Pulliam's demand for an apology, now offered one the league president wasn't there to hear, although it probably would have done little good. Nor, ultimately, would the leave of absence the magnates granted Pulliam later in the meeting.[84]

Unable for the moment to do anything further about Pulliam, the owners returned to the seemingly mundane subject of funding league administrative expenses, which was especially important to any clubs with financial problems. At present, each club was assessed 1/8 of the league's expenses, but Reds owner Garry Herrmann proposed charging each club a percentage of the costs, with the top clubs from the prior year paying the highest percentage. If adopted, Brooklyn's share would decline by about $1,500 from $4,650 to $3,150, an apparently small amount, but important in a world where every dollar mattered. Ebbets also liked the American League's system of assessing each team ten percent of its gate receipts and refunding any surplus equally to the eight clubs, a primitive form of revenue sharing. Throughout the debate, the Brooklyn magnate spoke fervently and eloquently of about how the contending clubs needed the second-division teams and should help them financially.[85]

Herrmann's proposal passed unanimously with New York not voting due to John Brush's absence. Although Charles Murphy, the outspoken Chicago president, claimed Brush wasn't present because he was "a very sick man," Ebbets thought the Giants owner's absence was due more to a "certain condition," probably his unabated anger at Pulliam over the Merkle game. Ebbets and Herrmann hoped the 7–0 vote would convince Brush to go along in spite of his reported objection that the proposal penalized a first-place club instead of rewarding its "business sagacity." Hopes were cheap, but no one who knew Brush had any illusions they had heard the last of the issue.[86]

CHAPTER VIII

"We gentlemen are the guardians of this great national game"

Now in his second decade as a baseball executive, Charles Ebbets' increasingly important role in league affairs couldn't hide the fact that his success or failure as an owner would ultimately be judged by his team's record on the playing field. One of the most important ways Ebbets could help the team be successful was by hiring good managers. Since, however, Harry Lumley was no better than Ebbets' second choice as Brooklyn's 1909 manager, it's unlikely anyone expected his hiring to produce immediate improvement. It was a pleasant surprise, therefore, when Brooklyn got off to a decent start, playing just under .500 ball through the end of May. Also gratifying, especially to Ebbets, were large crowds at the first two games, prompting him to promise he would give Brooklyn a park which could "accommodate any large size attendance" although he was not yet "in a position to tell" the location.[1] Any Dodgers fan who curbed his enthusiasm proved to be prudent, since the club came crashing down to earth in June, losing 15 of 16 games on a long road trip.

Watching his 1909 hopes unravel was bad enough, but Ebbets and his peers had other problems on their minds at a special owners meeting in Cincinnati on June 4. There were two important issues on the agenda, Harry Pulliam's return from his leave of absence and the breakdown of the new expense assessment system before it really got started. Under the new system, the 1908 pennant-winning Cubs had to pay the highest percentage of league expenses, with seventh- and eighth-place Brooklyn and Boston paying the lowest. Stopping the new system in its tracks was, predictably, John T. Brush, who thwarted the unanimously approved system (Brush was not present) by simply refusing to pay New York's share. Brush was joined in his opposition by the mercurial Charles Murphy, who changed his mind when he realized that under a revenue based system, the first-place club paid the highest amount even if it was less profitable than the second- or third-place team.[2]

Although Murphy and others expressed opinions, the real debate was between Brush and Ebbets, with the Brooklyn owner claiming the question was of greater importance than the relatively small amount of money involved. Rather, Ebbets insisted, the issue was what was best for the whole league, "not what is best as regards two or three or four of the clubs who may be fortunate enough to be in the first division." The Brooklyn magnate was not, however, wedded to the new system, continuing to prefer the American League's approach of assessing a percentage of gate receipts with any surplus returned equally to the clubs. Brush, however, argued that there was "no reason why the clubs that occupy this position [second division] should be subsidized," insisting that sharing in the gate receipts of road games gave second-division clubs adequate financial resources to improve their teams. Although Ebbets was obviously thinking first of the Dodgers, he also had the best interests of the entire league in mind, claiming, "I hope to God I am the fellow who pays the most." It was a heated debate but in the end, the magnates rescinded their February action and substituted Brush's proposal to assess a percentage of gate receipts (five percent in 1909), with any surplus to be returned in proportion to the amount paid in. The shift from charging each the club the same amount, regardless of its ability to pay, to a percentage of revenue was a partial victory for Ebbets.[3]

During the debate, in one of his embarrassingly effusive moments, Ebbets boldly predicted, "in the next five years, I tell you I will be among the top notchers."[4] Ebbets was doubtless glad the prediction wasn't made public, since Brooklyn finished June with a miserable 5–20 record, firmly ensconcing them once again in seventh place. July didn't see any improvement, but play on the field took a back seat to the tragic end to the sad story of Harry Pulliam, who committed suicide on July 29. Ebbets, for all his disagreements with Pulliam, attended the funeral and afterwards nominated John Heydler, league secretary-treasurer, to serve as president until the end of Pulliam's term in December.[5] Clearly 1909 was going to be the Dodgers' seventh consecutive second-division finish, and with Ebbets the sole constant, John Foster, writing in *Sporting Life*, didn't hesitate to find fault with his handling of the team. Part of the problem, Foster believed, was the club's practice of "clinging" to players "who have shown that they have outlived their usefulness."[6] Admitting Ebbets had spent money for new players, the writer placed the blame on poor talent evaluation, claiming management "doesn't get the right tips" on players.[7] Ebbets himself may have come to the same conclusion, since about that time the Brooklyn magnate first began employing scouts, especially Larry Sutton, who was reportedly "searching the Southern League [sic]."[8]

While it understandably drew little attention at the time, hiring Sutton was a brilliant decision on Ebbets' part and a key factor in turning around Brooklyn's baseball fortunes. Prior to the advent of scouts like Sutton, finding new talent was the responsibility of the manager, who had little time to observe prospects during the season, and/or the owner, who wasn't always a skilled talent evaluator. Even after clubs hired scouts, finding talent was nowhere near as scientific as in modern baseball because scouts could rely only on what they saw and heard, a far cry from the vast array of information available today. By 1910, Ebbets had four talent hunters in place: Sutton, former Brooklyn player Tom Daly, and two others who were "kept under cover for obvious reasons," adding an enticing cloak and dagger aspect to the process.[9] The most likely candidates for scouting positions were former major league players, but Sutton had little playing experience at any level. To Ebbets' credit, he somehow recognized Sutton's potential even though his 33 years in baseball were limited to umpiring and minor league managing. To be successful, a scout needed a free hand, since time and distance made it difficult to function effectively without autonomy. Sutton claimed that Ebbets was "the best man he has ever worked for," with instructions consisting solely of "Do as you please. Go where you please. But get me the players." Sutton didn't lack for imagination, as evidenced by a business card introducing himself as "Just Looking 'Em Over."[10] Time would show beyond any doubt that the Brooklyn scout was effective not just at looking, but at finding.

Whatever his shortcomings, Ebbets was no fool, so when another season went down the drain, he knew decisive action was necessary. Finding better players was the obvious priority, and one potential source was those warming other teams' benches. In late August, trying to open up this possibility, Ebbets threatened to buy up large numbers of minor league prospects unless his fellow magnates reduced the size of major league rosters.[11] Whether it was due to Ebbets' threats or not, in December, the owners cut roster levels to 25 from May 10 to August 20 and 35 the rest of the year, which the *Eagle* claimed put 250 players on the open market.[12] More importantly, Sutton's scouting in the Southern Association paid immediate dividends when Brooklyn acquired future Hall of Famer Zack Wheat and first baseman Jake Daubert from that circuit. Ebbets also wasn't kidding when he had warned Lumley to succeed or else, and the Dodgers skipper was released after just one season. Although names like John Ganzel and Willie Keeler appeared in the media, in the end Ebbets got the manager he had wanted a year earlier, but at no cost.[13] Free of his Boston contract, Bill Dahlen was hired with the traditional commitment that he was to have absolute control of "releases, purchases and trades."[14]

With his new manager in place and doubtless exhausted from another year of contentious league affairs and losing baseball, Ebbets spent most of November recuperating at Hot Springs, Arkansas. Returning for the December owners meetings, Ebbets called a press conference to campaign for a new league president. According to the Brooklyn magnate, he hadn't approved of John Heydler, even as an interim replacement, but went along to test Heydler's ability. Deeply dissatisfied with his handling of appeals of umpires' decisions, Ebbets wanted no part of electing Heydler to a full term and announced his support for John Montgomery Ward.[15] Going public was only part of Ebbets' strategy to replace Heydler, whom he labeled "an accidental president." Ebbets also took it upon himself to serve as a one-man, self-appointed search committee, to find a qualified candidate who could be elected without controversy and acrimony.[16]

Ebbets' search produced five possible candidates he then tested with six of the other seven owners (Brush was out of the country). Only two viable names emerged: James Hart, former Chicago Cubs owner, and Robert Brown of Louisville. Although generally acceptable, there were issues with both men, since Hart would insist on moving the league offices to Chicago and Brown had been out of baseball for 15 years. Ward's name was not on Ebbets' original list, but the former star player and baseball labor activist told the Brooklyn owner he was not only available, but interested. While Ebbets originally thought Ward was unacceptable to Brush, such was not the case, uniting the two magnates just as strongly behind Ward as they had been opposed on other issues. Like politics, baseball ownership made strange bedfellows.[17] Even with Brush's support, however, little was easy in baseball politics. Attempting a pre-emptive strike through the media, American League president Ban Johnson announced that Ward was so unacceptable that the American League would withdraw from the National Commission if he was elected.[18]

Whether or not Johnson's opposition swayed any votes, the first ballot produced a tie between Ward and Brown. Joining Brush and Ebbets in the Ward camp were Charles Murphy of Chicago and new Philadelphia magnate Horace Fogel. Backing Robert Brown were Garry Herrmann of Cincinnati, George Dovey of Boston, Stanley Robison from St. Louis, and Barney Dreyfuss of Pittsburgh. Of Brown's backers, Robison seemed the least enthusiastic, saying he would vote for Ward if he got six other votes. Trying to work toward that end, Murphy and Brush pushed Herrmann and Dreyfuss for an explanation of their opposition to Ward, but the two men refused. One possible explanation was concern over talk, attributed to Ebbets, that if elected, Ward would pick his own secretary-treasurer, putting Heydler out of a job. Ebbets vehemently denied the charge in a long, impassioned speech, arguing that the real issue was finding a president who would stop umpire favoritism.[19]

Interestingly, it was the umpire issue which united Ebbets and Brush, even though Ebbets claimed the Giants were favored by the arbiters, something Brush, unable to forget the Merkle incident, would never accept. Guessing, probably correctly, that some of the opposition to Ward was due to his work as a baseball union organizer, Ebbets defended Ward's part in the Brotherhood War. Courageously, especially considering the audience, Ebbets argued that the owners of that time (which included Brush) hadn't treated the players fairly. Ultimately, however, in spite of Ebbets' and Brush's attempts at persuasion, they couldn't convince their colleagues, and Ward directed Ebbets to withdraw his name. Having perhaps foreseen that this would happen, Brush had another compromise candidate in mind, former umpire Thomas Lynch, who presumably could handle umpires. Sensing some common ground, the magnates elected Lynch unanimously before even asking if he was interested.[20] Fortunately, Lynch quickly accepted, and Ebbets would learn to his cost that there was something more to the league president's job than handling umpires.

Amidst all the controversy of electing a new president, a gala dinner was held to honor Barney Dreyfuss and his champion Pittsburgh Pirates. During the speechmaking, Ebbets was called on to pinch-hit for the absent John Brush and made a remark that followed him for the rest of his life. Apparently speaking more or less off the cuff, the Brooklyn owner proclaimed that baseball "is in its infancy," a statement some claimed provoked gales of laughter and definitely attracted much newspaper comment.[21] Since the Mills Commission had recently "established" that baseball was invented in 1839, the reaction to Ebbets' suggestion that a 70-year-old game was in its "infancy," is understandable. If, however, Ebbets was speaking from the perspective of relatively new innovations such as the American League, the World Series and the beginning of a new generation of ballparks, his comments weren't that unreasonable.

After several days of intense debate, the magnates were more than ready to adjourn. Perhaps possessing more endurance because of his recent vacation, Ebbets used the waning moments to push adoption of a 168-game schedule. Unfortunately for Ebbets, Barney Dreyfuss, the other acknowledged schedule-making expert in the room, didn't think it feasible to play 168 games between mid–April and mid–October. Ebbets temporarily got around the objection with a motion to prepare a 168-game draft schedule, which, as Garry Herrmann reminded everyone, wasn't a commitment to adopt it. The motion was approved with dissenting votes from Pittsburgh and Boston.[22] The proposal's appeal to a majority of owners wasn't surprising, since 14 more games offered very real financial advantages. On the revenue side, extending the schedule added two more weekends plus the Columbus Day holiday, all conducive to good attendance.[23] On the expense side, player salaries were already paid through October 15, so there wouldn't be any added payroll cost. Furthermore, the extra games would be added to existing series so that railroad expenses wouldn't increase, leaving only hotels, meals and some additional game day expenses. Ebbets projected that Brooklyn would realize an additional $7,000–10,000 in gate receipts with minimal offsetting expenses, a healthy addition to the bottom line.[24]

With his usual diligence, Ebbets quickly prepared a 168-game schedule, supposedly devoting Christmas Day to the task.[25] Whether or not he actually worked on the holiday, the Brooklyn magnate certainly didn't procrastinate, sending each owner a draft schedule for comment by early January.[26] Having worked this hard and doubtless sincere in seeking input, Ebbets was understandably upset when Dreyfuss, the ideas leading opponent, gave his initial response to the media, not directly and confidentially to Ebbets.[27] As a result, Ebbets was, unfortunately, not in a receptive mood when he finally received Dreyfuss' three-page letter outlining his objections in detail. Concerned about too many doubleheaders, not enough open dates for makeup games, interference with the World Series, and the lack of consultation with the American League, the Pittsburgh owner remained opposed, but promised he would be "a good soldier" if outvoted.[28]

In his seven-page response,

Thomas Lynch, president of the National League, 1909–1913. Although Ebbets supported Lynch's election as a compromise candidate in 1909, the two men quickly became adversaries (National Baseball Hall of Fame and Museum, Cooperstown, New York).

Ebbets would have been far better advised to focus on the issues, but his temper got the better of his judgment. The Brooklyn magnate blasted Dreyfuss for not being a good committee member and for some "contemptible insinuations" that appeared in the media. To make matters worse, Ebbets also sent copies of his letter to the other National League magnates. It was particularly unfortunate because Ebbets had good answers to Dreyfuss' concerns, especially when he pointed out that only four of the additional 14 games would be crammed into the existing schedule, with the remaining ten games to be played over the extra week. Perhaps Ebbets' most powerful argument was that with the potential financial rewards, the league should try the 168-game schedule as an experiment and, if didn't prove successful, simply return to the 154-game version in 1911.[29]

Dreyfuss' opposition was hardly Ebbets' only challenge, since he also had to convince the equally formidable, and far less cooperative, Ban Johnson at a joint schedule meeting in Pittsburgh in late January. Getting the American League president's consent might have been impossible under any circumstances, but the public airing of the Dreyfuss—Ebbets disagreements meant Johnson was well aware of the divisions within the National League.[30] Johnson wasted no time expressing his opposition, but National League President Lynch convinced his counterpart to discuss both options.[31] This worked out to the senior league's advantage, since if Johnson wanted to avoid the 168-game schedule, he had additional incentive to cooperate on the 154-game version. As a result, the American League agreed to schedule Sunday games in Detroit and reduce conflicts in St. Louis, two major concerns of National League owners.[32] Although Johnson, Ebbets and Dreyfuss left the joint meeting still divided on the 168-game slate, everyone agreed that the 154-game schedule was the best ever.[33]

Even though Ebbets' 168-game schedule was still intact, it needed the approval of at least six other National League owners, which Ebbets probably recognized was unlikely. The debate at the February league meeting was long and bitter, lasting over four days, before the 154-game version was finally adopted unanimously. Although Ebbets went along, he gave full vent to his frustration before agreeing "to sacrifice myself."[34] Ebbets didn't come away totally empty-handed, however, since the approved schedule included games on Columbus Day, another of the Brooklyn magnate's pet projects.[35] Although defeated on the 168-game alternative, Ebbets still believed in the idea, predicting at the end of 1910 that "eventually every major league club will play 168 games."[36] It took over 50 years and expansion, but in the end, he got it just about right.

With league business over for the moment, Ebbets' next priority should have been the upcoming season, but the Brooklyn president first had to deal with rumors about his relationship with Cubs owner Charles Murphy, one of the "contemptible insinuations" Ebbets laid at the feet of Barney Dreyfuss.[37] The sinister suggestion was that Ebbets was somehow "under obligation" to the Chicago owner, prompting media speculation that Murphy or his financial backer, Charles Taft, owned stock in the Brooklyn club.[38] If so, syndicate ball was once again raising its ugly head in Brooklyn, talk Ebbets wanted stopped. To squash such speculation once and for all, Ebbets summoned reporters to his Washington Park offices and displayed all 2,500 of the Brooklyn club's stock certificates. Ebbets' statement confirmed that he was majority owner with 1,400 shares or 56 percent, followed by Medicus at 749 shares (30 percent) with most of the remaining stock owned by Charles Ebbets, Jr. (10 percent or 250 shares).[39]

Finally able to turn his attention to his team, Ebbets told the press he was pleased with the club's new players, and well he should have been.[40] Not only was Zack Wheat back for his first full season, Jake Daubert, the Southern Association's leading hitter in 1909, was the club's new first baseman. Brooklyn also strengthened itself behind the plate, adding Otto Miller, who although not as proficient as Daubert or Wheat, would play 13 seasons in Brooklyn.[41] Unfortunately, there was no immediate payoff from the new talent, and a 4–9 start put the Dodgers in last place at the end of April. Demonstrating little patience, the *Eagle* blamed the poor performance on low player morale due to salaries below those of comparable players on other clubs. Ebbets quickly denied the allegations, challenging the reporter to ask the players themselves, but the results of any follow-up weren't disclosed.[42] Ebbets did acknowledge that the club's payroll of $60,000, while "liberal" for a second-division club, was well short of the $90,000 typically paid by championship teams.[43] The situation improved when the club played around .500 ball in May and June, but summer saw the Dodgers hit the skids with a July–August record of 19–39, dooming Brooklyn to a ninth straight second-division finish. Even after another losing season, Ebbets, and some of the media, believed the roster was the most talented in recent years, and sufficient fans must have agreed since the season was reportedly a "most prosperous" one.[44]

Off the field, Ebbets didn't get off to a good start with new league president Thomas Lynch. In June, Ebbets sold Tom McMillan to Rochester without waiting for the conclusion of the ten-day waiver period, leading to a $500 fine from Lynch.[45] Extremely upset, Ebbets appealed to the league's Board of Directors in December. The Brooklyn owner didn't deny that he had broken the rules, but claimed Lynch had no constitutional authority to fine an owner. Lynch actually agreed with Ebbets about the fine, but said he imposed the penalty to "get some action and stop the practice." Not surprisingly, the board voted unanimously to rescind the $500 penalty.[46] Even so, Ebbets remained dissatisfied with Lynch's performance, and during the discussion of his re-election (with Lynch out of the room), the Brooklyn owner argued, somewhat contrary to his earlier position, that the league president had to do more than supervise umpires. In the end, Ebbets agreed to make Lynch's election unanimous, but helped thwart efforts to approve a multi-year term for Lynch.[47]

Although the 1911 schedule wasn't on the December agenda, the schedule-making process was still very much on the owners' minds. During the long and difficult discussion in February, John Brush proposed that the league presidents prepare the schedule rather than have club owners involved.[48] Now in December, the committee on the constitution brought the idea before the owners for a vote. Ebbets, while acknowledging past complaints of favoritism, argued that the schedule was "the most important proposition we have to deal with" and deserved the expertise of experienced schedule makers like Dreyfuss or himself. During the debate, Ebbets and Dreyfuss publicly reconciled, with Ebbets blaming his actions, to some degree, on "my stubborn disposition." Murphy also opposed the idea and it was defeated. The owners also decided to stick with 154 games in 1911, but Ebbets was successful in getting Columbus Day included on the schedule.[49] Lynch, however, had the final word, appointing Dreyfuss, but not Ebbets, to the schedule committee, angering the Brooklyn owner, who justifiably felt that his exclusion made him the scapegoat for the 1910 squabble. To the contrary, Ebbets claimed he had "at all times, done that which was best for the National League, according to my conscience," and his removal was "a deliberate slap at me, and I thank you for it."[50]

As Ebbets returned home to Brooklyn, he may have already begun to see the advantages of not being on the schedule committee. Relieved of that responsibility and with most of his players signed for 1911, Ebbets had little baseball-related work until the upcoming February owners meeting. Even though he had just been away, Ebbets decided it was time for another vacation, a cruise to Puerto Rico, presumably accompanied by Grace. Before leaving, however, he took a final shot at those trying to fill his large schedule-making shoes, saying he would be "satisfied with nothing short" of a perfect schedule.[51] When Ebbets returned at the end of January, he finalized a change in the club's front office by naming his son,

Charles Jr., his private secretary at a salary Charles Jr. claimed was "about double" his $1,500 municipal salary.[52] It was more than a little indiscreet for young Ebbets to publicly disclose his Dodgers salary to fans who would pay it and players who would remember it during their own salary negotiations. Both men probably hoped the move was a first step in planning for long-term Ebbets family ownership of the Dodgers, but sadly it was not to be.

Two months away from league meetings hadn't changed Ebbets' feelings about Lynch, with the Brooklyn owner criticizing the league president from almost the moment the February 1911 meeting began. After scoring on Lynch for failing to circulate the December meeting minutes, Ebbets used the schedule discussion to remind anyone who needed reminding that being "brutally removed" from the committee was a personal insult he wouldn't soon forget. Nor had Ebbets forgotten or forgiven Lynch for the "illegal" fine imposed in the McMillan affair, and Ebbets led the opposition to a proposed constitutional amendment which would have given the league president authority to fine clubs. Ebbets would have none of it and convinced the other owners to leave that power with the Board of Directors, so only owners could fine owners.[53] Clearly Lynch had made an implacable enemy in Ebbets to the point that the Brooklyn magnate opposed Lynch's re-election in December of 1911 because he "has not proven himself an able and efficient executive," an opinion he didn't hesitate to make public. Ebbets went so far as to nominate Robert Brown of Louisville to take Lynch's place, probably knowing full well that Lynch would be easily re-elected, which is exactly what happened.[54]

Charles Ebbets, Jr. (Library of Congress, Prints and Photographs Division, Bain Collection [LC-USZ62-94102]).

Even if Ebbets thought he was a better schedule maker than Dreyfuss, he couldn't complain about the reduced travel time in the 1911 schedule, which Dreyfuss predicted would save each club, including Brooklyn, $1,000–5,000 on railroad fares.[55] Ebbets' hard feelings may also have been somewhat mollified by the continuation of his practice of alternating the "plum" dates, but he must also have noticed that Dreyfuss hadn't ignored his own self-interest, scheduling the Pirates at home for all four holidays.[56] The fourth holiday was Columbus Day, which was once again on the schedule, if for no other reason because, according to Ebbets, Boston owner George Dovey claimed a Columbus Day doubleheader in Brooklyn had netted the beleaguered Boston franchise more money than "he had seen in a month."[57] Alas for Ebbets, Columbus Day wouldn't appear on the league's schedule again during his lifetime.

In preparing for the 1911 season, Ebbets decided to add an extended exhibition game tour to the standard spring trip, which meant all told the team would travel over 3,000 miles before the season even began, negating some of the reductions in regular season trips.[58] Ebbets and Dahlen continued to overhaul the roster, replacing the entire left side of the infield and one outfield spot, but unfortunately Eddie Zimmerman, Bert Tooley and Bob Coulson would not enjoy the success of Daubert and Wheat. Preparations for Opening Day were more hectic than usual due to emergency grandstand repairs mandated by the building inspector. Ebbets' short temper and sensitivity led to some unfortunate remarks when he blamed an unnamed "enemy" for the whole problem.[59] And his frame of mind didn't improve when at the end of July, the team was once again mired deep in the second division.

Eagle sports editor Abe Yager thought Ebbets was sunk "in the depths of disappointment" over another unsuccessful season (Brooklyn finished seventh). Dahlen was reportedly aggressively seeking trades, but as usual, other clubs wanted Brooklyn's best players such as Daubert and Napoleon Rucker.[60] Further convinced that finding new talent was the only solution, Ebbets joined Sutton on extended scouting trips in May and July, understandably focusing on the already fruitful Southern Association.[61] Brooklyn did sign two more players from that circuit, pitcher Frank Allen and third baseman J. Carlisle Smith. Both would enjoy major league success, although only for a limited time in Brooklyn.[62] The two players cost a combined $8,700, confirming that Ebbets was neither unwilling nor unable to spend money for players. Nor was this the limit of Ebbets' financial outlays for new players, since the club spent over $53,000 over the course of the season on drafted or purchased players.[63] Ebbets cast a wide net, looking for quality in quantity, and the 1911 draft produced results with the addition of future regulars George Cutshaw and the inimitable Casey Stengel.[64]

Another challenge facing Ebbets at the end of the 1911 season was the future of his ballpark, since the Washington Park lease expired in just two years. Even if another renewal was possible, the beginning of a new generation of brick and steel ball parks meant that Ebbets had to decide how his Brooklyn club would compete in the "arms race" to build these far more expensive state-of-the-art facilities. Needless to say there was no lack of speculation, including the depressing rumor that the Dodgers were headed back to East New York. Ebbets confirmed that site had been offered to him, but "asserted with great positiveness that he had not leased it."[65] It's almost impossible to believe Ebbets seriously entertained East New York, but the rumor provided a smoke screen for his real intentions. Sportswriter John Foster encountered Ebbets on the train to Philadelphia for the World Series, but got little out of the Brooklyn magnate other than that a new ball park would eventually happen. Reading between the lines, Foster said Ebbets' "encouraging manner" convinced him "something is doing."[66]

With another disappointing season behind him, Ebbets attended the minor leagues' annual meeting in San Antonio, Texas, something which would become part of his regular routine. Speaking to the assembled owners, Ebbets urged them to adopt sound business practices, especially establishing and honoring salary limits. The issue was significant for the financially fragile minor league teams since some owners regularly violated such agreements or understandings. Never lacking for practical solutions, Ebbets recommended that each owner be required to post a bond to be used if anyone violated the agreement.[67] While Ebbets was hardly a disinterested observer, his decision to attend the minor leagues' annual gathering is another example of his concern about every level of professional baseball.

Back in New York for the December 1911 owners meetings, Ebbets reported on behalf of the telegraph committee, which under his leadership successfully negotiated a $2,000 annual payment from Western Union for each club, up from nothing when Ebbets first got involved.[68] Still not satisfied and unable to get reliable data from his fellow club owners, Ebbets hired a private investigator. Ebbets' agent discovered that baseball scores and related information were key factors in enticing hotels, clubs, etc., to rent tickers from a Western Union subsidiary, which reportedly generated millions of dollars in revenue for the telegraph company. Naturally, little of the money found its way back to the baseball clubs. Ebbets believed the best way to get the maximum payment from Western Union was for the two leagues and the National Commission to approach the company collectively, but, once again and predictably, John Brush negotiated a separate deal for the Giants and Charles Murphy threatened to do the same for the Cubs.[69] Nothing was resolved at the December meeting, but Ebbets' report is further evidence of both his attention to detail and his commitment to improve every club's finances, not just his own.

The telegraph issue wasn't the only time Ebbets sparred with the outspoken Murphy. Apparently prior to the meeting, the Chicago owner made what Ebbets characterized as insulting comments about Ban Johnson, the equally outspoken American League president. Understandably, the Brooklyn owner believed it was in poor taste for a supposed National League leader to insult "the executive of a friendly body." Lecturing Murphy, and for that matter his colleagues, Ebbets argued that they were all "the guardians of this great national game," and Murphy's comments were far beyond the "joking point." Ebbets called for the Chicago magnate to be censured by his fellow owners, and while that didn't happen Ebbets clearly made his point.[70]

Also on the magnates' agenda were proposed changes to the National Agreement, and Ebbets had already sent detailed suggestions to his fellow owners a few weeks earlier. One Ebbets proposal may not have seemed significant at the time, but was ultimately Ebbets' greatest contribution not just to baseball, but all professional sports. Under the 1892 National Agreement, major league clubs were granted the right to choose or draft minor league players at "artificially low prices" in exchange for protection against player raids by major league clubs. Under the draft rules, each major league team submitted the names of the minor league players it wanted, and if more than one team wanted a player, the player was awarded by drawing team names from a hat or its equivalent.[71] The obvious disadvantage was that the best teams had an equal chance of getting the top prospects, limiting the lower-level clubs' opportunities to improve their teams. Ebbets proposed a more equitable system in which each club would be assigned a specific drafting position, and the clubs would draft 1–16 with the 16th club getting the first choice in the second round. At this point, Ebbets' idea wasn't fully developed, since he proposed assigning draft slots by lot, but he would make a final adjustment to his proposal which would eventually be adopted by every professional sport.[72]

Ebbets also strongly supported a proposal of Joseph O'Brien of the Giants requiring that all players released by major league clubs clear waivers in both leagues before they could be sold to a minor league team.

At the time, players who had been purchased were subject to waivers, but drafted players were not. Lynch opposed the idea, arguing for the club owners who might be able to get more than the $1,500 waiver price by selling or trading the player to a minor league team. Opposition from Lynch probably gave Ebbets even more incentive to support the change. The Brooklyn magnate's basic point was that bypassing waivers was unfair to the player, who might be able to stay in the majors presumably at a higher salary. Ebbets claimed that Lynch's position was simply "not fair" to the players, since "one of the objects of organized baseball is to see that the players are advanced in their profession." Once a player made the major leagues, Ebbets argued, the owners "should do all we can to retain him there as long as it is possible to do so." The proposal was approved, a victory for the players supported by an owner who cared about their interests.[73] It was no wonder that after the meetings adjourned, the *Eagle* commented that while the sports writers loved to kid Ebbets, everyone should recognize he was one owner who "studies baseball precisely 365 days per year."[74] Even while fighting for draft reform and players' rights, however, Ebbets' mind was very much on another subject, an historic announcement less than three weeks away.

CHAPTER IX

"A very important piece of news"

Not long after Christmas of 1911, Charles Ebbets invited a select group of men to a January 2 dinner at the Brooklyn Club. Although the Dodgers owner was supposedly as verbose as he was stingy, the reason for the dinner was a secret he had kept very close to his well-tailored vest. Once the news was out, however, Ebbets was counting on his guests to spread the word, and the guest list was designed accordingly. Among those who made their way to 129 Pierrepont Street that winter evening were the sports editors of Brooklyn's four daily newspapers, William Granger of the *Citizen*, Abe Yager of the *Eagle*, Leonard Woostor of the *Times*, and William Rafter of the *Standard Union*. Not losing sight of the wider baseball world, Ebbets also invited Damon Runyon and Grantland Rice, writers with a national audience.[1] Ebbets' choice of the format and the guest list allowed him to maintain confidentiality beforehand while facilitating maximum possible publicity afterwards. And any invitee, reluctant to venture out on a cold January night, was hard-pressed to resist a line on the invitation, printed in red no less, promising "a very important piece of news."[2]

Naturally, the tantalizing mention of important news quickly sparked speculation. Although Tom Rice of the *Eagle* thought the news was most likely "big improvements" at Washington Park, both the *Times* and *Citizen* were certain a new ballpark would be announced.[3] Never one to scrimp at entertaining, Ebbets gave his guests a "bounteous repast" including "solid silver cigarette cases" as souvenirs, but no one needed a memento to remember the occasion.[4] "With the ice cream," Ebbets made the "startling announcement"—Brooklyn was to have a new, state-of-the-art ballpark, news which was "greeted with a storm of applause."[5] Recognizing just how loyal Dodgers fans had been over more than a decade of second-division finishes, Ebbets told his audience, "Brooklyn has supported a losing team better than any city on earth."[6] In return, they were "entitled" to a "grounds and a home that will make them proud."[7] Ebbets also fully understood that the fans "want a pennant winner" and pledged he would "leave nothing undone toward accomplishing that object."[8]

While Ebbets' announcement of a new ballpark wasn't a complete surprise, the location was totally unexpected. William Granger of the *Citizen* called it such a surprise that "not one [guess] was close," a sentiment echoed by the *Standard Union* and the *Times*.[9] Bounded by Montgomery Street, Sullivan Street, Cedar Place and Bedford Avenue, Ebbets claimed the location had many advantages, especially access by public transportation. The new home of the Dodgers was reportedly within easy walking distance of eight street car lines as well as the Brighton Beach Elevated Railroad which, in turn, connected to 38 transfer lines, far more than at Washington Park. Always ready with a colorful metaphor, the *Eagle* said the site was so accessible, "Even a bigamist could ask no more avenues of escape or approach."[10]

Although few financial details were provided, the ballpark's total cost was estimated at between $650,000–$750,000, no small amount, especially with Ebbets' limited financial resources. Construction was to begin shortly, working towards a hoped-for but "doubtful" Opening Day of June 14 (Flag

EBBETS FIELD AS IT WILL APPEAR WHEN COMPLETED

Charles Ebbets' vision of the ballpark that bore his name (*Brooklyn Daily Eagle*, April 6, 1912).

Day), with August 27, the anniversary of the Battle of Brooklyn (Long Island), more likely (Ebbets was positive).[11] Whenever it opened, the park would have a double-deck grandstand of steel and concrete running from the right field corner to just past third base. From there, concrete bleachers would continue all the way to the left field foul line.[12] Although the original plan was to build bleachers in center field for total capacity of 30,000, no stands were built in fair territory, so total seating was closer to 24,000.[13] Although the modern memory of Ebbets Field is the small, intimate park of the 1940s and 1950s, the original layout, other than in right field, was the standard large outfield of the Deadball Era. While in right field, the fence was a mere 301 feet away (similar to Washington Park), the left field fence was a distant 419 feet, with the deepest part of center field a hard to imagine 507 feet.[14] One of the popular stories about the construction of Ebbets Field is that Ebbets and his architect failed to make provision for the media.[15] The reality is something different. While it's true that the original Ebbets Field didn't have a press box, it wasn't because anyone forgot about the newspaper men. Rather, Ebbets provided designated seating for the writers in the upper deck, which must have been more than adequate since when the park opened, the *Eagle* commented that "President Ebbets deserves a world of praise from the newspapermen for his new arrangement of the press box which has now become one of the most convenient in the country."[16]

Acquiring the site was neither cheap nor easy. In telling the story, Ebbets, Bernard J. York, his attorney, and Howard Pyle, a real estate broker, stressed that purchasing the 25–30 parcels had to be done without disclosing the intended use, or the land would have become too expensive.[17] Part of the strategy was the use of a shell corporation, with the innocuous name of Pylon Construction, supposedly chosen at random from the dictionary, as the buyer. Ebbets said site acquisition took over a year, although the Brooklyn owner had been planning the project for twice that long, even better evidence that he could keep a secret.[18] Included in the purchases was the now almost legendary parcel reportedly worth only about $100, for which a clever owner, sensing something was up, demanded and received $2,000. Far more impressive to the media, however, was the acquisition of "the Old Clove road" from the city without alerting speculators, a feat the *Eagle* said proved York was "some sort of wizard."[19] York was a long-time Brooklyn political leader, and his connections plus Ebbets' long involvement in Brooklyn politics seem to have been put to good use.

Pyle told the audience that Ebbets paid cash for the land, but the Brooklyn magnate's subsequent correspondence refutes that notion.[20]

Writing to Garry Herrmann about four months later, Ebbets said the total land acquisition cost was about $200,000, and the sellers took back-purchase money mortgages or notes for about half that amount.[21] In other words, only about 50 percent of the purchase price was paid in cash, with the balance due over a period of time or by a certain date. Since Ebbets used notes to finance much smaller transactions, it's no surprise that he relied on the tactic for a project far greater than anything he had previously undertaken. Ebbets' dependence on the sellers' willingness to take less than full payment at closing was an early sign of just how difficult financing the project would be. Of all the Deadball Era ballparks built on new sites, Ebbets had by far the most difficult time in acquiring the land, primarily because of the number of parcels involved. Most of the other magnates dealt with only one parcel, while the next-most complicated acquisition process was in Philadelphia, where Connie Mack and Ben Shibe had to deal with seven lots and only three owners.[22] And even if the large number of purchases didn't increase the cost, it was time-consuming, which hurt Ebbets in the long run.

With or without Ebbets' knowledge/permission, York recommended that the new ballpark should be called Ebbets Field.[23] The *Brooklyn Daily Times* quickly agreed, opening its account of the dinner by arguing, "Ebbets Field they should call it, and well deserved would be the honor" as "a fitting monument to his skill and tact, and capability."[24] A few days later, a reporter from the paper broached the idea to Ebbets, who, probably somewhat disingenuously, claimed he hadn't thought about the park's name, but believed it could cause "a great deal of worry to me" unless someone else made the decision. It wasn't surprising, therefore, that when the writer suggested letting the four Brooklyn dailies decide, Ebbets jumped on it as a "Good idea."[25] Whether or not that suggestion started the process, the four sports editors "considered the matter from every viewpoint" and unanimously agreed that it was the appropriate way to honor the Brooklyn magnate's "wisdom, enterprise and far-sightedness."[26] All of this may have been contrived to make it easier for Ebbets to do what he wanted to do all along, but it's hard to argue that the honor was inappropriate or undeserved.

While the location was reported to be a complete surprise, none of the writers shared why they were so shocked. One possible explanation was the amount of imagination it took to see the site as a baseball field, much less a state-of-the-art major league ballpark. York alluded to this in noting a large hole in the ground, which he labeled "the subway to China."[27] The metaphor apparently caught the creative imagination of Tom Rice of the *Eagle*, leading him to make his own personal inspection tour, which he all too willingly shared with his readers. First, the *Eagle* writer cautioned anyone contemplating a similar visit to make adequate preparations such as bringing a walking stick and wearing hip boots. His tongue now firmly planted in his cheek, Rice described a trolley ride to Flatbush Avenue followed by a long walk to Sullivan and Montgomery Streets, neither of which looked much like streets, the accompanying signage notwithstanding.

Once at the future home of the Dodgers, Rice sarcastically found the locale "pleasantly diversified" with the "rambling and picturesque homes of squatters" close to and even in "an amateur section of the Grand Canyon." The latter was the "subway to China" mentioned by York, the actual location of the home of a Mrs. Kennedy, so situated, Rice claimed, that at night, one could pass by without seeing it. Rice went on to describe streets which were models "of what a road should not be," leading to walking through mud on the way to "a lot more mud." Having shared these witticisms far longer and in more detail than Ebbets would have preferred, Rice became much more serious, noting darkly and all too prophetically that just grading the site would "require both time and money."[28]

Rice had correctly identified the first of the many challenges Ebbets faced in building the ballpark that would bear his name. The primary reason Washington Park was built so quickly in 1898 was that the land required little preparation, allowing construction to begin almost immediately. Not so with Ebbets Field, where the Bedford Avenue side of the site was as much as 16 feet higher than the Sullivan Street side, not to mention the "Grand Canyon" or "subway to China."[29] Before the field could be laid out and the stands built, the latter no small project by itself, the ground had to be leveled, including the construction of an abutment wall.[30] The site preparation might have been more time-consuming than complicated, but starting it depended on the weather, something neither Ebbets nor anyone else controlled. Although the *Eagle* optimistically claimed there was "good reason to believe that the weather would continue favorable," that was anything but the case.[31] January's and February's newspapers were full of headlines of brutally cold weather which froze tug boats in the East River and stopped oyster fishermen from plying their trade.[32] It was no surprise, therefore, that when the ground was tested in February, it was frozen down to at least 38 inches, sending "a cold chill down the presidential spine," which met another one coming up from his feet.[33] Of Ebbets' peers, only Barney Dreyfuss in Pittsburgh began construction in the winter, but the Pirates owner benefited from more favorable conditions and was able to finish the site work during January and February.[34] In Brooklyn, little or nothing could be done during that same period and the site work didn't begin until early March.

Finally on March 4, 1912, Ebbets, Borough President Alfred Steers and other dignitaries "wended their way through the cow paths and goat trails" to a platform set up for the ceremony. When the Brooklyn magnate turned over a symbolic shovelful of dirt with a "silver spade," some wag in the crowd suggested that Ebbets also "Dig up a couple of new players." It was a "cue for some merriment," but a reminder that a state-of-the-art ballpark didn't guarantee a winning team.[35] The luncheon which followed was the first in a series, typically scheduled to announce new construction contracts, but also a good way for Ebbets to keep his new park in the public eye. Although Ebbets and his architect, Clarence Van Buskirk, had previously visited a number of other parks, the two spent a good part of January on follow-up visits to five cities, including Pittsburgh, Philadelphia and Boston.[36] Ebbets paid so much attention to the details that Charles Jr. later claimed his father designed the park, using Van Buskirk only for the formal architectural drawings.[37]

Paying attention to detail is important, but also limits the number of tasks any one person can do well. Building a state-of-the-art ballpark, especially by a second-division team with limited funds, was a complex undertaking, and Ebbets made serious mistakes which cost him and the franchise in the long run. After another press luncheon, Ebbets told the *Brooklyn Daily Times* there were two ways he could manage the project—either hire a general contractor to coordinate all the construction contracts or serve as the general contractor and administer each contract himself. Ebbets went the latter route, claiming "this to be the better way" since it enabled him to "follow each detail personally."[38] Given his architectural background and his penchant for detail work, Ebbets might have been a good general contractor. Trying, however, to do that job on top of running a baseball club was more than any one person could do well, so something or some things didn't get the necessary attention. To his credit, Ebbets later manfully admitted he had "bitten off more than he could chew," but the admission was too late to prevent problems, especially financing the project.[39]

In early January, the total cost of Ebbets Field was estimated in the $650,000–750,000 range, but as late as May, Ebbets was using a figure closer to $525,000. Even at the lower cost, it was a bad sign that although the site work was well underway and construction about to begin, Ebbets didn't know how he was going to pay for it. Real estate projects are best financed with some combination of equity (the owner's money) and debt (borrowed money). Based on Ebbets' May 12, 1912, letter to Garry Herrmann, the Brooklyn owner had already invested $100,000 of his and/or the club's money in the project, which had paid about half of the land acquisition costs. If the figures in the letter are correct, the Brooklyn owner needed $425,000 to pay the balance due to the property owners and build his ballpark. The preferred approach would have been to take out a $425,000 mortgage loan with a long-term repayment schedule over 25 years or longer. With that commitment in place, Ebbets would have had little trouble arranging a construction loan to be replaced by the long-term mortgage when the construction was completed.

All Ebbets had in place, however, was a $100,000, two-year loan from Mechanics Bank (former Brooklyn stockholder and Ebbets friend George Chauncey was the bank's president). Ebbets proposed to fund the balance with a projected $50,000 profit for the 1912 season (which had just begun) and by selling $275,000 in bonds. Ebbets also told Herrmann that the contractors were committed to finishing by August 27, a little over three months away. Had the ballpark been finished anywhere close to that date, Ebbets would have been faced with a $325,000 bill and no money to pay it. It was a recipe for disaster, a problem with few solutions.[40] In his marriage to Minnie and his affair with Grace, Ebbets made important decisions while either not understanding or caring about their long-term implications. Faced with the most expensive and complicated project of his career, Ebbets seemed equally incapable or unwilling of taking a long-term approach.

Although the amounts of money involved wouldn't have helped Ebbets very much with his new ballpark, his actions at the February 1912 owners meeting were a sign of how much he needed money. During their deliberations, the magnates decided to take 25 percent from the National League champion's World Series share to pay league expenses, which would reduce each club's expenses by about $2,700. Not surprisingly, the idea was vehemently opposed by John Whalen, treasurer of the Giants (Brush was too ill to attend), supposedly because it would lessen a club's incentive to compete for the pennant, but more likely because of the high probability that it was the New York club which would suffer. Equally unsurprisingly, Ebbets favored the idea, because he said, the proposal "is right," but his self-interest was also obvious. Similarly, Ebbets bemoaned the fact that some clubs, especially New York and Chicago, opted out of the collaborative approach to Western Union negotiations, limiting the potential payout to the remaining clubs, especially Brooklyn. The owners

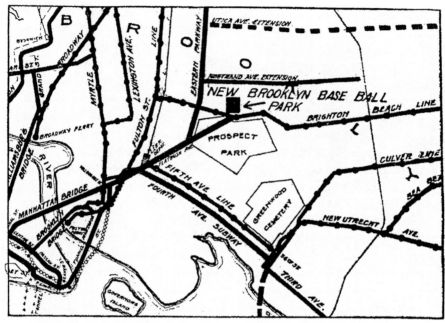

This shows the location of the ball park and the transit lines leading to it.

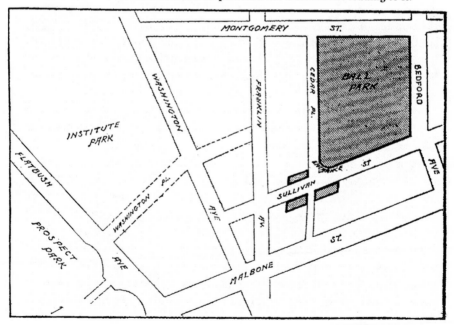

Tinted area shows property in Flatbush bought by the owners of the
Brooklyn baseball club for the erection of a great new ball park.

also approved the 1912 schedule which put Brooklyn in Chicago on August 27, creating a conflict with the second potential opening date of Ebbets Field, although an 1912 opening looked more and more unlikely.[41]

Winter was also the time to finalize the club's 1912 roster, but swamped with ballpark-related work, Ebbets looked up from "a desk full of plans for Ebbets Field" and told an *Eagle* reporter that manager Bill Dahlen had full control and would deservedly get all the accolades or blame. Ebbets did take time to praise his manager for almost completely turning over the roster, with only John Hummel and Napoleon Rucker remaining from Opening Day of 1909.[42] Additions for 1912 included second baseman George Cutshaw and third baseman J. Carlisle Smith, as well as pitcher Frank Allen, all of whom would have productive major league careers. Late in the season, they would be joined by aspiring dentist Casey Stengel, another important cog on the 1916 pennant-winning club. With their revamped roster in place, Brooklyn prepared to host the defending champion Giants in the last Opening Day at Washington Park, which proved to be memorable, but not in a good way.

If proof was required that Brooklyn needed a new ballpark, it was provided beyond any reasonable doubt at the April 11, 1912, opener. Whether because Giants fans couldn't wait for their own home opener or a distracted Ebbets failed to make adequate preparations, Washington Park was overrun by an estimated 50,000 people, more than three times the ballpark's capacity.[43] The gates opened at 12:30, and in no more than an hour, fans spilled from the stands on to the field. When Ebbets closed the gates shortly after 2:00, denying admission to some fans who already had tickets, 3rd Street remained a "solid black mass of fans" stretching all the way to the 5th Avenue "L."[44] Allowing fans to stand on the field was a common practice during the Deadball Era, but they were typically restricted to roped-off sections in foul territory or deep in the outfield. This time, however, the crowd wandered all over the diamond, and neither the "specials," hired by Ebbets, nor official police could force them to move off the playing area.[45] At one point, some Brooklyn players took matters into their own hands, forging a human chain linked by bats, and cleared part of the field.[46] Reluctant to cancel the game, perhaps as much for fear of provoking a riot as having to refund all that money, Ebbets and the umpires bade the game go on under extraordinary ground rules. As might

Opposite: **Map illustrating mass transit connections to Ebbets Field, so convenient, the** *Eagle* **believed, "Even a bigamist could ask no more avenues of escape or approach."** *Brooklyn Daily Eagle,* **January 3, 1912.**

have been expected, the result was less than artistic with the Giants hitting 11 doubles en route to an 18–3 rout of the Dodgers.[47] Speaking for all the sportswriters, who couldn't see without standing up (and then at risk of being pelted with apple cores and other items), the *Sun* labeled the game a "roaring farce," laying the blame on "gross mismanagement provoked by greed for gold."[48]

As unhappy as Ebbets was with the Opening Day disaster at his old ballpark, he faced more pressing issues with his new one. Although the possibility of Ebbets Field hosting any 1912 games seemed wildly optimistic, it wasn't necessary to build the entire ballpark. Finishing just the lower tier would have allowed some games at Ebbets Field that season, and excitement over the new facility would likely have drawn more fans than typically went to Washington Park. To that end, Ebbets made the playing field the first priority, but even that was no small matter. The work began by digging down three feet between the foul lines, over an area extending 145 feet from home plate. Once the dirt and other debris had been removed, 18 inches of stone were to be laid and then covered with nine inches of steamed cinders, "thoroughly wet and rammed." This would be followed by nine inches of top soil, producing, if all went well, a firm and well-drained playing surface.[49]

Before that work could even begin, however, the amateur "Grand Canyon" had to be filled in, which along with the rest of the site preparation wasn't finished until early May.[50] By then, Ebbets was dealing with nine to ten contractors, and it should have been no surprise when the project failed to go smoothly.[51] Problems included the unexpected, such as the discovery that a new sewer was required on Sullivan Street, something not easily or quickly remedied.[52] Fortunately, Borough President Steers was on board and helped facilitate both resolution of the sewer problem and approval of building plans.[53] No one, however, could do anything about the weather, which continued to delay the project. Heat was the problem in July, when truckmen refused to endanger their horses by having them move big loads in the extreme temperatures.[54] That problem might have seemed almost comical, but for Ebbets it was no laughing matter. Even laying the diamond didn't go smoothly as the contractor tried to use some rich black soil which while attractive would "hold water like a sponge." Fortunately, the mistake was discovered before it was too late, but it still cost the project time and money Ebbets didn't have.[55]

It was probably only a matter of time before labor unrest raised its ugly head, and sure enough a group of iron workers walked off the job because although the contract required union wages and union hours, it didn't mandate employment of union workers.[56] Fortunately, the walkout didn't last long, nor did it spread to other trades. At least the labor problems held off until the cornerstone was laid on July 6, on what the *Brooklyn Daily Times* claimed "was undoubtedly the greatest day of his [Ebbets'] life."[57] Once again Borough President Steers spoke, while President William Howard Taft and New York Mayor Gaynor sent congratulatory telegrams.[58] To help create a sense of community ownership of the new ballpark, Ebbets gave Brooklynites the opportunity to be part of the historic moment by signing rolls of paper to be deposited in the cornerstone.[59] Perhaps hoping for divine assistance, Ebbets asked the Rev. James Farrar, a member of an ecumenical clergy group which regularly sat behind third base, to be the keynote speaker.[60] It seems like Ebbets appeared upbeat, but as always appearances can be deceiving. A crisis was looming which threatened both the project and Ebbets' ownership of the Dodgers.

On August 3, less than a month after the groundbreaking, Julius Fleischmann, part-owner of the Reds, wrote to his partner Garry Herrmann, also the head of the National Commission. Fleischmann described a visit a week earlier from Ebbets, seeking money to finish his new ball park. Although Herrmann supposedly had agreed to a $25,000 loan, Ebbets had no success with Barney Dreyfuss or Charles Murphy and was reluctant to approach John Brush. Fleischmann offered the embattled Ebbets no assistance, saying that neither he nor the Reds would advance any money. Confirming the analysis earlier in the chapter, the Reds magnate said Ebbets had foolishly "let his contracts, without arranging the financial end of his business." As a result, Fleischmann believed Ebbets was "in a mighty bad fix regarding his finances and I can't see how he is going to get out of it." But as the Cincinnati owner knew full well, there was a solution, perhaps the only solution. Ebbets would have to give up control of the ball club in exchange for the money he needed so desperately.[61]

With Ebbets literally going door to door, asking, if not begging, for money, it's no wonder word of his financial woes leaked out. On August 19, Ebbets "wearily denied" rumors he would sell out to "Messrs. Weyburn and Livinston, two ambitious souls from Cincinnati," men supposedly "pestered with the baseball bug" and perhaps suggested by Herrmann or Fleischmann as potential investors. Doubtless trying to convince himself as much as anyone else, Ebbets insisted the club's finances "were never in better shape." Prudently, however, the hard-pressed magnate left himself an escape hatch, saying that if money was needed, he "could get an unlimited amount right here in Brooklyn."[62] Ebbets' claim that unlimited funds were available was a boast or wishful thinking, but clearly something was in the works. Only about a week later, the *Eagle* announced that Steve and Ed McKeever, supposedly "old personal, political and baseball friends" of Ebbets, were now his partners. The details of the transaction weren't disclosed, but the *Eagle* reported that while the McKeevers acquired some of Ebbets' stock, he remained in "full control," especially with regard to baseball matters.[63]

In his May 12 letter to Herrmann, Ebbets claimed that Henry Medicus owned 30 percent of the stock and he (Ebbets) held the rest.[64] Medicus had helped Ebbets out of a tight spot by buying out von der Horst, but the Brooklyn man was so much of a minority partner that Ebbets didn't even feel obligated to tell him about the new ballpark until just before the public announcement.[65] It's no surprise, therefore, that Medicus was expendable. Exactly how much the McKeevers paid for their half-interest is unknown, but only the net amount beyond what was needed to buy out Medicus could help Ebbets with his financial problems. The new money couldn't have been enough to finish Ebbets Field, since about a month later, the Guarantee and Trust Company lent the club $200,000.[66] Perhaps the addition of two prominent Brooklyn men as owners helped the club secure the loan. Although Ebbets and the McKeevers were to be equal partners, the *Eagle* claimed that Ebbets was in control of baseball operations and was the primary, if not only, club spokesman at owners meeting. The arrangement seemed to have worked reasonably well until Ebbets and Ed McKeever died almost simultaneously in 1925.[67]

At 58, Steve McKeever was the older of the two brothers, while Ed, only seven months younger than Ebbets, celebrated his 53rd birthday in March. Both McKeevers left school early to work at various jobs before joining forces as general contractors in 1890. Like Ebbets, Steve McKeever had been active in politics, serving on the city council with the Brooklyn magnate before reportedly declining a nomination for the state senate.[68] Ed McKeever's strength was supposedly his ability to reason "directly and mathematically," which served their business interests well when bidding for municipal sewer cleaning contracts.[69] According to a long, detailed 1898 article in the *Eagle*, the McKeevers were low bidders on an $8,000 contract, but ultimately collected $20,000. The McKeevers achieved low bidder status because they quoted an extremely low price for cleaning large pipes when almost all the actual work was done on smaller pipes at a much higher cost. Nor was the maximum contract price of $8,000 a problem since the brothers submitted a series of emergency invoices each just below the maximum allowed per invoice. Questioned by the media, Ed claimed that his company simply had greater knowledge of the work because they laid many of the pipes in the first place, and he couldn't "be blamed for taking advantage of what I know."[70] Nothing seems to have come of the paper's extensive investigative reporting. Steve McKeever was also familiar with the seamier side of municipal life, since in 1894 the *Eagle* reported that he had made a "surreptitious connection" of pipes between the Citizens' Electric Illuminating Company's boilers and the city water supply, allegedly giving the utility $25,000–30,000 worth of free water for more than five years.[71] While the two men had no experience running a baseball team, they certainly knew their way around Brooklyn and seemed well prepared to deal with baseball magnates.

Simultaneous with the *Eagle*'s announcement of Ebbets' new partners, the paper reported that the hoped-for September 5 opening wasn't going to happen due to the labor issues and delays in receiving materials.[72] A few weeks later, Ebbets confirmed the obvious: the park wouldn't open until 1913, and construction continued well into October.[73] While it was no comfort to the Brooklyn president, all of the issues with ownership and the ball park were a distraction from the team's continued subpar performance. After climbing to sixth place in June, by July the Dodgers were back in seventh, finishing 46 games behind the Giants. Rumors were heard in August about Dahlen's future, but Ebbets announced that the manager would be back in 1913 for what was likely to be his last chance.[74] Another 1912 development was Ebbets' and the McKeevers's late-season decision to buy a controlling interest in the Newark minor league club.[75] The investment was the last thing the three men needed, and it produced few, if any, benefits.

As 1912 drew to a close, Ebbets headed to the National League owners meeting, where he had the opportunity to introduce his new partners and show off his new ball park.[76] When it came to the annual election of the league president, Ebbets' low opinion of Tom Lynch hadn't changed, but recognizing the inevitable, he made the election unanimous. Far more important, however, was Ebbets' speech again advocating radical change in the minor league draft. The Brooklyn magnate still wanted draft slots assigned by club, but now proposed that the two last-place clubs be given the first choice within their respective leagues. Quite simply, Ebbets said, "The weakest club would come first in getting the men it wanted."[77] Here was Ebbets' greatest contribution to professional sports. At the time, the draft was limited to a relatively small number of minor league players, but it would expand to include amateurs and become an important part of every professional sport as a means not just to choose players, but also to maintain competitive balance. Ebbets may not have originated the idea of using the draft to help lower-level teams, but he never stopped fighting for it and, although it didn't happen quickly, he would ultimately prevail.

Most likely, Tom Rice of the *Eagle* attended the magnates' tour of Ebbets Field, which may have prompted him to push for a special Opening Day for Brooklyn's new ballpark. Under the standard schedule rotation, Brooklyn would open the 1913 season in Philadelphia while Boston would play at the Polo Grounds. Rice's first choice was a truly gala opening with the two-time defending league champion Giants, the day before New York hosted Boston. Recognizing, however, that Braves ownership might legitimately object to any diminished financial returns from Opening Day at the Polo Grounds, the writer suggested bringing in the Phillies for a one-game series again a day earlier.[78] Ebbets doubtless liked the idea and may even have suggested it to Rice, but having fought so hard for the "present rigid rotation in dates," Ebbets was reluctant to ask for special favors. Harry Hempstead of the Giants (Brush's son-in-law, in charge after the Giants magnate's death in November) was agreeable if the schedule could be arranged, although the alternative date with the Phillies seemed more likely to win the other magnates' approval.[79] Ebbets probably wasn't sur-

Ebbets Field shortly before its April 1913 opening (Library of Congress, Prints and Photographs [LC-DIG-ggbain-11612]).

prised to learn that Lynch opposed the idea, and he dismissed Lynch's opinion because he wasn't an owner and it was none of his business.[80]

While Ebbets' comment wasn't very diplomatic, he was correct. The decision rested with the magnates, and the matter came to a head at the February owners meeting. By that point, however, Ebbets had upped the ante considerably by scheduling two exhibition games with the New York American League club before Opening Day. Not only would the two exhibition contests generate additional revenue, they gave Ebbets a hedge against possible bad weather at a special opener. There was a limit, however, to Harry Hempstead's largesse, and when the magnates gathered on February 13, the Giants executive argued that the special opener on top of the weekend games was unfair. In response, Ebbets stressed how unusual it was for a seventh-place club to take on a project of this magnitude and, more importantly, reminded them that the new ballpark would make future visits to Brooklyn far more profitable for their clubs. In exchange, Brooklyn wanted a one-time accommodation, and his argument was persuasive since his fellow magnates agreed without a dissenting vote.[81]

By January of 1913, Ebbets had worked almost incessantly for an entire year on his new ballpark. Foolishly, the already overburdened magnate added to his workload by agreeing to write a multi-part history of baseball in Brooklyn (edited by Tom Rice) for the *Eagle*. The first installment appeared on January 8, and the series ran through March 11, which took the story only as far as 1899. The project was suspended and never resumed because Ebbets' health finally broke and, under doctor's orders, he took a cruise to New Orleans in mid–March. Although still concerned about finishing the park, Ebbets gave in when told that without some rest, he would be too sick to attend the opener.[82] The Brooklyn magnate's reluctance was understandable since Ebbets Field was still not finished, with the *Eagle* reporting a few days later that the rotunda floor had yet to be tiled, and various paving projects were also incomplete.[83] However unwillingly, Ebbets left everything in the hands of the McKeevers and Charles Jr. and when he returned, Brooklyn's new ballpark was ready for its gala opening.

About nine months earlier, the *Brooklyn Daily Times* had claimed that the laying of the Ebbets Field cornerstone was the greatest day of Ebbets' life, but that occasion must have paled in comparison with his feelings on the morning of April 5, 1913. Although the weather was a concern after some overnight rain, the historic day turned out to be "one of the nicest little spring days the oldest inhabitants of Flatbush could remember."[84] Not only would the new ballpark be put to the test, so would the capacity of mass transit to provide the promised convenient access. The latter challenge was more than adequately met when reportedly 10,000 people crossed the East River on the subway, albeit "bruised, and bumped on the cars to a fare-ye-well." Also tested was Brooklyn mass transit, as the Fulton Street and Brighton Beach lines "fairly groaned with the crowds" while trolleys were not neglected, carrying "their share of eager fans." Even with the convenience of subways and trolleys, a large number came by car, supposedly the "most elaborate motor display ever seen on this side of the river," to the point that some more sheltered Flatbush residents believed "there ain't that many machines [cars] made."[85]

Regardless of how they got to Ebbets' new ballpark, the "hurrying, chatty and happy" throng reached "the gates which open into the handsome lobby of the stadium." Although Saturday was typically a work day for most people, "the business of the city was summarily set aside shortly after noon" in honor of the occasion. By the time the gates opened, thousands were waiting to plunk down their hard-earned quarters not so much to watch a practice game, but to see the new ballpark. Perhaps mindful of the disaster at Washington Park a year earlier, about 150 police were on hand, but there were few problems until the gates opened. At that point, the ticket booths in the rotunda became a bottleneck, but the police solved the problem, at least temporarily, by opening and closing the gates to admit the crowd gradually. Once past the turnstiles, which functioned "like sluice gates of a dam," the crowd experienced the practical benefits of ramps over stairs on the way to their first glimpse of the field. Anticipating the thousands who would never forget their initial view of Ebbets Field, the pioneering fans gave "hearty shouts of approval" as they took their "first sweeping glance of Ebbets['] great new plant" and quickly proclaimed it "a wonder, and no mistake."[86]

Perhaps Ebbets' only disappointment was that although 24,000–30,000 fans were inside the park, another 5,000–10,000 were left outside, still holding money they would gladly have paid to get in. There were, however, some alternatives, including high ground supposedly once the site of "the famous Crow Hill Penitentiary," where some got a partial view for free. Even more frustrating for Ebbets were the budding entrepreneurs who built a temporary stand where an estimated "300 or more" paid to risk "breaking their necks to get a peek at the players from a distance of two city blocks." Any possible vantage point, even if offering only a partial view, be it "houses, barns, trees and telegraph poles," was "black with people [while] the few trees bent under the loads of boys and men."[87]

Left to right: Ed McKeever, Charles Ebbets and Ebbets' daughter Genevieve. Ebbets' youngest child is about to throw out the first pitch at the April 5, 1913, opening of Ebbets Field (Steve Steinberg Collection).

Game time was set for 3:00, but it was past that time when Ebbets, formally attired in a frock coat and bowler hat, walked to the flagpole with Jenny and Ed McKeever, followed by the Dodgers players. Resplendent in a "stunning coat of green" with matching green hat and white skirt, Jenny McKeever had the honor of raising the American flag, which was briefly delayed because the flag was left behind in the club's offices. The flag raising was accompanied by Shannon's Band, which played "The Star-Spangled Banner" while "Old Glory stretched full length in the Flatbush breezes." Sharing the honors with Mrs. McKeever was Ebbets' youngest daughter, Genevieve, who threw out the first pitch from beneath a "wide black hat with ostrich plume."[88] By then it was 3:30, but the clubs made up for the delay with a quick, low-scoring game. Brooklyn took a 2–0 lead into the ninth inning on inside the park home runs by Daubert and Stengel, but a throwing error by pitcher Frank Allen let the New York club tie the game in the ninth, setting the stage for a dramatic ending. With an appropriate sense of timing, the Dodgers did just that when J. Carlisle Smith drove in Zack Wheat with the winning run.[89]

The sudden ending generated "no little commotion" when fans realized they didn't know how to exit the park, but the special police and firemen quickly came to their aid. While Brooklyn and New York fans had different reactions to the outcome, there was unanimity that "Ebbets Field is the realization of a dream, something almost too good to be hoped for." Although Ebbets doubtless appreciated the compliments, the $20,000 in estimated gate receipts for an exhibition game warmed his heart beyond all measure as he remembered the small crowds and lean times at Washington Park. Proudly, the Brooklyn magnate proclaimed that Ebbets Field was "built for Brooklynites, by Brooklynites: is essentially a Brooklyn institution."[90]

Ebbets' foresight in hedging against bad weather for the special opener proved prudent when the temperature dropped to 37 degrees for the April 9 game with Philadelphia, understandably limiting the crowd to about 10,000. Mercifully, Ebbets kept the opening ceremonies "short and simple," with Borough President Steers throwing out the first pitch, and the teams hustled through the game in only one hour and 33 minutes. Although there was ample sunshine, the "chilly raw winds" kept many people standing, stamping their feet and clapping their hands in a vain effort to stay warm. Unfortunately for Nap Rucker, the change of venue didn't change his hard luck when the Brooklyn ace suffered another tough loss, 1–0 on an unearned run. Praise for the ballpark, however, continued unabated, with the *Philadelphia Inquirer* lauding the "awe inspiring grandstand" in "an athletic enclosure second to none."[91]

Even with two celebratory dates in the books, Ebbets wasn't about to miss the opportunity to boost attendance with other special occasions of his own design, beginning with the "regular opening day" on April 18. Also featured were the May 10 observation of Ebbets' 30 years in baseball, "Ballpark Dedication Day" on July 15 and "Battle of Long Island Day," only a year late, on August 30.[92] The May celebration may not have been solely Ebbets' idea, since the Brooklyn magnate's friends and associates honored him with a testimonial dinner that night.[93] Priced at $2 with informal dress to encourage maximum participation, the sponsors hoped for 1,000 attendees at the new Hotel Shelburne in Brighton Beach.[94] The date was literally the 30th anniversary of Ebbets' first day in baseball, reportedly the "longest term of service" with one club.[95] The organizers' hopes were more than realized by a crowd of over 1,000, "shouting loud approval every time the name of Ebbets was mentioned." So large was the turnout, which included players from the Dodgers, Reds, Cubs, and Giants, some had to sit on piazzas, dubbed "the bleachers." Ebbets was presented with a diamond pin in the shape of a baseball diamond by Steers, who spoke as did a number of other friends and dignitaries. Modestly, Ebbets claimed the new park was created by "many brains" and told his fellow Brooklynites, "Through my entire career I have believed that if I did what was right and endeavored to deliver the goods the Brooklyn public would stick to me."[96]

No new ballpark could open without encountering problems, and such was the case on April 26 when the *Eagle* reported "Fans, in near riot, mob Ebbets Field." A huge crowd tried to attend a Brooklyn-Giants game, but multiple problems left 10,000 fans outside. The biggest difficulties were the limited number of entrances and ticket lines blocking the entrance of fans who already had tickets. Shortly thereafter, Ebbets remedied the situation by adding four new entrances plus an exit in center field.[97] While these steps were necessary, as the season went on Ebbets didn't have to worry about big crowds, since the team's performance deteriorated as the season progressed. Perhaps caught up in the excitement of the new ballpark, the Dodgers were in third place at the end of June, seven games over .500. July, however, saw the bottom drop out once again as an 8–20 record sent the club plummeting into the second division, ultimately finishing sixth, 34½ games behind first place New York.

Dahlen paid the price, with Yager noting in *Sporting Life* that having put together an improved roster, the Brooklyn manager showed he didn't "know what to do with it when he had it."[98] Ebbets fired Dahlen in November amidst rumors of a playing manager, possibly first baseman Jake Daubert.[99] Ebbets instead went in a different direction, bringing in Wilbert Robinson, the last manager he would ever hire.[100] Robinson quickly and correctly identified pitching as a major priority and said, "Shortstop is our weakest point," a gaping hole the new skipper hoped to fill by making "a deal for some good, seasoned player."[101] Although the 1913 season saw little success on the field, a state-of-the-art ballpark along with a new manager suggested things might be looking up for the Dodgers. Unfortunately, however, more hard times lay head for both Ebbets and his Brooklyn ball club.

CHAPTER X

"An outside organization antagonistic to us coming into Brooklyn"

With his ballpark finally finished and a new manager in place, Ebbets turned his attention to the December 1913 National League owner's meetings at the Waldorf Astoria in New York City. Ebbets' first priority was replacing league president Thomas Lynch, who consistently opposed the Brooklyn magnate, including what seems like spite-driven opposition to the "special" Opening Day at Ebbets Field. Fortunately, other magnates also wanted Lynch out, especially Phillies owner William Baker who, more importantly, had a viable candidate, John Tener, Governor of Pennsylvania. Unable to succeed himself as governor, Tener not only had executive experience, but played major league baseball in the late 1880s. Better still, Tener was not just electable, he was very interested, if he could be chosen without the divisiveness of past elections. Equally anxious to avoid repeating that experience, the owners elected Tener without incident. Since the new president couldn't take the position full-time until he left the governor's office, secretary John Heydler would oversee league affairs in 1914.[1]

Ebbets' second priority was the previously mentioned radical reform of the minor league draft. Under the current system, teams in need of a shortstop (like Brooklyn) had to submit the names of multiple shortstops, hoping a random drawing of team names (as opposed to players' names) would give them at least one of their choices. This led to the submission of excessive draft lists of 30–40 players, plus secret agreements that a team would draft players it didn't need or want and then sell or trade them to the club that did. Far more important, however, than a more efficient system was what Ebbets rightly called "the great good" of giving teams at the bottom of the standings the opportunity "to strengthen their respective clubs and thus in a broader manner, strengthen their leagues."

Pirates owner Barney Dreyfuss agreed that the current system was broken and suggested that Ebbets submit his plan in writing for consideration by both leagues in February. The only negative voice was Garry Herrmann, who predicted that clubs might try to finish lower in the standings to get a better draft position or, as Charles Murphy suggested, would be accused of doing so, even if it wasn't true. Herrmann also believed the larger number of players available under the current system gave second-division teams a better chance to upgrade their rosters than Ebbets' more quality-focused approach.[2] The magnates deferred the issue until February, but Ebbets got further support from *Sporting Life*, which argued that Ebbets' plan was "infinitely superior to the present lottery system" and should be tried.[3]

Unfortunately, for unexplained reasons, the owners failed to discuss the subject in February, but support continued to build with the *Eagle* reporting that American League owners Robert Hedges of St. Louis and Connie Mack of Philadelphia supported Ebbets' proposal.[4] Even with the growing support, draft reform didn't come before the owners for another two years, probably because the Federal League war took priority. In February 1916, however, with baseball peace finally restored, Ebbets again pushed his plan, which the National League magnates adopted unanimously over the objections of John B. Foster. The former sportswriter, now Giants club secretary, considered it unfair to the players who, he believed, were entitled to have a chance to go to a good team. National League approval sent the proposal to the American League and the National Commission (which administered the draft) for their consideration.[5]

The American League owners approved Ebbets' plan, but for undisclosed reasons, it wasn't accepted by the National Commission, although Fred Lieb's claim that Ban Johnson opposed it is probably the best explanation.[6] After 1916, Ebbets' proposal seldom appeared on the National Commission's agenda and wasn't approved when it did.[7] Attention to draft reform was likely diverted by the United States' entry into World War I. The draft then became a moot point when the minor leagues opted out of that portion of the National Agreement in January of 1919, and full minor league participation in the draft wasn't restored until 1931, six years after Ebbets' death.[8] Ebbets did, however, have the satisfaction of seeing his ideas gradually go into effect during the early 1920s, when some minor leagues resumed participation in the draft.[9] Far beyond his sight, however, Ebbets' basic idea became a fundamental part of all professional sports.

In December of 1913, however, Ebbets had no idea his draft reform proposal would take so long to be approved. When the owners meeting adjourned, Ebbets had good reason to be pleased, not just with the progress of his pet reform, but also because he had with one stroke filled the biggest hole in his club's lineup, or so he thought. When he was hired as Brooklyn manager, Wilbert Robinson said he hoped to solve the short-stop problem by acquiring a veteran. Little did the new skipper realize that a candidate would become available who could turn a glaring weakness into a strength. Pleased with a fourth-place finish in 1912 and hoping for better things in 1913, Cincinnati Reds club president Garry Herrmann had hired future Hall of Fame shortstop Joe Tinker as his player-manager, reportedly for a $10,000 salary. Although the hiring seemed to make a lot of sense, the Reds played poorly under Tinker, with the latter grousing to the media about a lack of control. When the club finished seventh, Herrmann didn't hesitate to cut his losses, notifying Tinker he wouldn't be back, prompting the disgruntled shortstop to insist that he would play only in Pittsburgh or Chicago. In spite of Tinker's statement, prior to the owners meeting, Herrmann and Ebbets discussed a possible deal, with the Brooklyn magnate reportedly offering $25,000 to Herrmann, who wanted players as well as money.[10] No agreement was reached, and it appeared the deal was dead.

Dead, that is, as long as at least one of the parties remained rational. During a break in the owners meetings, Herrmann was apparently feeling pleased with himself after acquiring shortstop Buck Herzog from the Giants, a sense of self-satisfaction most likely fueled at the hotel bar. Herrmann's ebullient mood, along with the presence of the media, made for a highly combustible atmosphere. Whether someone else threw a match or Herrmann ignited the conflagration himself, the Cincinnati magnate began mocking the absent Ebbets' sincerity. Throwing caution to the winds, Herrmann claimed that Ebbets' offer for Tinker was nothing more than a bluff, intended to get the Brooklyn club "some free advertising."

Knowing a big story when he saw one, a sportswriter found Ebbets and told the Brooklyn owner about Herrmann's comments, including the latter's challenge to make the deal right then and there. Predictably and understandably, Ebbets was filled with righteous indignation, his ire also perhaps fueled by a drink or two. Joining the group which was probably growing by the moment, Ebbets suggested discussing the transaction in private, but Herrmann challenged Ebbets, saying, "Let's make this deal in public." The Reds owner continued to badger Ebbets, who wasn't about to back down to a public challenge to his integrity, especially when he both wanted and needed Tinker. They agreed on a $25,000 purchase price, with $10,000 to go to Tinker, the whole deal contingent on the star shortstop signing a Brooklyn contract. At the urging of Barney Dreyfuss, the agreement was reduced to writing, and Ebbets had solved his shortstop problem, or so it seemed.[11]

The "baseball men" in the group reportedly "swarmed about Ebbets and warmly congratulated him" on a "great deal," supposedly the "biggest deal, financially, ever recorded in the history of the game."[12] The positive reaction was understandable since Ebbets not only acquired one of the game's best players, he did so without giving up any players in return. Regardless of how Ebbets and Herrmann felt at the time, however, it's probable both of them had second thoughts the next morning, especially Herrmann. Supposedly while Herrmann was brow-beating Ebbets, Harry Stephens, the Reds' secretary and representative of the Fleischmann interests in the club, tried at least to delay the deal. Stephens knew his bosses well, since a few days later the *Eagle* reported that Herrmann's partners were balking because they wanted players as well as cash for someone of Tinker's caliber.[13]

While Ebbets probably wasn't troubled with remorse about acquiring a .317 hitter who led the league's shortstops in fielding, the Brooklyn owner still had to sign the reluctant Tinker. Two days later, Ebbets wrote to his new shortstop, expressing pleasure at the written report that Tinker "would be pleased to come to Brooklyn," which sounds like more than a little wishful thinking on Ebbets' part. Making sure to remind Tinker that the $10,000 was the "largest bonus ever paid to a ball player," Ebbets suggested meeting in Indianapolis on either December 20 or 21 to sign a contract, even though "there was no killing hurry."[14] Ebbets' missive apparently crossed in the mail with a telegram from Tinker, who was apparently displeased at not hearing directly from Herrmann or Ebbets. Not sounding at all anxious to play in Brooklyn, the disgruntled shortstop challenged Ebbets to "send me your highest terms for three years."[15]

Ebbets' willingness to travel to the Midwest a few days before Christmas shows that the Brooklyn owner understood full well that the deal was far from done. Ebbets planned to go to Indianapolis after stopping in Cincinnati to deliver the $15,000 purchase price to the Reds owners and, if necessary, assuage any lingering doubts on Cincinnati's part.[16] Ebbets didn't make the trip, however, which Tinker apparently learned not from Ebbets, but through the media, something unlikely to make him any more willing to join the Dodgers. On December 21, however, according to Tinker, Wilbert Robinson told him by phone that Ebbets was "sore" about the "highest terms" telegram, and his mind was made up about Tinker's salary. Robinson asked for Tinker's "ideas," which prompted a demand of not less than $7,500 per year. In response, the Brooklyn manager said he wanted Tinker to get the maximum he could, but Ebbets wasn't likely to change his mind.[17] The Brooklyn magnate later told his fellow owners that he decided not to go to Indianapolis, thinking it better to "just let Mr. Tinker rest awhile."[18]

Even so, Ebbets wasted little time confirming Robinson's message, writing Tinker two days later that his demands were unreasonable. The Brooklyn club president claimed Tinker never made that kind of money with the Cubs and argued that a $7,500 salary wouldn't be fair to the "men on our team with ability equal to yours" (presumably Wheat and Daubert), who didn't make as much. Rather, Ebbets insisted, the $10,000 Tinker was to receive from the purchase price plus a $5,000 annual salary will "compensate you in a great fashion." Ebbets offered Tinker a three-year contract and, if the terms were agreeable, suggested that Tinker come to the February 9 owners meeting (at the club's expense) to sign the deal. The Brooklyn magnate further recommended keeping the salary issue out of the newspapers and closed by wishing his still-hoped-for new player "a Merry Christmas and Happy New Year."[19] In spite of Ebbets' supposed desire for confidentiality, the next day's *Eagle* reported that the Brooklyn owner wasn't about to give in, since no major league team would pay Tinker more and it wasn't clear that the new Federal League had enough money.[20]

Any doubts on the latter score were quickly erased on December 30 when the *Eagle* published a telegram from Tinker announcing that he had signed with Chicago of the new league for "terms much better than Brooklyn."[21] In an affidavit later filed in the Federal League's antitrust lawsuit, Tinker claimed that the salary was $12,000 a year for three years, far more than not only what Ebbets offered, but also more than Tinker himself had demanded.[22] Although Chicago sports writer George Rice claimed that Tinker signed with the Feds because of the lack of response to his initial telegram, it's far more likely that Tinker stuck to his position of not playing in the East and was richly compensated for it.[23] Even with the announcement, Ebbets didn't give up, meeting with Tinker in Chicago in mid–January and later agreeing to the $7,500 salary demand, all predictably in vain.[24] Understandably, Ebbets wanted the $15,000 purchase price back from Cincinnati, something the Reds owners inexplicably and unreasonably refused to do. Ebbets brought the matter to the National League's Board of Directors in June, which deferred action until after the season, but the two owners reportedly "settled out of court so to speak." The details of the settlement were never made public.[25] While Ebbets may have made some errors along the way, his failed courtship of Tinker showed Brooklyn fans that their owner was far from reluctant to spend large amounts of money to improve their ball club.

If nothing else, Tinker's defection proved beyond any doubt that the Federal League threat was real, the last thing Ebbets needed right after building an expensive new ballpark. While the recent "explosion in baseball profits and franchise values" was good news for the current owners, the boom times also attracted other middle class businessmen looking for a good investment opportunity. Since there were more interested buyers than potential sellers, the logical step was to start a new league. In March of 1913, under the leadership of John Powers, the Federal League was formed with franchises in six Midwestern cities. Although initially the group didn't aspire to major league status, the situation changed in August when the far more aggressive James Gilmore assumed the league presidency. The new league's outlook became even brighter (and worse for Ebbets) when Ned Hanlon, part-owner of the Baltimore Federal League club, and supposedly still harboring a grudge against Ebbets, convinced the very wealthy Robert Ward to go head to head against Ebbets in Brooklyn. Ward, who provided significant financial support for the new league, quickly demonstrated his financial wherewithal by spending over $200,000 to build the third and final incarnation of Washington Park, literally from the ground up.[26]

With the December owners meetings behind him, Ebbets took a three-week cruise to Puerto Rico, although it's doubtful he got much rest with a baseball war looming on the horizon. Literally hours after his return, the Brooklyn owner left home again on a long trip which took him as far west as Kansas City and as far south as Atlanta to sign 16 of his 18 targeted players, a number to multi-year contracts. Demonstrating that he could be discreet when necessary, Ebbets wisely made the trip without fanfare, traveling as he put it without "a brass band" since "such is a foolishness." Needless to say, the signed contracts didn't come cheap, which added to the new park and the loans to the minor league Newark club put even more pressure on the Brooklyn club's finances. Having made his own pre-emptive strike, Ebbets claimed that the new league wasn't really a threat, but acknowledged that the Brotherhood and American League wars had taught him "never to underestimate an enemy."[27]

As expected, the Federal League was the primary issue facing the National League magnates at their February 1914 meeting. If the prospect of another baseball war wasn't bad enough, the bungling of Cubs owner Charles Murphy seemed about to give the new league the gift of another star player. Described as "self-important" and "meddlesome," Murphy informed his colleagues that Cubs manager, future Hall of Famer Johnny Evers, had resigned and Murphy, therefore, had no obligation to pay the balance of his five-year contract. However, when they looked at the details, the horrified magnates discovered that Evers hadn't resigned and was negotiating with the Federal League's Chicago club.[28] In the chair when the owners discussed the impending disaster, Ebbets blasted Murphy for his incompetent actions, telling the embattled magnate he had put the league in "a terrible position." The only solution was to move Evers to another club, with the league guaranteeing his $40,000 contract. At one point in the debate, Ebbets angrily told Murphy that having put the league in a bad position, "you have to take, in a measure, what we want. It is seven clubs you got into the hole damn it!"[29] In the end, Evers went to Boston with a guaranteed contract, and shortly thereafter, Murphy was forced to sell his interest in the Cubs.[30]

Having had more than his fill of baseball wars, Ebbets was also giving some thought about how to achieve a better, more structured relationship with the players. While still in the chair, Ebbets wondered aloud about the possibility of bringing the Players Fraternity into the National Agreement. It was, Ebbets acknowledged, a "radical step," but one which would bind the players and owners together. Not surprisingly, the idea made little headway, but Ebbets urged its consideration, since "Baseball is a big proposition. It is very important to the players, that one thing in it, and if they were part of the National Agreement, there might be far more satisfaction to all concerned."[31] Once again, Ebbets seems ahead of his time, speculating about some kind of contractual relationship with the players as a group.

Ebbets, in spite of his dismissive public comments, was quite concerned about what must have seemed like a gun pointed at his head by the Federal League and Hanlon.[32] In response to the new league's decision to put a franchise in Brooklyn, Ebbets intended to take the offensive against the far wealthier Wards. The Dodgers president wanted to offer "continuous baseball" at Ebbets Field, with an International League team playing home games there when Brooklyn was on the road. Ebbets claimed that local fans and, more importantly, the media demanded more baseball, and if they couldn't get it at Ebbets Field, it would open the door to "an outside organization [i.e., the Feds] antagonistic to us coming into Brooklyn."[33] The Dodgers owners wanted the Jersey City International League franchise to shift to the supposedly more profitable Newark market, allowing Ebbets and the McKeevers to move the Newark team, which they controlled, to Brooklyn.[34] While it has been alleged that Ebbets' outrageous demands on the owners of the Jersey City team killed the deal, it wouldn't have mattered since the National League owners turned the request down by a decisive 6–1–1 vote.[35]

It's unclear if "continuous baseball" at Ebbets Field would have made a difference, but the 1914 season was a disaster at the new Ebbets Field box offices, threatening to undermine everything Ebbets had worked so hard to build. Although both teams drew large crowds for their home openers, attendance dropped quickly and drastically.[36] One source puts the Brooklyn Federals' total attendance at just over 77,000, while the Dodgers didn't do much better at 122,671, a mind-boggling decrease of 64 percent from 1913, one of the deepest drops in the National League, which fell 41 percent in total.[37]

In his book about the Federal League, Daniel Levitt estimated that major league clubs had average operating expenses of $140,000 and assumed ticket revenue averaging 70 cents per admission. Using those figures, the Brooklyn Federal League club lost over $85,000, although there might have been even more red ink at Washington Park since all ticket prices were cut to 25 cents at the end of June.[38] Applying the same formula to the Dodgers' 1914 attendance produces a loss of about $54,000, although this was offset somewhat by renting Ebbets Field for other purposes, such as vaudeville productions, movies, boxing matches and football games.[39] Even with some additional revenue, however, 1914 was a bad year financially for the Dodgers. Just how bad was seen in a September 20 telegram Ebbets sent to Herrmann, asking or begging for immediate payment for a player transaction plus renewal of an outstanding note because he was "straining every condition to close [the] season."[40] At season's end, the Dodgers owed almost $4,700 to the National League, which the club still hadn't paid by the December league meeting, not a lot of money, but an embarrassment for Ebbets.[41]

Absorbing a big loss in Brooklyn was bad enough, but Ebbets and the McKeevers had another money-losing venture on their hands. Back in 1911, Ebbets purchased a minority interest in the Newark International League franchise for $9,000. When the McKeevers bought into the Brooklyn franchise in 1912, they also invested in the Newark club, and after Ebbets purchased additional shares, the three men held a controlling interest.[42] No rationale was offered for the investments, but it was probably the same good economic times in baseball which attracted investors to the Federal League, plus the possibility of using the Newark club as an informal "farm team." It seemed like a good investment in 1913 when the Newark club realized a $26,000 profit, but that same year, the National

Commission ordered major league clubs to sell any minor league holdings by January 1, 1914. Ebbets claimed that he and his partners tried to comply, but when an attractive offer of $60,400 for their interests wasn't extended to co-owners George Solomon and Henry Medicus, the Dodgers owners felt it wasn't honorable to abandon the two men. If so, Ebbets and the McKeevers, or rather the Brooklyn club, paid a high price for their principled stand, because the minors suffered even more than the majors in 1914, with Newark attendance frequently not even covering the visiting team's guarantee.[43] In 1914, the Newark franchise cost the Brooklyn club (not the owners) $34,000 in loans to cover operating losses.[44] Since there was little likelihood the loans could be repaid, the Dodgers' total 1914 losses were in the $90,000 range. The combination of an inflated wartime payroll, an expensive new ballpark, and declining ticket sales was driving the club towards the precipice of financial disaster.

If Ebbets didn't have enough problems, an apparently innocent action on his part almost led to a players' strike. In July of 1914, Ebbets placed Clarence Kraft on waivers, and when no major league team claimed him, he was released to the Newark club. Although Kraft wasn't in demand by major league teams, Nashville of the Class A Southern Association insisted it had first call on his services. Playing for Class A Nashville instead of Class AA Newark meant a pay cut for Kraft, which he was understandably reluctant to accept. Since recent negotiations between the players' union and the National Commission (known as the Cincinnati Agreement) gave players the right to play in the highest league that wanted them, Kraft appealed to the National Commission. But it turned out that if a player was originally drafted from a Class A league (which Kraft was), that league had first rights, so the commission had no choice but to award him to Nashville. This infuriated not just Kraft but also union head Dave Fultz, who believed the Cincinnati Agreement eliminated the earlier provision in practice, if not by written agreement. Fultz and the union threatened to strike if the ruling wasn't changed, a confrontation the always pugnacious Ban Johnson supposedly welcomed. To their credit, the National League leadership was too smart to risk a strike, so the Newark club (financed by Brooklyn loans) paid Nashville $2,500 for the rights to Kraft, another expense Ebbets and the McKeevers didn't need.[45]

Already burdened with added payroll expense from his whirlwind 1914 signing tour, Ebbets still had to deal with possible 1915 defections, which meant signing promising pitcher Jeff Pffefer to a two-year contract.[46] In the end, the only Brooklyn defections were Frank Allen, Bill Fischer and Jack Dalton, all losses the club could withstand. Ebbets had clearly learned from prior baseball wars and, in spite of his reputation for cheapness, paid the price necessary to keep his team together. As early as June of 1914, however, the Brooklyn owner knew full well that there was only one solution. Speaking at a special owners meeting that month, Ebbets warned his fellow magnates, "you are not going win the law courts," nor, he believed, would they prevail in constant competition for players. Rather, Ebbets argued, "you have got to get these people and get some kind of compromise. I do not see how you can win without it."[47] Ironically, Robert Ward, the owner of the Brooklyn Feds and a major financier of other Federal League clubs, also wanted a peace agreement, but in the end, "neither side had yet suffered enough to reach a settlement," so the war continued.[48]

Unlike Ward, Ebbets couldn't fall back on his own personal wealth, so the Brooklyn magnate and the McKeevers were forced to seek help (money) from their fellow National League owners, beseeching them in late January for a $7,500 loan plus more time to pay the club's 1914 league obligations. Although the loan was approved, the terms demonstrated the magnates' concern about the Brooklyn club's finances, since Ebbets and the McKeevers had to endorse the notes personally.[49] While $7,500 in 1915 was a more substantial amount than today, it wasn't even close to the value of the franchise, including the new ballpark, but the club's finances were so uncertain that the three men had to put their personal assets at risk. Perhaps the stringent requirement was a good thing if it discouraged future loan requests, since the Brooklyn club would have more than enough trouble repaying this one.

Faced with financial problems and an uncertain future, Ebbets and the McKeevers reorganized their corporate structure in early 1915. When the club was founded, it was incorporated in New York. In 1892, however, like many businessmen of the day, the Brooklyn owners took advantage of New Jersey's more liberal corporate laws, and the club had operated under a Garden State charter ever since. According to Ebbets, however, New York laws had been "greatly" changed so there was no need to continue the New Jersey corporate status. As part of the change, Ebbets and the McKeevers formed not one, but two corporations. The perceived need for separate corporations, one to own Ebbets Field (Ebbets-McKeever Exhibition Company) and another to own the ball club (Brooklyn National League Baseball Club) was likely an important motivation for the restructuring. Incorporation is almost always intended to limit liability, and keeping the ball park separate from the team protected their most valuable asset, Ebbets Field, from the ball club's creditors, a prudent move given the current operating losses. Ironically, considering what the future held, the restructuring was also supposed to anticipate the deaths of the owners, facilitating either continuing the business or "all the partners selling together." Equally owned by Ebbets and the McKeever brothers, the property assets were valued at $700,000, perhaps some indication of the total cost of the relatively new ball park.[50]

Also equally owned was the baseball team, capitalized at $300,000 in common stock and $250,000 in eight percent preferred stock, with the assets likely limited to player contracts and the estimated value of the franchise. If the motivation for the preferred stock wasn't obvious when the restructuring was announced, it became crystal clear two weeks later when the *Eagle* announced a supposed baseball first. A "financially strong major league club" (Brooklyn) was offering to sell $100,000 of the preferred stock in $100 increments, paying an eight percent dividend and redeemable in three years. Either the paper didn't know the club's true financial condition or it was trying to help Ebbets raise some badly needed money. Also facilitating the sale, again perhaps unknowingly, was the *New York Tribune*, which claimed that Ebbets had been "importuned" for years to sell stock to the public, but had been reluctant, supposedly because some might feel it was due to financial problems.[51] Ultimately, about $10,000 was raised, and while it must have helped, at the end of December 1915, the $7,500 debt to the National League remained unpaid.[52]

Some of Brooklyn's financial problems were due to the Newark club's dire condition, where to make a bad situation worse, if that were possible, there was now going to be head-to-head competition with a Federal League franchise. Finally, in early April of 1915, Ebbets and the McKeevers threw in the towel, effectively giving the franchise to Solomon and Medicus for $1.[53] Even at that price, it was a lost cause, and on June 30, the Newark franchise was forfeited to the International League. Not only had Ebbets and the McKeevers suffered personal losses of about $30,000, there was no hope of recovering over $75,000 in loans from Dodgers funds.[54] The personal losses were one thing—Ebbets and the McKeevers had every right to put their own money at risk anywhere they chose—but pouring money badly needed in Brooklyn into a black hole in Newark wasn't a responsible use of club funds. After everything he had gone through to pay for his new ball park, Ebbets should have known better.

In the end, the International League was forced to pay $12,000–15,000 of the failed club's debts, which didn't exactly endear Ebbets to league president Ed Barrow, especially when, a year later, the Brooklyn magnate tried to recover some of the Dodgers' loans after the Newark franchise was sold for $25,000. Recognizing that the International League was entitled to recoup its expenses, Ebbets asked for the difference, since without the loans from the Dodgers, the unpaid bills would have been even higher. Predictably, Barrow was outraged, calling the amount "ridiculous" while implying that Ebbets and the McKeevers were trying to recover some of their personal investments. Equally incensed, when Brooklyn's claim reached the National Commission, was Ban Johnson, who denounced the 1915 ownership transfer as "a fraudulent transaction" and insisted that the Dodgers weren't entitled to a dollar. Far more objective were the other two members of the National Commission, John Tener and Garry Herrmann, who, although uninterested in helping the Brooklyn owners recover their personal investments, found no evidence of fraud and acknowledged the tangible financial assistance Brooklyn gave the Newark club. Brooklyn's claim was approved by a 2–1 vote, but in 1918, Ebbets was still seeking a reduced settlement of $5,000.[55]

Fortunately for Ebbets, dramatically improved on-the-field performance in 1915 sparked a turnaround in the club's finances. While the Brooklyn Federal League club's 1915 attendance was so pathetically low, Ebbets' called it "a joke," Dodgers attendance more than doubled, falling just below the 1915 National League average of 300,000.[56] Applying Daniel Levitt's estimates of club operating expenses and average ticket prices, Brooklyn had a 1915 profit of $68,000, more than the higher end of Fred Leib's $25,000–50,000 contemporary estimate.[57] On top of this good news was even better news when the Federal League owners sued for peace in December of 1915.[58] The combination of better financial results and an end to the final baseball war of Ebbets' career meant that he and his club had once again averted disaster. Although the final peace agreement allowed defectors to the Federal League to return to organized baseball, Ebbets honored his pledge not to take back the "jumpers" since, as he told his fellow owners, the Brooklyn public would "rebel against us" because they believed "if they [the defecting players] had remained with us, we might have won the championship."[59]

Ebbets' claim that Brooklyn might have won the 1915 pennant wasn't as ridiculous as it might sound, because some of his and Robinson's personnel moves began paying off. In his 1914 inaugural season as Brooklyn manager, Robinson kept Hi Myers, who had been farmed out every year since 1909, on the major league roster, and he became a valuable addition to the outfield. Robinson and Ebbets were also well aware that pitching was a major need, and the first piece of the puzzle was Jeff Pfeffer, who was acquired in 1913 and joined the rotation in 1914. Robinson's first

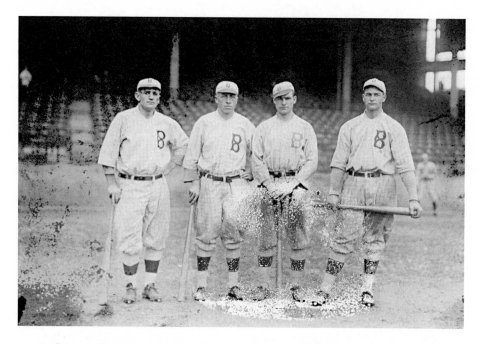

Left to right: Casey Stengel, Jimmy Johnston, Hi Myers and Zack Wheat, Brooklyn's 1916 National league championship outfield, all acquired by Ebbets, most with the assistance of top scout Larry Sutton. Ebbets would have contract issues with all but Myers (Library of Congress, Prints and Photographs Division, Bain Collection [LC-DIG-ggbain-22985]).

Dodgers squad—he would manage 18 in all—got off to a 5–3 start, but Brooklyn went 32–46 over the next three months, dropping all the way into last place on July 31. Perhaps having adjusted to their new manager, the club rebounded in the second half with a 38–30 record, finishing fifth, only three games out of the first division, the club's best finish since 1907.

While Brooklyn's improved second-half play doubtless pleased Dodgers fans, they had witnessed similar second-half spurts before only to have their hopes dashed the following year. The discerning Brooklyn fan could, however, have found even more reason for optimism in the unexpected, some said miraculous 1914 pennant race. Ever since Hanlon's Brooklyn club won the 1900 flag, Chicago, New York or Pittsburgh had won 13 straight National League pennants, and 1914 started out as if it would be no different. On July 4th, the three-time defending champion Giants were once again in first place, obscuring the overall tightness of the race, with last-place Boston only 15 games out of first. From that point, the Braves went on their miraculous pennant-winning run, climbing to fourth place in just four days and tying New York for first on August 26. Although the two clubs were still tied on September 8, Boston pulled away to capture the National League flag by 10½ games, going 65–19 after July 8.

An important part of Boston's 1914 success was their acquisition of Brooklyn third baseman J. Carlisle "Red" Smith. Although Smith hit .293 for Brooklyn in 1913, he reportedly never accepted Robinson as manager because he wanted Jake Daubert to get the job. Smith was hitting only .245 in August when Ebbets released him on waivers due to fears he would jump to the Federal League. While some Brooklyn fans likely questioned the release of Smith, a far better question was: if hapless Boston could defy expectations and win the pennant, why not Brooklyn?[60] Regardless of what Smith thought of Robinson, Ebbets was so confident he had finally found the right manager that he signed his new skipper to a three-year contract at the end of June even though the club was mired in last place. According to Abe Yager, it was the first time a last-place manager was rewarded with a contract of that length.[61]

The club's financial problems notwithstanding, Ebbets and Robinson continued to upgrade the roster for the 1915 season. Still appropriately worried about the chronic problem at shortstop, Ebbets built depth and created competition between Ollie O'Mara and Ivy Olson by claiming Olson on waivers from Cleveland. Ebbets then made what Tom Rice called "a sheer baseball gamble," signing former Athletics ace pitcher Jack Coombs, who had suffered from serious, if not life-threatening health issues.[62] One move that didn't work out was the September 1914 draft of Louisville pitcher Fred Toney. As required by the rules, Ebbets sent a $2,500 check, payable to the Louisville club, to the National Commission, which was to hold it until Toney signed a Brooklyn contract. Toney, however, demanded $4,500 a year for two years, an amount Ebbets couldn't afford to pay even if he wanted to, which he didn't. Unfortunately, Ebbets failed to cancel the draft within the prescribed time, which left Louisville without the player or the $2,500. Eventually the National Commission sent the check to Louisville, but Ebbets stopped payment, beginning a dispute that lingered into 1915. While Ebbets tried to argue that since Toney hadn't signed, the National Commission shouldn't have released the check, it was another example of Ebbets' unfortunate sloppiness in player transactions. In the process, he lost a solid major league pitcher in Toney.[63]

When the Dodgers were in seventh place at the end of June, after losing 15 of 21 games on a long road trip, it seemed unlikely that 1915 would see the long-hoped-for pennant in Brooklyn. Fortunately, however, as in 1914, the league was very balanced, so when on returning to Ebbets Field, the Dodgers suddenly regained their "batting eye," they quickly made up ground by taking eight of nine games from New York and Boston.[64] In the next game against the Cubs, Chicago got off to a 7–1 lead, which had to have some Brooklyn fans thinking the club had reverted to form. Such thoughts were, however, more than a little premature, since Brooklyn rallied to win in the tenth inning, prompting Rice to predict, "If this thing keeps up the doctors will have to hold their vacation plans in abeyance" since "they will be needed to look after Brooklyn National fans overcome by the excitement."[65]

On July 10, Brooklyn swept a doubleheader from the first-place Cubs, moving into third place, just three games out of first. Hoping for a repeat of 1914, Rice noted that Brooklyn was ahead of the Braves' miracle pace.[66] After winning 14 of 18 from the visiting Western clubs, Brooklyn headed west themselves in early August, with a much better result, finishing the trip just a game below .500. Still trying to upgrade the pitching, Ebbets acquired veterans Larry Cheney (Cubs) and Rube Marquard (Giants), hoping they had something left in their arms. League-leading Philadelphia came to Ebbets Field right after Labor Day for the first meaningful September games in Brooklyn in a long, long time, only to be swept by the hard-charging Dodgers. Brooklyn was now on the brink of first place, and a September 8 doubleheader sweep of Boston and a Philadelphia loss at the Polo Grounds would have put the Dodgers on top. But on a day when "wait till next year!" was probably heard for the first time at Ebbets Field, Brooklyn, in Rice's words "cracked," losing both games.[67] Although the season was far from over, the Dodgers' chance was gone, and Philadelphia went 18–6 down the stretch to finish ten games ahead of third-place Brooklyn, back in the first division at last. 1915 had seen a second straight outsider crash the pennant-winning party. Would 1916 see another? And could that lucky club be Brooklyn?

CHAPTER XI

"A wide smile on his face and giving the glad hand to all comers"

Although championship seasons by the upstart Braves and Phillies should have convinced the baseball world that parity was the new order of the day in the National League, stereotypes die hard. At least that's what Charles Ebbets found at the December 1915 owners meeting, when some magnates scoffed at the very idea that his Brooklyn club might be a 1916 contender.[1] Less cynical observers, however, would have considered the club's 1915 third-place finish and the benefits of a full season from veteran pitchers Rube Marquard and Larry Cheney as sufficient basis for hope in Brooklyn. At the same time, any such optimism had to be tempered by the Brooklyn outfield's poor 1915 performance, since none of the three starters—Zack Wheat, Casey Stengel or Hi Myers—hit over .258. Wheat's subpar performance was the most mysterious since he was and would be a consistent .300 hitter.[2]

Unwilling just to hope the incumbents returned to form in 1916, Ebbets tried to bolster his outfield by adding Jimmy Johnston, a promising player from the Pacific Coast League. Already in San Francisco for the minor leagues' annual meetings, Ebbets was in the right place at the right time to negotiate with Johnston. When the two men met on November 22, 1915, however, the Federal League, although on life support, had beaten Ebbets to the punch by signing Johnston to a two-year contract at $4,000 per year without the right to release him on ten days' notice. At the same time, Johnston was well aware of the very tenuous nature of the Federal League and quite willing to listen to Ebbets. The Brooklyn magnate matched the two-year contract with a slightly lower salary of $3,600, but wouldn't waive the ten-day clause. Instead, Ebbets guaranteed Johnston a $3,000 salary should he be sent to the minors. Ebbets' offer wasn't enough to close the deal, but the two men agreed to meet again in Atlanta near Johnston's off-season home.[3]

Instead of waiting for the meeting in Atlanta, however, Ebbets sent his prospective player a "contract on the terms we agreed" even though no such agreement existed. When Johnston understandably declined to sign the contract, the whole matter might have become a typical player-owner negotiation, but unfortunately for Ebbets, good long-term news created a short-term problem. The peace agreement with the Federal League suddenly legitimized the soon-to-be defunct league's player contracts, which meant the Newark Federal League franchise owned the rights to Johnston. Muddying the waters even further, and weakening his case in the process, Ebbets had reimbursed the Newark Feds for a $1,000 advance paid to Johnston and received in return Johnston's contract, endorsed to Brooklyn. Ebbets' action strengthened the argument that if Brooklyn wanted Johnston, Ebbets had to honor the more favorable Newark contract. Nor was Johnston without legal assistance, since Dave Fultz of the Players Fraternity backed the player's appeal to the National Commission. Although Ebbets insisted he had a binding agreement with Johnston, without a signed Brooklyn contract, Ebbets' case was extremely weak. Under the circumstances, American League President Ban Johnson urged the equivalent of an out-of-court settlement rather than a hearing before the commission. Ebbets was smart enough to know when he was beaten, so when Fultz proposed a two-year contract at the lower $3600 annual salary, but without the ten-day clause, the Brooklyn magnate jumped at it.[4]

Ebbets was wise to compromise, since Johnston would have a productive major league career, helping Brooklyn win two National League pennants and making the ten-day clause more than a little academic. The episode is instructive as to how Ebbets negotiated player contracts, an aspect of his job which would become increasingly public. Most disturbing was Ebbets' unwillingness to accept that he had no agreement with Johnston, verbal or otherwise. His mishandling of the Johnston case was painfully reminiscent of the Toney episode, another example of what seems like an uncharacteristic lack of attention to detail. However, Fultz's claim that the Brooklyn owner wanted Johnston to give up a two-year guaranteed salary for the risk of no salary at all was neither accurate nor fair.[5] Ebbets wanted to preserve the ten-day clause, which he considered "essential to the life of the game," but the Brooklyn owner addressed the player's concern with a guaranteed $3,000 salary should Johnston not make the major league club.[6] Nor was Ebbets' offer of $400 less than the

Federal League proposal (money Johnston had no chance of collecting) necessarily unfair. Johnston was an unproven rookie who under Ebbets' offer would earn only about $900 below the major league average.[7] Also interesting, although it was obviously said for effect, was Fultz's description of Ebbets as "a man of much will power," who "does not allow his purposes to be thwarted by any weak opposition."[8] In this case, at any rate, it's hard to fault Ebbets' offer to his prospective player.

While resolving a controversy of his own making, Ebbets was also busy attending the February owners meeting and preparing for the annual spring trip. Spring training had become more expensive since Wilbert Robinson wanted to prepare his veteran pitchers properly for the rigors of a 154-game campaign. With Ebbets' agreement, Robinson sent six pitchers and two catchers to Hot Springs, Arkansas, for two weeks of extra training before joining the full squad in Daytona, Florida. Ebbets' approval of the plan was another indication of his willingness to spend money to bring Brooklyn a pennant. Although Ebbets and Robinson had added depth to the pitching staff, there were still major problems on the left side of the infield, where the choices were Ivy Olson or Ollie O'Mara at shortstop and Mike Mowrey or Gus Getz at third. In the end, there was no clear winner at either position, so Robinson kept all four, which meant the club carried only four outfielders, with newcomer Jimmy Johnston filling the fourth and final spot.[9]

Optimism about the Dodgers' 1916 chances wasn't limited to Brooklyn, since *The Sporting News* predicted that if the "hitting was up to form" and the "pitching what it should be," Brooklyn appeared to be the best team in the National League.[10] The Dodgers' success would depend in large measure on veteran pitchers Jack Coombs and Rube Marquard. If both men came anywhere near Coombs' 1915 record of 15 wins and a 2.58 ERA, the outlook was very promising.[11] The club's performance on the three long Western road trips was also a concern, since an abysmal 5–16 record on the initial 1915 Western swing proved too much to overcome.[12] It was with a sense of guarded optimism, therefore, that Brooklyn opened the season on April 12 before 15,000 fans at still relatively new Ebbets Field. After the obligatory players parade to the flag pole, the crowd watched Brooklyn get off to a bad start, losing 5–1, partially due to some sloppy defense, doing nothing to allay concerns about the Dodgers' fielding.[13] Writing far more prophetically than he could have known, Tom Rice fell back on an old adage, claiming that if a "bad beginning makes a good ending," the Dodgers "should have the National League pennant clinched by July 4th." Rice was echoing, probably unknowingly, similar sentiments from an unnamed *Eagle* writer in Brooklyn's 1899 pennant-winning season.[14]

While neither Brooklyn nor anyone else would clinch the pennant by Independence Day, the Dodgers took over first place on May 1 and maintained their position throughout a successful Western trip. Ahead of second-place New York by 1½ games on May 29, Brooklyn hit a temporary road block, losing three of five to Boston, who would prove to be the Dodgers' season-long nemesis. Ebbets' club rebounded, however, during a long home stand against the Western clubs and was still in first place on June 22, even after losing three of five games to Philadelphia. Although pleased at being in first place, Ebbets was less than thrilled with the 15 games lost to bad weather just two months into the season. Since most of the postponed games were made up as single-admission doubleheaders, the Brooklyn club had reportedly lost $30,000–50,000 in gate receipts.[15] Things looked brighter financially, however, after a June 24 Saturday doubleheader with the Giants which the *Eagle* headlined as the "Largest [crowd] in Brooklyn's Baseball History." Although no official figures were announced, Ebbets put the crowd at over 30,000, which overflowed into temporary outfield bleachers the Brooklyn president hoped would be needed again in October.[16] The huge throng was rewarded by a sweep of their arch rivals behind major contributions from Coombs and Marquard. A few days later, Brooklyn left on a month-long road trip, including their second visit to the West, with a 3½ game lead on the second-place Phillies.

The Dodgers spent the next month on the rails and in hotels, beginning with a visit to Boston, where once again they struggled, losing three of five to the Braves. Brooklyn quickly turned things around, however, taking three straight at the Polo Grounds before heading west, where they enjoyed another winning trip. As a reward, Ebbets bought every player a Palm Beach suit, hardly the behavior of a stingy owner.[17] Part of Brooklyn's success was thanks to continued effective outings by Coombs and Marquard, and the Dodgers arrived back in Brooklyn in late July, four games ahead of both Boston and Philadelphia.[18] Another important contributor was new acquisition Jimmy Johnston, who played so well after Hi Myers injured his ankle that once Myers recovered, he couldn't get back in the lineup.[19] With two of the three grueling Western trips successfully completed, Dodgers fans had good reason to be optimistic. While Ebbets, obviously, had little to do with the club's day-to-day success, the roster was still his responsibility, and the Brooklyn magnate's first move was more defensive in nature. In July, Slim Sallee, a capable pitcher for the Cardinals, became available, and while Brooklyn didn't need pitching help,

Ebbets and Robinson wanted to keep him away from Boston and Philadelphia. Whether or not it was the decisive factor, Ebbets' reported $7,500 offer supposedly drove up the price, and in the end Sallee went to the Giants for over $10,000.[20]

Although Ebbets and Robinson believed they had sufficient pitching, shortstop remained a major concern. Not only was help available, but ironically the potential source was another unsuccessful Cincinnati player-manager, this time in the person of Charles "Buck" Herzog. By mid–July, the Reds were mired in last place and drawing poorly, making Herzog and his prickly personality, not to mention his high salary, very expendable.[21] Unfortunately for Ebbets, history repeated itself since the Reds owners, as with Tinker, wanted players, not money or at least not just money. As early as July, the *Eagle* confirmed both Ebbets' interest in Herzog and Cincinnati's demand for second baseman George Cutshaw in return.[22] Ebbets was unwilling to make a trade that he considered to be the exchange of one star player for another, and also reportedly felt it unfair to send Cutshaw from first to worst.[23] Ebbets made a counteroffer of $25,000 and an unnamed player, because the Dodgers' need had become even more pressing due to the subpar "work of O'Mara and Getz." The Brooklyn owner didn't even get a response, and Herzog went to the Giants as an ever-present reminder of what might have been.[24] There was also newspaper speculation that Brooklyn might acquire St. Louis phenom Rogers Hornsby, but the future Hall of Famer was not for sale.[25]

Even with the chronic weakness at shortstop, Brooklyn continued to play well, going 14–3 against the visiting Western clubs, but did little to increase their lead since Boston, Philadelphia and New York all won 13 games from the hapless visitors.[26] Still the race seemed to be going Brooklyn's way as they prepared to close out the long home stand with a four-game series against Boston, beginning with an August 12 doubleheader. The Braves were in second place, five games behind, giving Brooklyn the opportunity to put some real distance between themselves and the pesky Boston club. That's certainly what the fans were hoping for when a huge crowd filled Ebbets Field, to the point that one-dollar reserved seats in the upper tier "never sold so fast."[27] The massive throng must have been on the brink of exploding when their hometown heroes carried a 4–1 lead into the ninth inning, only to see Boston rally for a 5–4, heartbreaking Brooklyn loss. It got worse in the second game, since not only did Boston win again, but first baseman Jake Daubert injured his leg, putting the hard-hitting Dodger out of action for over three weeks. At least the Dodgers managed to split the last two games with Boston before leaving home on an epic 28-game road trip to all seven league cities, still in first place by three games.

Brooklyn's almost month-long quest for the 1916 National League pennant began with 15 games in the West, where they went 9–6 even without Daubert. Concern about exactly how long the first baseman would be out led Ebbets and Robinson to trade catcher Lew McCarty to the Giants for the star-crossed Fred Merkle.[28] Although Brooklyn was finished in the West, they still had 13 consecutive road games against much tougher opposition. Brooklyn headed to Philadelphia two games ahead of Boston, five up on Philadelphia and 15 on the Giants, who were a distant fourth and two games below .500. Beginning on September 1, Brooklyn had five games with the fading Phillies, which gave them a chance to finish off the defending National League champions once and for all. The 1916 pennant race was far from over, however, and the situation changed quickly and dramatically when the Phillies swept all five games. In the process, Philadelphia made up the entire five-game deficit, tying them with the Dodgers, just percentage points behind now first-place Boston. Ebbets' club was out of first place for the first time in over three months and headed into a tight race to the bitter end.

It was hard to find a silver lining in the Baker Bowl debacle, but at least the Dodgers got Daubert and Johnston (who had been out for about two weeks) back for the stretch run.[29] Now tied for second, the Brooklyn club dragged itself out of Philadelphia and headed for New York for four games against the struggling Giants. The Dodgers stopped the bleeding by splitting the series, but Philadelphia won three games in Boston and took over first place. Trailing Philadelphia by 1½ games, the Dodgers headed for Boston and four crucial games with their nemesis, the still very much alive Braves. Considering Boston's season-long dominance of Brooklyn, the first-place Phillies had good reason to believe they could expand their lead against the floundering Giants. By September, however, John McGraw had finished rebuilding his team, and the reconstructed Giants routed Philadelphia's ace, Grover Cleveland Alexander, in one game and swept a doubleheader the next day. No one knew it, but McGraw's club had launched a record-setting 26-game winning streak (a mark that still stands). More importantly for Brooklyn fans, their team finally mastered the Braves, taking three of four from Boston, putting the Dodgers back in first place and headed home for their last 24 games.[30]

Before the contending clubs squared off in two season-ending series, the Western clubs came east in a final, fruitless attempt to impact the National League pennant race. Once again, the Eastern clubs dominated and by September 27, Brooklyn led Philadelphia by 1½ games and Boston by 3½. The big change, however, was that it was now a four-team race after the Giants ran roughshod over the Western clubs to close within 6½ games of first place after trailing by 15 games on August 30. The last weekend of the season found all four contenders in New York, Boston for four games at the Polo Grounds and Philadelphia at Ebbets Field for three games against first-place Brooklyn. Although the Giants had fattened up on the weak Western clubs, McGraw's men showed they were for real by sweeping both ends of a doubleheader from Boston as their winning streak hit 25. Meanwhile at Ebbets Field, Alexander won his 32nd game, defeating Brooklyn, 8–4, to bring Philadelphia within a half-game of first. Perhaps the only surprise was that Brooklyn scored four times, since the Phillies' ace recorded 16 shutouts over the course of the season, like the Giants' winning streak still a major league record.

After a day of rain, doubleheaders were scheduled for Saturday, September 30, with first place in the balance in Brooklyn. At the Polo Grounds, the Giants won their 26th consecutive game, pushing Boston to the brink of elimination before finally losing in the nightcap. In Brooklyn, Ebbets chose, with Philadelphia's permission, to play a separate admission, morning-afternoon twin bill. Supposedly all the reserved seats had been sold for the scheduled Saturday game, prohibiting the use of rain checks from Friday's rainout, although some speculated that Ebbets was trying to maximize his revenue. If so, it didn't work because whether due to fan resentment or the cold weather, only about 7,000 fans saw Philadelphia easily win the morning game, 7–2, and move into first place by a half-game. With their club out of the lead and Alexander on the mound for Philadelphia in the second game, the outlook for the 16,000 Brooklyn fans in attendance couldn't have been much bleaker, but the Dodgers, like their owner, were a resilient lot. After allowing a first-inning run, Marquard dominated the Phillies, while Casey Stengel broke a 1–1 tie with a home run over the right field fence, putting Brooklyn in the lead for good on the way to a 6–1 victory. For the third time since May, the Dodgers had responded to being knocked out of first place by quickly reclaiming the top spot.[31]

Back in second place, the Phillies headed home to Philadelphia to finish the season with six games with the Braves, while the Dodgers prepared for four games against the Giants at Ebbets Field. By this point, the Giants had been eliminated, and Boston, four games off the pace, had only a slight mathematical chance. Brooklyn's lead over Philadelphia was a slim half-game, and the math was simple, Philadelphia had to win two more games than Ebbets' club or the 1916 National League pennant came to Brooklyn. Alexander was back at it again on Monday, shutting out and eliminating Boston, but the Braves came back to win the second game, helping Brooklyn, which was locked up in a tight pitchers' duel with the Giants. Having won a crucial game with Marquard on Saturday, Robinson trusted Brooklyn's fortunes to another veteran, Jack Coombs, before a big Monday "wash day" crowd of 15,000. Pitching for the Giants was the previously unheralded Ferd Schupp, who had been at the heart of the Giants' record streak, winning six games, but even more impressively, allowing only three runs while pitching four shutouts. Schupp pitched well once again, giving up just one run in his seven innings of work, but Coombs was even better, shutting out the Giants, 2–0. Ebbets, his club and the people of Brooklyn were on the brink of their first league championship since 1900.[32]

After Monday's games, the Dodgers' path to the pennant was clear, but fragile. A Brooklyn win and two Phillies losses gave Ebbets' team the flag, but the opposite result put the Dodgers back in second place. Since the Phillies were playing another doubleheader on Tuesday, their first game began earlier than the Brooklyn—New York single affair at Ebbets Field. The Phillies lost the opener while a back-and-forth contest developed in Brooklyn. The Dodgers fell behind, 4–1, early, tied the game at 5–5, and took the lead for good on the way to a 9–6 victory. Having done their part, the Dodgers withdrew to their dressing room to await word from Philadelphia. Shortly after 5:30, a reporter raced in with news of a Phillies loss and a National League pennant in Brooklyn. Needless to say, a celebration broke out, which was matched by fans waiting outside in the gathering dark.[33]

Nothing, however, was simple in 1916, and controversy erupted after John McGraw stormed off the field in the fifth inning, complaining that his players weren't trying. Naturally McGraw's behavior led to media speculation about gambling interests as well as the supposed desire of the Giants players to help Brooklyn or hurt Philadelphia. Nothing came of the incident or the speculation, and regardless of what happened in that game, the pennant was in Brooklyn, where it belonged. Second-place Phillies actually won one more game than in their pennant-winning 1915 campaign, but Brooklyn won 14 more, primarily because of the pitching staff Ebbets and Robinson had so laboriously put together. Especially of note was the performance of Cheney and Marquard, who won 31 games between them.[34]

Winning the 1916 National League pennant was without question a high point of Ebbets' long tenure as Brooklyn Dodgers president. Yet his appearances in the story of the dramatic pennant race have been limited, which is a reflection of the owner's role. Ebbets played a major part in putting together the Brooklyn roster, but once the season began, he had little impact on what happened on the field. One of the highest tributes paid to Ebbets' contribution to the 1916 championship season, probably offered unintentionally, was a widely circulated newspaper article describing how it cost only $20,000 to put together the Brooklyn roster.[35] While this can be seen as another example of Ebbets' cheapness, it's more of a compliment to Larry Sutton's ability to find relatively unnoticed prospects and Ebbets' decision to hire Sutton in the first place. Then as now, building a championship team at low cost was no small accomplishment.

Once the pennant was in hand, however, there was much to do and little time for Ebbets to do it, since the World Series began just four days after Brooklyn's pennant-clinching win. Ebbets had already waived his chance to open the Series in Brooklyn if Detroit or Chicago were the opposition and, in the end, it also proved more practical to let Boston host the

Left to right: Ebbets, manager Wilbert Robinson, Steve McKeever and Ed McKeever, ready to accompany their team to Boston for the opening of the 1916 World Series (Library of Congress, Prints and Photographs Division, Bain Collection [LC-DIG-ggbain-22956]).

first two contests.[36] According to the *Eagle*, it was the "most trying period of his entire career," made even more difficult by "almost unbearable" pain from an ear affliction which supposedly "threatened [Ebbets] with deafness in one ear." Even so, the paper claimed that Ebbets enjoyed the moment, walking around the club offices "with a wide smile on his face, and giving the glad hand to all comers."[37] Nowhere near as pleasant for the Brooklyn owner, however, was the controversy over ticket prices for the World Series games scheduled at Ebbets Field.

While World Series ticket prices ranging from $1 to $5 seem absurdly cheap today, the cost was four to five times 1916 regular season prices, and although basically unchanged from 1915, there was a controversial difference in Brooklyn.[38] At issue was the decision to charge $5 for reserved seats in the front rows of the lower and upper grandstand, seats which cost only $3 for the 1915 fall classic and would have remained the same had Boston or Philadelphia won the 1916 National League pennant.[39] The media wasted no time heaping criticism on Ebbets, led by Fred Lieb of the *Sun*, who felt Ebbets "has pulled another 'bone'" with a ticket price structure "far in excess of anything ever asked for world's series tickets." Lieb also complained that Ebbets' regular season prices were bad enough, since Brooklyn's average ticket price was "more per head than any major league owner." Warming to his task, the *Sun* scribe reminded the about-to-be-fleeced Dodgers fans that Ebbets was the magnate who had tried to convince the other owners to eliminate 25-cent seats. In addition, Lieb considered the price scale a poor business decision since the players were the primary financial beneficiaries of a short Series, while in a longer one, Ebbets' share would have been just as good at the old prices.[40]

Initially Ebbets tried to make the National Commission the scapegoat for the unpopular decision, which was duplicitous on his part since a September 18, 1916, letter from Ebbets to Garry Herrmann strongly suggests that the Brooklyn owner had more than a little to do with the decision.[41] Ebbets' next line of defense was the imaginative, but nonsensical claim that the higher prices were necessary to uphold the borough's "civic pride" because Brooklyn wouldn't want the gate receipts at the embarrassingly low levels of Philadelphia in 1915. Unsurprisingly, Lieb thought such an occurrence unlikely to cause Brooklynites any loss of sleep.[42] Ebbets was on far firmer ground when he pointed out the embarrassingly low attendance at some games during the heat of the pennant race, crowds he estimated as low as 2,000–3,000. It was an argument few wanted to hear, but Ebbets appropriately argued that the club had a right, if not a responsibility to recover "the tremendous outlay" it took to build a contender.

Supporting Ebbets was the *Eagle's* Tom Rice, who said he first identified with "the indignant yeomanry, who arose and called Charles H. Ebbets names," but after considering the "pitifully small attendance" at some games, had changed his mind.[43] Ebbets, it's important to note, didn't increase the price of a World Series bleacher seat, so he wasn't cutting off the average fan, but taking his chances with how much those who could pay, would pay. If Ebbets was really greedy, he would have jumped at Boston owner Joseph Lannin's suggestion to move Brooklyn's home games to the larger Polo Grounds, a move the Boston owner said could be masked as a National Commission decision to spare Ebbets any adverse reaction.[44]

The controversy notwithstanding, by Friday, October 6, it was time to leave for Boston. Ebbets spent the morning in his office, protected by "a husky doorman" from well-wishers, especially those seeking free tickets. Around 11:00, the Brooklyn owner came out of his office, "screwed his pain-racked face into a smile" and climbed into one of a fleet of 18 cars carrying the Dodgers to Grand Central Station and the 6 1/2-hour train ride to Boston.[45] The convoy made a triumphant procession through the streets of Brooklyn, cheered on by office workers while trolleys stopped to smooth their passage. Ebbets waved his hat to the crowds, but on closer view, his face "was a study." After receiving so much criticism about ticket prices, the Brooklyn magnate didn't seem to know how to respond to cheers which were "like water to a man on a desert [island]."[46] Once on the train, Ebbets was one of the last to remove his "black cutaway coat," due to his habitual insistence on "being dignified."[47] Upon their arrival in Boston, the Dodgers headed for the Brunswick Hotel to get ready for the big day.

As defending World Series champions, the Red Sox were understandably favored to repeat, but on a perfect fall day in Boston, the Dodgers were ready for the challenge.[48] Practicing what he preached, Red Sox owner Lannin shifted Boston's home games to far larger Braves Field, but to the chagrin of the owners, and especially the players, the crowd was some 6,000 short of capacity even with no increase in ticket prices. Going to the bottom of the seventh inning, the game was a close, low-scoring contest with Boston ahead, 2–1, but at just the wrong time, Brooklyn's suspect infield defense came unglued, leading to three runs on just one hit. Trailing 6–1 going to the ninth, while some of the crowd headed for the exits, Brooklyn staged a desperate rally, scoring four times and loading the bases for Jake Daubert, one of Brooklyn's best hitters. Alas, it was not to be, as Daubert was nipped at first base by a fine throw from Boston shortstop Everett Scott, a painful reminder of what good defense could do.[49] Not only did Ebbets have to endure the tough loss, he was suffering from vertigo and pain in his head and left ear. Although told by local physicians to go back to New York, the Brooklyn magnate refused.[50] Ebbets' frustration boiled over when he encountered Lannin in a hotel lobby and berated the Boston magnate for the poor seats given to the Brooklyn party. Ebbets threatened to repay Lannin in kind when the Series shifted to Brooklyn, but apparently nothing came of it.[51]

After the mandatory off-day on Sunday, the weather changed for the second game, turning cloudy with rain in the area. In spite of the less favorable conditions, there was a much larger crowd in place when Boston's Babe Ruth, making his first World Series start, threw the first pitch. Brooklyn got off to a good start two batters later when Hi Myers hit one past the Red Sox outfielders with plenty of room to roll in expansive Braves Field. By the time the ball was retrieved, Myers had crossed the plate with an inside-the-park home run, giving Brooklyn pitcher Sherry Smith a 1–0 lead. Boston tied the game in the third inning, aided by a bad play by second baseman Cutshaw, and the game remained tied going to the bottom of the ninth. The Red Sox almost won the game in what would come to be called walk-off fashion, but were thwarted when Hi Myers, having the best Series of all the Dodgers, threw out the potential winning run at the plate. The game went into extra innings, and as the 14th inning began, the gathering dark made it clear that this was the last inning. A tie would be a big problem for those who had checked out of their hotel rooms, since the game would be replayed the next day in Boston. Fortunately for those worried about spending the night on the streets of Boston, the Red Sox scored the winning run, a second straight heartbreaking loss for Brooklyn.[52]

Although the Dodgers' long train ride home was reportedly upbeat, any optimism must have been tempered by the frustration of two close loses to heavily favored Boston. When Ebbets awoke the next day, he not only found his team down two games to none, but also faced weather conditions far from conducive to a large crowd, with heavy winds and temperatures below 50 degrees. Temporary bleachers had been erected to expand the park's capacity to about 26,500, but Ebbets could hardly have been surprised by a less than capacity crowd estimated at 21,000. The weather, along with the 2–0 deficit, didn't help, but there was no denying that the furor over ticket prices hurt sales, with "yawning gaps" in the supposedly outrageously priced $5 seats.[53]

Empty seats or not, this was the first World Series game ever played at Ebbets Field, and Robinson went with Jack Coombs (4–0 in World

Series starts) against Boston's Carl Mays. The latter turned out to be very hittable as Brooklyn scored four times, highlighted by Ivy Olson's triple in the fifth inning. Just when it looked like Brooklyn would win easily, however, Boston rallied in the sixth and seventh innings, drawing to within one run and prompting Coombs to remove himself from the game. While there had to be more than one Brooklyn fan preparing for another heart-breaking loss, Jeff Pfeffer took over and stopped Boston cold for Brooklyn's first-ever World Series victory at Ebbets Field.[54]

If Ebbets harbored any illusions that the empty seats were due to the weather, he was disabused of that notion when ideal conditions the following day attracted only a slightly larger crowd of about 21,700. Brooklyn got off to an even faster start in the fourth game, scoring twice in their first at-bat and threatening for more before Boston closed out the inning. Unfortunately, that was the high-water mark for Brooklyn, both for the game and the Series. Boston quickly took back the lead in the top of the second when Larry Gardner hit a home run (his second in two days) off Rube Marquard. Unlike Brooklyn, the Red Sox were far from done offensively, expanding their lead to 6–2 to take a stranglehold on the Series. Recognizing that the game was over and the Series probably not far behind, Wilbert Robinson honored long-time Dodgers pitcher Napoleon Rucker by having him pitch the last two innings.[55]

Since there were no travel days, the two teams headed to Grand Central Station for the overnight trip to Boston. The Red Sox were understandably feeling good about themselves, while at least some of the Dodgers must have felt that the trip was pointless. One person who definitely didn't share that view, even if he wasn't optimistic about his club's chances, was Charles Ebbets, to whom the extra game was especially important, no matter the outcome. By splitting the two games in Brooklyn, the Dodgers guaranteed at least one game where most of the financial rewards went to the two owners, and gate receipts of almost $84,000, the largest of the Series, were no small matter to Ebbets. Ironically, the game was played on Columbus Day, the holiday Ebbets had long struggled to add to the National League schedule.[56] The game itself was more than a little anti-climactic since poor Brooklyn defense, led by shortstop Ivy Olson's two errors on one play, handed Boston the winning runs on the way to a 4–1 victory to close out the Series.[57]

Although the World Series loss was disappointing, 1916 was one of Ebbets' best seasons in baseball, both on and off the field. Winning Brooklyn's first pennant since 1900 rewarded the club's long-suffering fans, who, in turn, made the season a financial success. Low attendance was admittedly a problem during the last weeks of the pennant race, something *Sporting Life* attributed to residual damage from the Federal League war and Ebbets' failure to sign big names like Joe Tinker, Buck Herzog and Heinie Zimmerman. Although these factors supposedly made fans believe Ebbets wouldn't spend the money to build a pennant winner, 447,747 of them still made their way to Ebbets Field, a 50 percent increase over 1915. If, as Ebbets claimed in a July 8 letter to his fellow owners, a club's annual operating costs were about $240,000 ($100,000 more than Levitt's estimate for a few years earlier), and using Levitt's 70-cent average admission price, the 1916 regular season generated a profit of just over $73,000. Added to the club's World Series share of $68,289, it was a level of profitability almost unthinkable just two years earlier.[58] As the off-season began, there were multiple rumors Ebbets would sell his interest in the Brooklyn club, speculation fueled by his understandable statement that "I need a rest badly."[59] Once rested, however, with historic profits and a National League pennant to his credit, Charles Ebbets, a baseball lifer if there ever was one, wasn't going anywhere.

CHAPTER XII

"A man who can do that has more than twenty-five cents in his pocket"

No matter how satisfied Charles Ebbets was with his club's 1916 profits, his subsequent actions confirm that he remained concerned about the Dodgers' finances, which was prudent since the team's on-the-field success would be difficult to sustain even for one season. Brooklyn's National League pennant-winning team, especially its pitching staff, was built to win in 1916, which combined with the rebuilt Giants' late-season success, made a repeat performance very unlikely. To make matters worse, without the uncharacteristically high 1916 revenues, Ebbets still had to meet a payroll inflated by the Federal League war. Finally, although Woodrow Wilson was re-elected on a platform of continued neutrality, the risk of the U.S. being drawn into World War I was growing. Ebbets knew far too well from his 1898 experience the devastation that even a small conflict could wreak upon the national game. Much of Ebbets' attention over the next three years would be spent on these issues, until the realization of a long-time goal finally solidified the team's finances.

Ebbets began addressing financial issues at the December 1916 owners meeting by resuming his crusade to eliminate, or at least drastically reduce, the number of 25-cent seats at National League parks. Although some owners considered ticket prices a local issue, Ebbets reminded them that below-market prices also hurt the visiting club. Nor did Ebbets believe affordability was an issue, since the fan who could spend three hours at a baseball game "has more than twenty-five cents in his pocket." The Brooklyn owner also shared examples of how to work towards this worthy goal, describing how he reduced the number of cheap seats at Ebbets Field by persuading the local building inspector to order him to put aisles through the 25-cent stand. The tactics not only reduced the number of cheap seats, but also deflected any potential criticism elsewhere. While he didn't ask for formal league action, Ebbets insisted that the combination of "cheap rates and high salaries" simply "does not jibe." In essence, Ebbets was arguing that major league baseball clubs offered a quality product and were entitled to charge a fair price for it. Although no action seems to have been taken, there was general agreement with Ebbets' position.[1]

Additional revenue was important, but Ebbets' primary goal was to cut payroll, which was a league-wide concern. According to a *New York Times* article, the 1916 season was the "most costly in the history of baseball," with the average National League payroll escalating to almost $97,000.[2] Although the same writer believed Brooklyn was slightly below that figure, Ebbets claimed that Brooklyn's 1916 salaries and bonuses totaled $125,000.[3] Not surprisingly, the magnates wanted salaries closer to pre-Federal League levels, but as Tom Rice wrote in the *Eagle*, Ebbets was in the highly "embarrassing position" of trying to cut the salaries of players who had just won the National League pennant.[4] Even so, Ebbets' stated goal was to reduce his player payroll to about $90,000, still above the supposed break-even point for a club finishing lower than third. To achieve his objective, the Brooklyn magnate concentrated on 11 unnamed players he claimed had used the Federal League to successfully negotiate a higher salary or at least a multi-year contract.[5] While most of the discussions were conducted in private, negotiations with Casey Stengel and Zack Wheat became sufficiently public to offer insights into Ebbets' approach to salary negotiations.

Stengel was apparently one of Ebbets' primary targets because, according to the Brooklyn owner, Stengel had used the Federal League war to negotiate his salary from $3,000 to $5,300, an increase of over 75 percent.[6] Although not a Dodgers star like Wheat or Daubert, Stengel yielded to no one in aggressively standing up for himself and wrote Ebbets of his dissatisfaction with the proposed $2,000 salary cut, a letter the Brooklyn owner termed "impudent." The disgruntled player also went public, arguing through the *Eagle* that while a cut would have been reasonable if the club had a bad year financially, the players made Ebbets a "goodly sum of money" in 1916, so a "nice little increase" was only fair.[7] Unimpressed, Ebbets met with Stengel in St. Louis and reminded the unhappy player that although he had been ill for a good part of the 1915 season, Ebbets paid him his full salary, something the Brooklyn owner had no contractual obligation to do. Supposedly the lecture left Stengel "somewhat chastened," but chastened or not, he remained unsigned when spring training began.[8]

It took outside intervention to get negotiations re-opened when, in a move hard to imagine today, Abe Yager of the *Eagle* wired Stengel on behalf of the sports writers attending spring training, urging him to come to camp. Although not entirely pleased with third parties getting involved, Ebbets met with Stengel. While it took several sessions, Stengel reportedly signed for a $3,600 salary plus a $400 bonus if he hit over .300.[9] While only limited salary data exists, the available information confirms that Stengel used the Federal League war to his full advantage. Not only was Stengel's 1916 base salary almost exactly the same as Wheat's, he made more than Philadelphia's Gavvy Cravath ($4,800) and Fred Luderus ($4,500), both of whom had better career numbers. Stengel's salary was also in the same range as Art Fletcher ($5,500) and George Burns ($5,500) of the Giants, who were also more productive than the Brooklyn player.[10] Stengel can't be faulted for taking advantage of his opportunities, but with the Federal League option removed, Ebbets had the right to negotiate a lower, but hardly unfair contract.

Ebbets also wanted Zack Wheat to take a pay cut, but although Wheat was "very much dissatisfied," at least he didn't attempt to negotiate through the press.[11] The Brooklyn star also met with Ebbets in St. Louis, but as with Stengel, nothing was resolved.[12] With no agreement in sight, this time it was Ebbets who went public, claiming that his star player received two salary increases during the Federal League war, the second of which was 25 percent higher than the first. According to Ebbets, Wheat wanted another 20 percent increase in 1917 while Ebbets offered a lower salary, but the ability to make up the reduction in performance bonuses.[13] Prudently, Ebbets let the media, and therefore Wheat know that he was willing to compromise, prompting the Brooklyn left fielder to come to spring training without a contract.[14]

After further negotiations, Wheat avoided a salary reduction, settling for his 1916 salary, reportedly $5,300 with a bonus for another .300-plus season in 1917.[15] Although Wheat also used the Federal League war to his advantage, targeting him for a salary reduction reflected poor judgment on Ebbets' part. Wheat, with four .300 seasons behind him, was not only far more valuable to the Dodgers than Stengel, but was, in 1916 at least, one of the most valuable players in the entire National League. Using the sabermetrics Wins Above Replacement (WAR) tool (which admittedly wasn't available to Ebbets), Wheat was worth six more wins than his replacement player, the second-highest figure for all everyday players, with only Art Fletcher of the Giants higher.[16] It could even be argued that Wheat was a little underpaid since Burns and Fletcher of the Giants both made $5,500 even though their statistical performance wasn't as good.[17]

Why Ebbets targeted Wheat is unclear, but regardless of the reason, a contentious relationship with the club's best player wasn't in the Brooklyn owner's or the club's best interest.

Exactly how close Ebbets came to his $90,000 goal isn't known, but he seems to have avoided the increases which typically accompanied a pennant-winning season. At first glance, "rewarding" pennant-winning players with salary cuts seems to combine ingratitude with cheapness, but further consideration tempers that view. Regardless of whether the players deserved the higher, Federal League-driven salaries, the larger question was whether Brooklyn and similar clubs could generate sufficient ticket sales to cover the higher expense. "Big market" teams like the Cubs and Giants probably weren't at risk, but clubs like Brooklyn, whose revenue was vulnerable to forces like war, economic downturns or poorly performing teams, could have difficulty just meeting payroll. Nor was the issue just meeting current operating expenses, since excessive payroll cost made it difficult for clubs to afford new talent. In Brooklyn, Ebbets and the McKeevers were the only ones responsible for the financial viability of the Dodgers, and they were wise to pay attention to their largest cost.

While the Brooklyn squad, satisfied or not with their contracts, prepared for the opening of the 1917 season, another of the potential nightmares on Ebbets' financial horizon became real when the United States entered World War I. Since the slaughter in Europe had gone on for almost three years with no end in sight, even the most naïve owner knew that this war would have far greater effects on major league baseball than the Spanish-American War, which, although far less encompassing, devastated baseball attendance. Having experienced first-hand the dire effects of that conflict, Ebbets, more than any other owner, had good reason to fear what this cataclysmic conflagration meant for his club and the rest of major league baseball. Ebbets' fears quickly became tangible, in the form of a ten percent war tax on admissions, which Ebbets labeled "confiscation" since the clubs already paid income and corporation tax. In the end, a joint committee of both leagues decided to dodge the "bullet" by passing the tax on to the fans, accepting the risk that higher ticket prices would deter some of them from coming to the ballpark.[18]

The tax took effect in 1918, making Ebbets understandably even more concerned about player salaries. Seeking a collective solution at the December 1917 owners meeting, the Brooklyn owner urged the magnates to adopt a $60,000–70,000 salary limit or cap which, based on a survey of club payrolls, would have required major cuts. Nothing came of the proposal, but it was only the first salvo in Ebbets' campaign on that front.[19]

Although anxious to cut or at least limit his own payroll, Ebbets wisely decided not to seek broad salary reductions for 1918. According to the *New York Tribune*, Ebbets wrote to 26 players, asking them what they considered "equitable remuneration under war conditions," and got 15 responses, most of which he considered "satisfactory."[20] Whether due to the different approach, the wartime conditions or the team's poor 1917 record, there was only one difficult negotiation, but unfortunately, it was again with Zack Wheat. This time, the Brooklyn star went public, calling Ebbets "one of the most unappreciative creatures in the world."[21] It's hard to find fault with Wheat's attitude since Ebbets again showed poor judgment, demanding that the future Hall of Famer accept a salary reduction of about $500 after hitting .312, third-highest in the National League.[22] Surviving comparative salary data supports Wheat, since his salary wasn't even keeping pace with Burns ($6,000) and Heinie Zimmerman ($6,500) of New York, both of whom hit less than Wheat. Also weakening Ebbets' position, unlike many of his peers, Wheat had other options since he could devote himself year-round to his farm. Fortunately, Wilbert Robinson reportedly intervened, and Ebbets finally agreed to continue Wheat's 1917 salary of $5,800.[23] Ebbets' concern about 1918 player payrolls would prove to be well-founded, but once again he made a poor decision in how he handled Zack Wheat.

Although the 1917 season turned out to be business as usual, the government issued a "work or fight" edict effective September 1, 1918, which Fred Lieb predicted meant there would be no baseball in 1919 unless the war ended first.[24] The more pressing problem for the owners was what to do about the balance of 1918 schedule. While there was little chance of breaking even financially, Ebbets wanted to play the full schedule, even if it meant using replacement players, to at least offset some of the financial losses. In a remark he would live to regret, the Brooklyn magnate also warned that if the season ended early, the owners would be liable for the salaries of players exempt from military service.[25] In the end, the magnates decided to end the regular season on September 1, and by mid–September, Ebbets Field was being used to store war-related supplies.[26]

Unfortunately for Ebbets, Jake Daubert paid attention to the Brooklyn owner's comments about unpaid salaries. Ebbets' unwillingness to pay salaries he couldn't offset with revenue is understandable, but as with Wheat, Ebbets should have been more prudent in dealing with one of Brooklyn's best players. After Ebbets rejected Daubert's claim for the $2,150 balance of his $9,000 salary, the Brooklyn first baseman appealed to the National Commission, which supported Ebbets.[27] Daubert was not easily deterred, however, and took the matter to court, where he was represented by John Montgomery Ward, which was bad news for Ebbets.[28] Although Daubert's position was both legally defensible and reasonable, his actions apparently angered Ebbets so much that by early December 1918, the Brooklyn owner "intimated pretty plainly that Jake has played his last game in a Brooklyn uniform."[29] Ebbets had unwisely backed himself into a corner and traded his unhappy ballplayer to Cincinnati for outfielder Tommy Griffin, hardly an exchange of equal value. The lawsuit was settled for $1,500 to be paid in $500 increments, but Ebbets proved to be less than a gracious loser, since as of late August of 1919, he had yet to make the final payment.[30]

While the war created many problems for major league baseball owners, the conflict also gave Ebbets and his peers the opportunity to reopen the Sunday baseball question. The subject had apparently arisen in 1916 when Ebbets claimed that fans were requesting Sunday games, a question the Brooklyn owner suggested the legislature allow local communities to decide for themselves. Claiming he was neutral, which was highly unlikely, Ebbets said he would be bound by the wishes of people of Brooklyn.[31] As the military buildup got underway, war relief became a pressing issue, so Ebbets and other owners tried to link Sunday baseball with a good cause, doubtless believing that even without any financial return, the move would build popular support for playing on the Sabbath. Ebbets and the McKeevers decided to host a concert of patriotic and sacred music on Sunday, July 1, 1917, followed by a Brooklyn—Phillies game moved up from the following day. Admission would only be charged for the concert, with the proceeds going to various war relief organizations.[32]

Local officials were not, however, impressed with the Brooklyn owners' supposedly selfless action. After the authorities confirmed that admission was, in fact, being charged for the baseball game, Ebbets and Wilbert Robinson were arrested and later convicted of violating the Sunday baseball prohibition.[33] The convictions, at the same time John McGraw and Christy Mathewson were acquitted for playing a similar game in Manhattan, were the last straw for Ebbets and the McKeevers, who finally took public ownership of the fight for Sunday baseball.[34] First came ill-advised support for Sheriff Edward Riegelmann's opponent in the upcoming borough president's election because of Riegelmann's enforcement of the Sabbath law, support criticized by the *Eagle* and rejected by his opponent.[35] While their political campaigning did little for the cause, the three men were not discouraged, and at the end of November they sent a letter to Brooklyn clergy explaining their support for Sunday baseball.[36] Although playing on the Sabbath was still beyond the pale, the issue was publicly joined, and since wartime typically brought social change, there was some basis for hope.

Little went right for Ebbets in 1917 and 1918, including his club's won-lost record. Trying to defend their championship with basically the same roster, Brooklyn played close to .500 ball through the end of August, but was no better than sixth place. The team's performance dropped off in September, and the Dodgers finished the 1917 campaign in seventh place, 26½ games behind first-place New York. Dan Daniel, writing in *The Sun*, called it a "terrible fall" for a team "with substantially the same set of men."[37] Although Stengel would later argue that the acrimonious salary negotiations hurt the team's performance, that can't be the complete explanation, since Jake Daubert's average fell 55 points even though his multi-year contract preserved his salary.[38] Quite simply, a team built to win in 1916 did just that, and a repeat performance was highly unlikely. Regardless of the cause, Daniel concluded, "The Brooklyn club is sadly out of gear, and if Ebbets expects to pay expenses next season he had better start overhauling soon."[39]

Ebbets took that advice and also avoided difficult 1918 salary negotiations with Stengel by trading his discontented right fielder and second baseman George Cutshaw to Pittsburgh. In return, Brooklyn obtained pitchers Burleigh Grimes and Al Mamaux along with infielder Chuck Ward, a move praised by Tom Rice, especially since three Brooklyn starting pitchers had already been taken by the military.[40] Ebbets claimed the trade was part of a longer-term strategy, arguing "it was just as well that we should get rid of some of our veterans" in order "to bring Brooklyn another pennant winner in a reasonable time."[41] Although Rice and Ebbets were both positive about the transaction, there had to be Brooklyn fans who questioned trading two regulars for pitchers whose recent performance wasn't that good. Grimes' 3–16 mark in his first full major league season was hardly encouraging, and while Mamaux won 21 games in both 1915 and 1916, he dropped off to 2–11 in 1917 with an un–Deadball Era-like 5.25 ERA. The move smacked more of getting rid of Stengel, who had obviously worn out his welcome, than the first step on the path to another pennant, and Ebbets even admitted that the Mamaux acquisition was done "purely on a speculation."[42]

Stengel's place was taken by Jimmy Johnston, who proved a more than adequate replacement, but the only other major 1918 move was signing 38-year-old Mickey Doolin, who hit .179 in his final major league season. Fortunately, the acquisition of Grimes paid off immediately when he went 19–9 with a 2.13 ERA, or the team's record might have been even worse than 1917. Brooklyn lost nine straight games to start the season before playing roughly .500 ball over the abbreviated campaign, finishing fifth, 25½ games behind the first-place Cubs. Far worse for Ebbets, however, was the attendance, since only 83,831 fans paid their way into Ebbets Field, drowning the club's financial ledgers in red ink.[43]

While no one knew it on September 1, the fighting stopped just two months later, ensuring that there would be a 1919 baseball season, although its parameters were murky. Concerned about the uncertain transition from war to peace, the magnates, to their regret, took the conservative approach and opted to play only 140 games.[44] The majority of National League owners now also shared Ebbets' concern about salaries and voted 6–2 (New York and Chicago against) for a self-imposed cap of $11,000 per month of the playing season. To show they were serious, the magnates also mandated a $5,000 fine for any violation of the rule.[45] Whether they realized that this meant sharing their financial information with other clubs, or at least the league office, isn't clear, but the salary limits weren't well received, with sportswriter Fred Lieb predicting they would likely lead to a players' strike.[46] Just a few days later, on reflection and after further discussion, the owners replaced their earlier action with a $70,000 limit, which applied only to players not yet under contract, watering the idea down enough to avoid controversy, but also having little, if any, impact on salaries.[47]

Even though World War I was over, Ebbets could have been forgiven for feeling discouraged about the future of his baseball team. The National League's senior owner with 35 years in baseball, Ebbets must have wondered if his club would ever be financially secure. Having survived four baseball wars and one world war, built two ballparks and won three pennants, his club couldn't attract even 100,000 in paid admissions in 1918. Another season like that would ruin him, but unbeknownst to Ebbets, two important factors were about to bring a sea change to baseball finances. Perhaps recognizing what they lost in the abbreviated 1918 season, fans returned to the ball parks in droves in 1919, leading Fred Lieb to predict that seven of the eight National League clubs (St. Louis was the eighth) would be profitable.[48] In New York, however, the surge in attendance was due to something much more important than renewed passion for the game—the realization of one of Charles Ebbets' long-time goals.

Although the local authorities quickly stopped the 1917 Sunday benefit games, the arrests in Brooklyn and New York led to favorable press coverage and contributed to a shift in the attitudes of elected officials. For over 20 years, attempts to pass Sunday baseball laws in the New York state

——1919——
National League Schedule
As Revised and in Effect May 19, 1919

[Form Copyrighted by Charles H. Ebbets.]

	AT BOSTON	AT BROOKLYN	AT NEW YORK	AT PHILADEL.	AT PITTSB'GH	AT CINCINN'TI	AT CHICAGO	AT ST. LOUIS
April 19	Brooklyn (2)			New York		St. Louis	Pittsburgh X	
23	Brooklyn			New York		St. Louis	Pittsburgh	
24	Brooklyn X			New York		St. Louis	Pittsburgh	
25	Brooklyn X			New York		St. Louis	Pittsburgh	
26	Brooklyn X			New York X		St. Louis	Pittsburgh	
27						Pittsburgh	St. Louis	
28	New York			Brooklyn		Pittsburgh X	St. Louis X	
29	New York X			Brooklyn		Pittsburgh	St. Louis X	
30	New York			Brooklyn O		Pittsburgh X	St. Louis	
May 1		Boston X	Philadelphia X			Chicago X		Cincinnati
2		Boston	Philadelphia			Chicago		Cincinnati
3		Boston	Philadelphia			Chicago		Cincinnati
4		Boston	Philadelphia			Chicago		Pittsburgh
5						Chicago		Pittsburgh
6		Philadelphia				Chicago		Pittsburgh
7		Philadelphia X	Boston X			Chicago X		
8		Philadelphia	Boston		St. Louis		Cincinnati X	
9		New York X		Boston X	St. Louis X		Cincinnati	
10		New York X		Boston X	St. Louis X		Cincinnati	
11		New York				St. Louis	Pittsburgh	
12		New York	Chicago	Boston X	Pittsburgh	Chicago		
13	St. Louis	Cincinnati	Chicago	Pittsburgh				
14	St. Louis	Cincinnati	Chicago	Pittsburgh				
15	St. Louis X	Cincinnati	Chicago	Pittsburgh				
16	St. Louis	Cincinnati	Chicago	Pittsburgh				
17	Pittsburgh	Chicago X	Cincinnati X	St. Louis X				
18		Chicago	Cincinnati					
19	Pittsburgh	Chicago	Cincinnati	St. Louis				
20	Pittsburgh	Chicago	Cincinnati	St. Louis				
21	Pittsburgh	Chicago	Cincinnati	St. Louis				
22	Cincinnati	Pittsburgh	St. Louis	Chicago				
23	Cincinnati	Pittsburgh	St. Louis	Chicago				
24	Cincinnati	Pittsburgh	St. Louis	Chicago				
25		Pittsburgh	St. Louis					
26	Chicago	St. Louis	Pittsburgh	Cincinnati				
27	Chicago	St. Louis	Pittsburgh	Cincinnati				
28	Chicago	St. Louis	Pittsburgh	Cincinnati				
29	Philadelphia		Brooklyn		Cincinnati			
A.M. 30	Philadelphia		Brooklyn		Cincinnati			Chicago
P.M. 30	Philadelphia		Brooklyn		Cincinnati			Chicago
31	Philadelphia		Brooklyn		Cincinnati			Chicago
June 1		Philadelphia	Boston			Pittsburgh 2		Chicago
2	Brooklyn 2		Philadelphia 2				Pittsburgh 2	Cincinnati
3	Brooklyn 2		Philadelphia				Pittsburgh	Cincinnati
4	Brooklyn 2		Philadelphia				Pittsburgh	Cincinnati
5					New York	Brooklyn	Boston	Philadelphia
6					New York	Brooklyn	Boston	Philadelphia
7					New York	Brooklyn	Boston	Philadelphia
8								
9					New York	Brooklyn	Boston	Philadelphia
10					Brooklyn	New York	Philadelphia	Boston
11					Brooklyn	New York	Philadelphia	Boston
12					Brooklyn	New York	Philadelphia	Boston
13					Brooklyn	New York	Philadelphia	Boston
14					Philadelphia	Boston	New York	Brooklyn
15						Boston	New York	Brooklyn
16					Philadelphia	Boston	New York	Brooklyn
17					Philadelphia	Boston	New York	Brooklyn
18					Boston	Philadelphia	Brooklyn	New York
19					Boston	Philadelphia	Brooklyn	New York
20					Boston	Philadelphia	Brooklyn	New York
21					Boston	Philadelphia	Brooklyn	New York
22						New York	Brooklyn	Pittsburgh
23				Boston		Chicago 2		Pittsburgh
24		New York 2		Boston 2		Chicago		Pittsburgh
25		New York		Boston		Chicago		Pittsburgh
26		New York				Pittsburgh 2	St. Louis 2	
27	New York				Cincinnati		St. Louis	
28	New York 2		Philadelphia 2			St. Louis	Pittsburgh	
29			Philadelphia					
30	New York			Brooklyn	St. Louis		Cincinnati 2	
July 1	Philadelphia			Brooklyn	St. Louis		Cincinnati	
2	Philadelphia			Brooklyn	St. Louis		Cincinnati	
3	Philadelphia			Brooklyn	Chicago	St. Louis		
A.M. 4		Boston		New York	Chicago	St. Louis		
P.M. 4		Boston		New York	Chicago	St. Louis		
5		Boston 2		New York	Chicago	St. Louis		

legislature had floundered against the resistance of upstate Republicans. By 1918, however, the media, labor, progressives and the movie industry, along with the state's three major league clubs, coalesced around a proposed law which would allow local communities to decide the issue. A 1918 attempt, called the Lawson Act, failed, but a year later, with New York City Democrat Al Smith in the governor's chair, Manhattan State Senator Jimmy Walker successfully moved a similar bill through both houses of the state legislature. Smith signed the bill on April 19, 1919, and the New York City Board of Alderman unanimously approved Sunday baseball (64–0) just ten days later.[49]

At least one sports writer believed the Walker bill was the metaphorical equivalent of the last-minute arrival of the cavalry at Ebbets Field. Writing in the *New York Tribune*, William O. McGeehan claimed that without Sunday baseball, "it was doubtful as to the existence of Brooklyn as a big league club worthy of consideration" to the extent that in fighting for the bill, "the Brooklyn people were fighting for their lives."[50] Regardless of the accuracy of those sentiments, Ebbets wasted no time shifting a game to the first available Sunday and was rewarded with a crowd of 22,000 without any advanced ticket sales.[51] Recognizing that the law created new "plums" in the schedule, the National League magnates called a special meeting on May 13 and awarded Brooklyn 13 home Sunday dates, with the Giants limited to ten because they shared the Polo Grounds with the Yankees.[52] It was almost an incalculable windfall for Ebbets which would offer even greater benefits when future schedules could be designed knowing that Sunday games were legal in New York City.

The fans who put down their quarters (at least two for the most part) to watch Sunday baseball without fear of interruption saw a somewhat retooled Brooklyn roster. Faced with a gaping hole at first base after parting with Daubert, Ebbets purchased veteran first baseman Ed Konetchy from Boston, agreeing to pay the salary the first baseman was demanding from the Braves owners.[53] Also new to the club was right fielder Tom Griffin, acquired in the Daubert deal, which enabled Wilbert Robinson to move the ubiquitous Jimmy Johnston to second base. Returning from military service were pitchers Jeff Pfeffer, Leon Cadore and Sherry Smith, giving Brooklyn back its deep and talented pitching staff. With a more competitive lineup, the Dodgers finished two games below .500 in 1919, ending the season 69–71, in fifth place, not great, but a basis for hoping better days were ahead. More importantly from Ebbets' perspective, peace, renewed fan interest and Sunday games increased attendance more than four times the abysmal 1918 totals, to over 360,000.[54]

Just as Ebbets started to feel better about his baseball fortunes, the Brooklyn magnate's dysfunctional personal life came out in the open, possibly because of a media account some nine months earlier. On Christmas Eve of 1918, the *Eagle* reported, probably innocently, that Mr. and Mrs. Ebbets were almost run down by a man attempting to steal a horse and wagon.[55] Unfortunately for Ebbets, the woman wasn't Mrs. Ebbets, or at least not Minnie Ebbets, the magnate's legal wife. Two days later, the "real" Mrs. Ebbets not only denied she was present, but complained that reports of her being with Charles had become a "serious annoyance."[56] Whether she was finally fed up with losing her public identity to another woman or for other reasons, possibly financial, Minnie filed for divorce in early September of 1919.[57] Obtaining a divorce in New York in 1919 was no easy matter, since the state law was the "most restrictive" in the nation, with adultery the only legal grounds, which was undeniably true in the Ebbets' situation. Even, however, when adultery was proven or admitted, judges could deny a divorce if the person seeking to end the marriage had, among other things, "condoned the offense."[58] In the Ebbets' case, the length of their separation as well as the lack of a defense from Charles and/or claims for alimony from Minnie made the judge skeptical about the entire proceedings.[59]

Not only did the divorce application make the unfortunate situation public, testimony disclosed severe divisions within the Ebbets family. Obviously on Minnie's side, daughter Anna Ebbets Booth claimed that she asked her father to end his relationship with Grace Slade and was told to "mind her own business." On another occasion, Anna said she put Grace out of the stand at Ebbets Field, only to be put out herself.[60] While there was no mention of his testifying, Charles Jr. also reportedly took his mother's side in the squabble either at that time or a later date.[61] In the divorce proceedings, the estranged couple asked the court to terminate the marriage and endorse a settlement of $6,500 a year for 12 years, along with the payment by Charles of $1,800 in legal fees.[62] The judge, however, would have none of it, arguing that Minnie gave "passive acquiescence" to the situation for too long, thereby condoning it, and only wanted the divorce because she couldn't "get along" on her allowance while Grace "sported an automobile and apparently reveled in luxury."[63] Instead, Minnie sought a legal separation and finally, in early 1920, the two sides agreed to an out-of-court settlement reportedly equal to Minnie's initial demand.[64]

The Ebbets' divorce circus finally came to an end through a ploy commonly used to circumvent New York's rigid divorce law. In September of 1921, Ebbets and Grace were "caught" by a private detective in the Ten

Eyck Hotel in Albany, with Grace registered as Ebbets' wife. The "discovery" gave Minnie new grounds to reopen her divorce action which, to no one's surprise, Ebbets didn't defend, and by the end of December the two sides agreed on financial terms. While the settlement was sealed, Minnie's lawyer told the *Tribune* it was for $6,000 per year, most likely at this point for life.[65] In addition to resolving the financial issues, the settlement permitted Ebbets and Grace to "regularize" their relationship, which they did by marrying in early May of 1922.[66] With his marital issues finally resolved, the 62-year-old Ebbets would have been well advised to think about the long-term future of his ball club.

CHAPTER XIII

"1920 will be the most wonderful season in the history of our great National game"

When the settlement with Minnie moved Ebbets' personal problems out of the public eye, his attention turned to the February 1920 owners meeting and the upcoming season. At the owners conclave, the Brooklyn magnate finally realized his longtime goal of eliminating 25-cent admission prices throughout the National League. In place of the old 25/50/75 structure, the owners approved a new 50/75/1.00 scale.[1] Less than two weeks later, Ebbets announced new ticket prices at Ebbets Field which, by absorbing the war tax, actually reduced the cost of some seats.[2] In addition to higher ticket prices, Brooklyn's 1920 finances would also benefit from the first schedule intentionally designed to take full advantage of Sunday baseball in New York, with 19 Sabbath "plums" awarded to Brooklyn.[3]

Although the 1919 World Series fix had occurred six months earlier, the National League magnates were blissfully ignorant of the impending crisis when they debated candidates to replace Garry Herrmann as head of the National Commission. Ebbets suggested New York State Senator (and future Mayor of New York City) Jimmy Walker, who sponsored the Sunday baseball bill, but considering his scandal-plagued future, it's probably just as well the idea didn't go anywhere. Above all, Ebbets wanted someone who wasn't intimidated by American League president Ban Johnson. Having had more than enough of the imperious Johnson, the Brooklyn owner argued that it was time for the National League magnates to "stand firm and stop the dictating by Mr. Johnson." Ebbets also wanted to change the selection process so all the owners had a vote, rather than leaving the decision solely in the hands of the two league presidents, anticipating how modern-day commissioners are elected.[4]

Whether it was because of improved club finances or simply a desire

181

to avoid salary squabbles, Ebbets had signed all but eight of his players before the February owners meeting even began. Fred Lieb believed Ebbets was ahead of the other owners in signing players because of a "liberal policy of salary raises." According to Ebbets, he decided to offer increases which averaged 30–33⅓ percent because of the high cost of living.[5] To no one's surprise, Zack Wheat wasn't among the signed, but when he and Ebbets reached an agreement with little drama, it was clear that Ebbets was serious about getting his roster in place.[6] Among the unsigned were pitchers Jeff Pfeffer and Sherry Smith plus right fielder, Tom Griffin. For the two hurlers, the issue was money, with Pfeffer admitting he wanted more than the 30 percent increase offered by Ebbets. Media accounts suggested that Ebbets was trying to trade the recalcitrant pitchers, but fortunately the parties came to terms without breaking up the Dodgers' talented pitching staff.[7] Griffin, who had been acquired in the Jake Daubert trade, wasn't holding out for more money, but had decided to give up baseball for "the stockbrokers' game."[8]

Convincing Griffin to change his mind or finding a suitable replacement was essential if the Dodgers were to compete for the 1920 National League pennant. Brooklyn's greatest weakness was still the infield, but without Griffin, Wilbert Robinson had little choice but to play Jimmy Johnston in the outfield, weakening the infield even further. Although the problem wasn't solved by the end of spring training, optimism still abounded in the Brooklyn camp. Manager Wilbert Robinson's confidence so impressed the *Eagle's* Abe Yager, the writer picked the Dodgers to win the National League pennant with a 95–59 record.[9] Nor was belief in Brooklyn's chances limited to local, and perhaps less objective, observers. Robert Maxwell of the *Philadelphia Public Ledger*, who had seen seven of the eight National League teams during spring training, considered Brooklyn the "dark horse" behind defending champion Cincinnati, due to Brooklyn's pitching, which Maxwell rated second to none. The Philadelphia writer, however, shared the doubts about the club's "wobbly infield," especially Chuck Ward, the presumptive shortstop.[10] The optimism rubbed off on Ebbets, who told Frank Lane of *Baseball Magazine* that he believed "1920 will be the most wonderful season in the history of our great National game" and, if the Dodgers avoided injuries, Brooklyn would "surely land in the first division" and might even win the pennant.[11]

Optimism is always cheap in spring training, but a 10–6 record on a barnstorming trip north with the Yankees and their new star Babe Ruth gave even the most cautious Dodgers fan reason to believe in the club's prospects.[12] Opening Day saw the season get off to a good start when

10,000 fans watched Brooklyn defeat the Phillies, 9–2, behind Leon Cadore. Although higher ticket prices boosted Opening Day gate receipts, expenses also increased due to a new requirement that game balls be replaced at what the *Eagle* called the "slightest provocation." All told, 34 balls were used on Opening Day, twice the past average, with a projected full season's cost of over $3,000 per team, something the detail-oriented Ebbets was certainly watching.[13] If Ebbets had any worries about the relatively small Opening Day attendance, they disappeared when an estimated 56,000 fans crammed their way into Ebbets Field for the first two Sunday games.[14] Nor was there any cause for concern about the team's early performance, since the Dodgers won eight of their first 12 games, good enough for second place on April 30.

Although baseball has experienced many changes since 1920, one constant is that no team goes through the long season without hitting bumps in the road. It would have been difficult, however, for anyone to anticipate the nature of the Dodgers' initial 1920 rough patch. It began innocently enough on Saturday May 1 before a minuscule crowd of 2,500 "frost bitten and damp" fans at cavernous Braves Field. With Leon Cadore opposing Joe Oeschger, Brooklyn took a 1–0 lead in the fifth inning, but Boston tied it in the sixth. Neither team scored over the next three innings, sending the game into extra innings, which was nothing out of the ordinary. What happened, however, not just unusual, but historic since the two clubs went on to play 17 extra innings before the game was finally called for darkness after 26 innings, a record that still stands. Incredibly even for the time, both pitchers went the distance. Neither manager had incentive to make a change as Cadore allowed only two Boston hits over the last 13 innings, while Oeschger did even better, holding Brooklyn hitless over the last nine innings. During the Deadball Era, pitchers sometimes started both ends of a doubleheader, a Herculean feat in its own right, but Cadore and Oeschger went further than any pitcher before or since, just one inning short of pitching three games in one day.[15] No one familiar with baseball of the period would be surprised that it took just three hours and 50 minutes to play 26 innings.

The ordeal, however, was far from over for the Dodgers, who boarded a train for the overnight trip to Brooklyn and a Sunday date with the Phillies. The legalization of Sunday baseball in New York City, while it remained prohibited in Pennsylvania and Massachusetts, set the stage for what effectively became one-game series where clubs traveled overnight to play a Sunday game in Brooklyn or New York and then got back on the train. That was hard enough, but this trip was even more difficult since after the marathon in Boston and the train ride to New York, the Dodgers played and lost a 13-inning game to the Phillies.[16] At least playing "only" 13 innings on Sunday kept the game to two hours and 15 minutes before the exhausted Brooklyn players made a return trip to Boston.

By the time the Dodgers arrived back in Boston, the fatalistic among them probably expected the worst, and they weren't disappointed when it took 19 innings to play and, of course, lose the Monday game, 2–1. The losing pitcher was left-hander Sherry Smith who went the distance just as he had in the 14-inning, second-game loss in the 1916 World Series, also played at Braves Field. All told, Brooklyn scored a grand total of five runs, only three of which were earned, in the equivalent of more than six games. There was one positive to the long and unproductive weekend. Having seen enough of Chuck Ward at shortstop, Robinson put Pete Kilduff at second and moved Ivy Olson to short, in what proved to be the next-to-the-last step in getting Brooklyn's best possible lineup on the field.[17]

Mercifully, the next day's game was rained out, leaving Ebbets and Robinson with an offense that couldn't score and two pitchers exhausted from their marathon outings in Boston. Fortunately, the club stopped the bleeding by splitting four games with the Giants and Phillies, followed by a satisfactory 5–4 record on their first Western trip. Throughout May, Brooklyn's position shifted within the first division, reaching as high as second, but no worse than fourth. Winning five straight at the end of the month got the club back into second place on May 31, only a half-game behind the surprising Chicago Cubs. The outlook improved even more when the last gap in the starting lineup was filled after Tom Griffith decided the stock market could wait and rejoined the team.[18] With Griffin in right field, Johnston was moved to third base, where along with Ed Konetchy at first, Kilduff at second and Olson at short, Brooklyn had an infield which, although far from perfect, was the best Ebbets and Robinson could manage.

Brooklyn continued to play well, and on June 6, they were in first place with a one-game lead over the Reds. During a home stand against the Western clubs, however, the Dodgers went just as fast in the opposite direction, losing eight of 11, dropping to third place in the process. The overall June record was a subpar 12–16, consistent with the club's mediocre play of the past few seasons, and the Dodgers bore little resemblance to a pennant contender. About the only high point came off the field when the Rev. Edward W. McCarty, pastor at the Church of St. Augustine in Brooklyn, celebrated the 50th anniversary of his ordination at Ebbets Field.

Another clergy friend of Ebbets, the Roman Catholic priest consistently supported Sunday baseball even though he couldn't get to the ballpark himself.[19]

Fortunately, any Brooklyn fan who worried about the club's poor performance in June could take solace from the National League standings, which on July 1, 1920, revealed a wide-open race with only eight games separating seventh-place New York and the league-leading Reds. Fortunately for the other seven clubs, including Brooklyn, John McGraw's team was in a rebuilding mode, featuring "an unstable mix of youngsters and veterans."[20] Two talented, but sleazy players, Heinie Zimmerman and Hal Chase, were no longer with the Giants, and New York became even more shorthanded after they lost their young star, Frankie Frisch, to an emergency appendectomy.[21] With the Giants at less than full strength and the front-running Reds playing slightly behind their 1919 pennant-winning pace, the door was open for another team. The question was whether Ebbets' club could be that team.

When they won seven of eight games in early July, the Dodgers suggested that the answer might be yes and left on their second Western trip only a half-game out of first. Western trips meant playing 15 to 20 consecutive road games while spending days and nights on the railroad and in hotels, all without air conditioning. The challenges posed by the travel alone made a .500 record more than satisfactory, but the Dodgers stayed hot, going 13–7, and moved into first place. While it was more than a little premature, Brooklyn's strong play apparently inspired Tom Rice to ask Ebbets about the process for buying World Series tickets, although it's also possible the conversation was a contrived announcement to Brooklyn fans. Ebbets claimed to have learned from his 1916 experiences, and if the Dodgers were National League champions, the Brooklyn magnate wanted to give priority to the "thick-and-thin fans." As a start, Ebbets asked fans to save rain checks from the upcoming 22-day home stand. The more rain checks, the better the chance to get World Series tickets. It was, Ebbets acknowledged, an imperfect system, but the Brooklyn magnate believed those who had proven their loyalty "should have first crack" at tickets. Offering additional incentive to buy tickets over the next three weeks would also help regular season attendance, a further benefit which doubtless didn't escape Ebbets' notice.[22]

There is no logical reason to believe that World Series talk in July actually hurt the Dodgers' play on the field, but baseball isn't always logical, and the club struggled through the home stand and left on the season's final long road trip in second place. The team's mediocre performance also raised the hackles of fans who remembered past disappointments all too well. Their discontent boiled over on August 7 after an embarrassing 7–0 defeat to the Pirates when, according to Charles Mathison in the *Sun*, the Dodgers were "hooted by the irate fans." The boos, however, were only a prologue to a scene almost unimaginable today where "several hundred fans" cornered Ebbets in the grandstand for 30 minutes and unleashed a barrage of critical questions at the Brooklyn owner, including "What's the use of us hoarding rain checks for a world's series?"[23]

Perhaps to everyone's surprise considering Ebbets' sometimes volatile nature, the Brooklyn president was "equal to the occasion," answering every question put to him. Ebbets began with one of his time-honored responses to demands for better players, offering to "make it worth your while" (pay them) to anyone who could tell him where to get a good catcher. The besieged Brooklyn magnate also mentioned injuries the fans might not have known of and noted that Brooklyn's pitching problems were hardly unique. Ebbets was also adamant that Robinson had full control and the owners didn't interfere. Having, at least for the moment, silenced the fans, Ebbets turned his attention to a small boy who said in a squeaky voice that he would "like to ask a question." Perhaps guessing what was coming, Ebbets told the young man to go ahead, and the boy unsurprisingly asked for a free pass to the next day's game. Since the boy was, as Ebbets put it, in his "infancy as a baseball fan," and doubtless because he recognized the public relations value, the Brooklyn magnate granted the request.[24] It sounds like Ebbets' handling of the disgruntled fans was masterful, but any respite from fan negativity was short-lived.

During August, the Dodgers bounced back and forth between first and second before finishing the month in the lead, but just a scant half-game ahead of the Reds. By that point, however, the Giants had turned things around, and McGraw's club was only 2½ games off the pace. Headed into September, Brooklyn had played better on the road, something Rice without hesitation blamed on "a certain sort of Brooklyn fans" who "denounce them [the players] without mercy for the slightest misplay, and never hand them a word of encouragement, if things are breaking badly." It was too late, Rice lectured his readers, to add new players, even if they were available, which they weren't. In his many years of covering baseball, the writer claimed he had never seen a contending team treated as badly as the 1920 Brooklyn club. To back up his opinion, the *Eagle* writer quoted Ebbets and Robinson, who agreed that the behavior of "a loud-mouthed minority," a group Ebbets said the club didn't want as fans, was hurting the team's morale. Something had to change, Rice insisted, or "such fans

Temporary seats at Ebbets Field for the 1920 World Series (Library of Congress, Prints and Photograph Division, Bain Collection [LC-DIG-ggbain-31275]).

will come pretty near, if not entirely, to costing Brooklyn a pennant," something that would be "unique in the annals of baseball."[25]

Whether this was Rice's personal agenda or he was providing a forum for ownership, the message was a clear call for loyalty to the Brooklyn club as they headed into the home stretch. Although only 6,000 fans showed up for the next home game, many had obviously gotten the message. Rice praised the "change of attitude" which began with a big round of applause when the team took the field, creating an atmosphere similar to "the loyal rooting of a college football crowd."[26] The idea that fans could make the difference in a major league club winning the pennant is more than a little difficult to accept, but regardless of the reason, the Dodgers turned things around, going 12–2 against the Western clubs. Brooklyn's hot streak obviously made it easier for the fans to be positive, but Rice claimed that even mental mistakes such as bad base running no longer produced the usual storm of abuse.[27] Nor did the *Eagle* writer hesitate to remind readers that the change in fan behavior came right after his article, accompanied by improved play he labeled simply "astonishing."[28]

Winning also helped build attendance, with 25,000 watching Brooklyn sweep a doubleheader from St. Louis on September 11 while the Reds dropped two games, giving Brooklyn a three-game lead.[29] Some in the large crowd watched from temporary bleachers, seats which hopefully would be needed for a World Series in Brooklyn. That possibility became even more likely just two days later when the Dodgers swept another doubleheader, this time from the Cubs before a third consecutive crowd of over 25,000, a far cry from the disappointing crowds of the 1916 pennant race.[30] Cincinnati was now five games back, effectively knocked out of the race, leaving the Giants as the only potential challenger. A successful challenge, however, required that Brooklyn lose some games, but the Dodgers refused to cooperate, winning 23 of their last 29 to finish seven games ahead of second-place New York. In the process, the Brooklyn club made a prophet out of Abe Yager, not only by winning the pennant, but coming only two short of his projected 95 wins.[31]

September of 1920 was one of the best months the Dodgers ever enjoyed in Brooklyn, but sadly, the biggest scandal in baseball history eclipsed Brooklyn's second National League pennant in five years. Just as the Dodgers got hot in early September, Chicago newspapers reported an attempt to fix a Phillies—Cubs game, and shortly thereafter a Cook County Grand Jury was formed to investigate gambling in baseball. In late September, "Shoeless" Joe Jackson and Ed Cicotte admitted their part in the plot to fix the 1919 World Series, and the details of the Black Sox scandal began to unfold.[32] Not only did the scandal take the spotlight away from the Dodgers' National League championship, rumors that the same gamblers were also out to fix the 1920 World Series put the Brooklyn club under the magnifying glass. King's County District Attorney Harry E. Lewis had "no evidence," but "acting on general principles," set out to investigate the allegations.[33] To Ebbets' credit, he pledged full cooperation, and shortly thereafter, Ebbets, Robinson and a dozen players met with Lewis, testifying that no bribes had even been offered, much less accepted. A large crowd cheered the players as they left the meeting, confirming that Brooklyn's fans still believed in their team.[34]

Defeating the Cleveland Indians in the World Series, however, promised to be far more difficult than answering questions about non-existent bribes. In winning its first American League pennant, the Indians, led by player-manager Tris Speaker, overcame not only the defending American League champion White Sox and the improved Yankees, but the tragic death of their shortstop, Ray Chapman, from a Carl Mays pitch. Cleveland found a more than adequate replacement in Joe Sewell, who Ebbets "graciously" permitted to play in the Series even though he joined the club after the August 30 deadline.[35] Recognizing the potential financial benefits of a longer Series, the magnates had expanded the fall classic to a best-of-nine format in 1919 and continued the practice in 1920, with the first three games to be played at Ebbets Field. Whether or not Ebbets made the ticket-buying process more fan-friendly, there seems to have been minimal complaints about ticket prices, especially compared to 1916.[36] Brooklyn had eight players on its roster who were reprising their World Series appearance of four years earlier: pitchers Marquard, Pfeffer and Smith, along with five members of the starting lineup, Wheat, Myers, Johnston, Miller and Olson, so a shortage of post-season experience was neither a concern nor an excuse.[37]

Unlike 1916, there were no reports of large sections of empty seats at Ebbets Field when 23,573 fans watched Brooklyn drop the opener, 3–1, as Stanley Coveleski bested Robinson's somewhat surprise starter, Rube Marquard.[38] Perhaps Wilbert Robinson was saving his ace, Burleigh Grimes (23–11), in case of a first-game loss, and Grimes proved to be a stopper, throwing a seven-hit shutout in Brooklyn's 3–0 victory. Having tied the Series, Brooklyn wasted no time jumping out to a 2–0 lead in Game 3, going on to a 2–1 win behind Sherry Smith, probably the most poorly supported pitcher in World Series history. Probably wisely assuming he wouldn't get much support, Smith allowed just three hits and one unearned run. In what was a bad omen for Brooklyn, former teammate "Duster" Mails came on in relief for Cleveland with one out in the first inning and allowed just three hits and no runs over the next 6 2/3 innings. As the two clubs left on the long train ride to Cleveland with Brooklyn ahead two games to one, the Dodgers' camp was optimistic, with Ebbets reportedly allowing "encomiums" about his players to "roll off his silver tongue like pebbles roll down steep mountainsides."[39]

Ebbets, however, probably used something other than an encomium to describe Rube Marquard when the Brooklyn pitcher was arrested for ticket scalping before the fourth game. According to Marquard's biographer, the pitcher was in the lobby of Cleveland's Winton Hotel when, in response to a question, he offered a "Brooklyn acquaintance" tickets at something above face value. Unfortunately for Marquard, he was overheard by a detective looking for ticket scalpers and ended up in a Cleveland police station. After going free on his own recognizance, Marquard appeared before a judge the next day and tried unsuccessfully to talk his way out of the charges before being fined all of $1 and $3.80 in court costs, which he quickly paid.[40] Apparently Marquard didn't take the whole thing very seriously, which Tom Rice thought was a big mistake considering how strongly Ebbets, the McKeevers and league president Heydler, not to mention "the army of 400 newspapermen here feel on the subject."[41] Ebbets' own feelings were well known since about two weeks earlier, the Brooklyn magnate told a group of scalpers outside of Ebbets Field that he wished he could give them "a licking."[42] Rice incorrectly thought that if Marquard was convicted, he was "through as a major leaguer," but his spot on the Dodgers' roster was another matter because Ebbets was already saying he was "through with Marquard absolutely," and he kept his word by trading the pitcher to Cincinnati that winter.[43]

Meanwhile, at the ballpark, Robinson took Tom Rice and others in the media by surprise when he named Leon Cadore as Brooklyn's Game 4 starter. The decision quickly came back to haunt Robinson when Cadore lasted just one inning in a 5–1 defeat, tying the Series at two games apiece.[44] The next game made baseball history not once, but twice, when, as Rice reported, Brooklyn was on the wrong end of "the most remarkable game in the history of the World Series." First, Elmer Smith put Brooklyn in an almost inescapable hole with a first-inning grand slam off Grimes. Then, when Brooklyn tried to climb out of that same hole with 13 hits, they were turned aside by three double plays and the only triple play in World Series history, an unassisted one at that, by Cleveland second baseman Bill Wambsganass.[45] While that game was clearly the most memorable of the Series, it was the next day's contest which doomed Brooklyn. In a matchup between Sherry Smith and "Duster" Mails, the former Dodger proved his third-game relief performance was no fluke by shutting out Brooklyn, 1–0, on three hits. Smith wasn't far behind, allowing just one run on seven hits, but once again the Brooklyn left-hander was doomed by a lack of offense from his teammates. In his three World Series starts, Smith's "support" consisted of three runs. It remained only for Cleveland to finish the job, which they did the next day, 3–0. Graciously, Ebbets made a brief speech from the stands, acknowledging that the best team won and leading three cheers for Speaker and the victorious Indians.[46]

Although Ebbets had to be disappointed at his club's second World Series defeat, he had good reason to be pleased with the off-the-field results. After drawing a record-breaking regular season attendance in excess of 800,000, Brooklyn enjoyed additional revenue from seven World Series games.[47] Based on media reports, the club's World Series share was just over $100,000, almost all of which went directly to what had to have been a record bottom line.[48] While the *Eagle* claimed the club made a

$700,000 profit, that was based on an attendance estimate of one million fans, which was off by about 200,000. So the $189,785 figure released years later to the Celler Committee was probably more realistic.[49] Credit was due to Robinson and the players, but also to Ebbets, who built his second National League pennant-winning club in five years, largely by hiring one man who could find talent (Larry Sutton) and another (Wilbert Robinson) who could develop and manage it. Since the period from 1915 through Ebbets' 1925 death was dominated by the New York Giants (five pennants), it's easy to overlook that in the same time span, Brooklyn was more successful than any of the other six clubs. It was in no way a dynasty, but the combination of good scouting and trading succeeded twice and, as we shall see, came extremely close another time. After years of second-division finishes, Charles Ebbets, with help, had given Brooklyn competitive baseball.

CHAPTER XIV

"Tell the fans that I am in baseball until I die"

If Ebbets' 61st birthday in October of 1920 didn't remind him that he was getting on in years, the Brooklyn magnate received a wakeup call the following January, when bronchitis confined him to his home for over three weeks.[1] At least the illness wasn't made worse by contentious contract negotiations, primarily because higher profits enabled Ebbets to reward his pennant-winning team with raises ranging from 10–45 percent. Thanks to Sunday baseball and higher ticket sales, the club's finances had been stabilized, and Ebbets was comfortable sharing the box office success with his players. According to the *Eagle*, the lower percentages went to the club's stars, with the higher amounts offered to those who "blossomed last year" like Pete Kilduff.[2] Naturally, the raises were well received, and by the eve of spring training, only five players remained unsigned, including, to no one's surprise, Zack Wheat, along with another soon-to-become-chronic holdout, Burleigh Grimes.[3] A closer look at Ebbets' negotiations with both men over a multi-year period give a sense of the Brooklyn owner's treatment of his players.

Although Wheat started out looking for a $7,000 raise to $15,500, which would have put him at the rarefied levels of Ruth and Speaker, in the end the Brooklyn star came to terms relatively easily.[4] In mid–March, Wheat wired Ebbets that he would accept an $8,800 salary if the Brooklyn owner added a $1,000 bonus should the club finish third or higher. Ebbets was in transit so Robinson, understandably anxious to get his star player in camp, accepted Wheat's demand even if he had to pay the bonus himself.[5] While the 1921 contract negotiations with his star outfielder had been less difficult, Ebbets was apparently weary of the annual squabble. Wheat had another good year in 1921, hitting .320, but after the season, Ebbets told Garry Herrmann that he was ready to part company with the future Hall of Famer because Wheat had "been too long in Brooklyn" and would be happier closer to his Missouri farm.[6] Fortunately for the team, not to mention the Brooklyn fans, nothing came of this.

After another .300 season in 1922, Wheat, nearing the end of his career, understandably wanted to make as much money as possible and reportedly demanded a $10,000 salary for 1923, a raise of $1,200.[7] Predictably but not understandably, Ebbets refused to grant the request and this time suggested publicly that Wheat might "be benefitted by a change to another team."[8] By late March, Wheat was willing to settle for a $500 increase which Ebbets, again showing little judgment and less grace, refused to grant. The situation reached the point where the other Dodgers players were reportedly willing to come up with the $500 to keep their heavy-hitting teammate.[9] Fortunately, the matter was worked out and while the details weren't announced, James Murphy of the *Eagle* claimed that if Wheat didn't get his $500 increase, he at least got a two-year contract.[10]

In spite of hitting over .300 every year from 1920 to 1923, it appears that Wheat received only one $800 raise during that time. But when Wheat hit .375 in 1923, although he played in fewer than 100 games, and duplicated the feat in 1924, he was rewarded with total raises of $5,700, putting his 1925 salary at $14,000. Evaluating Wheat's salary is difficult because of both the lack of reliable data and the challenge of identifying another player as a reference point. The best candidate seems to be Ross Youngs, another Hall of Fame outfielder, who like Wheat hit over .300 throughout the five-year period and has comparable WAR figures. Although Youngs made considerably less money than Wheat in 1920 ($7,500/$5,500), over the next three years the Giants outfielder received $5,500 in raises while Wheat was limited to one $800 increase. In each of those campaigns, Youngs was an important contributor to a pennant-winning and very profitable team. Beginning in 1924, however, Wheat not only caught up, but by 1925 was earning more than Youngs ($14,000/$13,750). The analysis suggests that while Wheat may very well have deserved more money sooner, he ultimately wasn't underpaid by Ebbets. At the same time, however, Ebbets' seemingly grudging attitude toward Wheat doesn't reflect well on the Brooklyn owner, and it's easy to see how it could have contributed to his cheapskate image.[11]

While in 1921 Grimes' resume didn't come close to Wheat's long and distinguished record, the pitcher aggressively demanded a 150 percent increase from his $5,200 1920 salary, which the *Eagle* claimed would put his compensation close to long-time star pitchers Grover Cleveland Alexander and Walter Johnson.[12] Recognizing that Grimes deserved more money, Ebbets reportedly offered the pitcher a $7,500 salary plus a $1,500 bonus if he performed as well in 1921. Understandably uncomfortable with the vague standard for the potential bonus, Grimes wanted $12,000 in straight salary.[13] The pitcher missed all of spring training, showing up at Ebbets Field when the team returned north, where he and Ebbets reached an undisclosed agreement. Grimes' biographer puts the 1921 figure at $9,000 in salary plus a $1,000 bonus for winning 25 games, while the Haupert database reports $7,500, the latter a 44 percent increase, certainly not an unreasonable reward for Grimes' 1920 performance.[14]

If Ebbets was getting tired of arduous salary negotiations, he got no relief from Grimes in 1922, when the right-hander again demanded more money. The spitballer didn't lack for evidence to support his case, since although Brooklyn fell from first place to fifth, Grimes' 22–13 record and 2.83 ERA almost mirrored his 1920 performance. After supposedly first offering a $10,000 salary, Ebbets again shifted to a salary plus bonus arrangement which could reach the same amount, but after back-to-back 20-win seasons, Grimes reasonably believed his compensation shouldn't depend on bonuses.[15] Fortunately and unusually, the negotiations didn't drag out, ending with a mid–March compromise for a $9,000 salary and a $1,000 bonus "if in the estimation of the club's owners, the pitcher's work is satisfactory." Perhaps both men were tired of the drama, since they also agreed to a two-year contract, thus avoiding further negotiations until 1924.[16] Perhaps even more surprisingly, those negotiations went relatively smoothly, and Grimes was signed for the 1924 season by the end of February.[17]

After winning 21 games in 1923, Grimes supposedly wanted an increase to $12,500 while Ebbets offered $11,000. The two sides ultimately agreed on an $11,250 salary, a 25 percent increase, bringing Grimes' salary close to Wilbur Cooper, Eppa Rixey and Alexander, three of the league's highest-paid pitchers at $12,000 apiece. While Alexander was reportedly paid $12,000 a year throughout the five-year period, Rixey and Cooper, like Grimes, received annual raises until by 1924, the two made $750 more than the Brooklyn pitcher.[18] Considering the relatively small difference between Grimes' compensation and that of the other three pitchers, Ebbets certainly paid his pitcher a competitive salary, and Grimes' lack of a long-term record like Wheat's plus his prickly personality, rather than Ebbets' cheapness explains, if not excuses, the difficult negotiations. The relatively easy signing of Grimes for 1924 was not, however, a harbinger of things to come, since sadly Ebbets spent most of his last few months as a baseball owner in difficult and unpleasant salary negotiations.

Ebbets' long-term negotiations with Wheat and Grimes lay in the future, however, when Ebbets and Robinson prepared for the 1921 season by making only minimal adjustments to their pennant-winning club. The most significant change was the replacement of Ed Konetchy at first base with Ray Schmandt, who would prove to be a more than suitable replacement. While there was little change in Brooklyn's offensive production, the Brooklyn pitchers, other than Grimes, failed to match their 1920 performance. Although Brooklyn started out hot, going 10–5 in April, an 11–17 mark in May sank them to the bottom of the first division, and they fell even further in June. Symbolically throwing in the towel that same month, Ebbets traded pitcher Jeff Pfeffer to St. Louis, which the *Eagle* believed marked the beginning of another rebuilding process.[19] Basically a .500 club, the 1921 Dodgers ended the season in fifth place, 16½ games behind a soon-to-become-dominant Giants team. In what had become almost an annual ritual, the off-season brought rumors that Ebbets intended to sell his ownership position in the club, which, as in the past, Ebbets denied.[20]

In spite of the fifth-place finish, Ebbets and Robinson made only two major roster changes for 1922, including another ill-fated attempt to solve the chronic shortstop problem. In January, Brooklyn sent Pete Kilduff, one of the keys to the 1920 pennant-winning club, along with catcher Ernie Krueger plus $7,500 in cash to Cincinnati for Sam Crane. Crane was to be the new shortstop so Ivy Olson could move to second, but the newcomer performed so poorly that he soon lost his job. Fortunately, rookie Andy High proved proficient at third, allowing Jimmy Johnston to shift to short, where he became a serviceable replacement.[21]

Ebbets and Robinson also considered another possibility at shortstop which not only didn't come off, but again illustrated Ebbets' proclivity for sloppiness in player transactions. In late 1921, Ebbets asked Philadelphia owner William Baker about his plans for veteran shortstop Art Fletcher. According to Baker, he told Ebbets that he wanted Fletcher to make his own decision without interference from any other club, which Ebbets said he understood. Needless to say, Baker was furious when he learned that Wilbert Robinson had subsequently approached Fletcher, either with Ebbets' blessing or without him objecting. According to Ebbets, Robinson claimed he had been given permission from Philadelphia manager Irvin "Kaiser" Wilhelm, and although Ebbets asked if Baker knew about it, the Brooklyn owner didn't bother to make sure. Baker complained at length at the February 1922 owners meetings, but after Ebbets admitted his mistake, no league action was taken. Like the earlier sloppiness with the Johnston and Toney transactions, Ebbets' failure to pay attention

Left to right: Pat Moran, Wilbert Robinson and Charles Ebbets, December 1921. Note Ebbets' weight especially compared to Robinson, who was the regular butt of jokes on the subject (National Baseball Hall of Fame and Museum, Cooperstown, New York).

to detail in player transactions was in sharp contrast to his approach to other issues.[22]

The other problem position was catcher, where Otto Miller, after years of dedicated service, was at the end of his career. The solution, although it proved to be only partial, fortuitously produced an upgrade of unimaginable proportions in Brooklyn's pitching staff. Ebbets and Robinson believed that Hank DeBerry of New Orleans of the Southern Association was the best option at catcher, but DeBerry wouldn't sign unless the Dodgers also acquired a 31-year-old, well-traveled pitcher named Dazzy Vance. According to Vance's biographer, Ebbets was supposedly unwilling to acquire Vance until Robinson convinced him, but the source is Frank Graham's history of the Dodgers, which provides no supporting evidence.[23] If Ebbets sometimes believed he was unlucky, this was one time the fates were on his side, because no one would have predicted that an unknown in his early 30s would go on to a Hall of Fame career.

Although Vance needed a little time to adjust to the major leagues, Brooklyn still got off to a good start in 1922, and by early July 1 was only 5½ games out of first place. During a disastrous road trip, however, the club lost 14 of 18 games, due at least in part to injuries to Grimes, DeBerry, Griffin and Johnston, dropping them to sixth place and effectively out of the race.[24] If Ebbets thought Grimes' two-year contract meant a respite from problems with his star pitcher, he was disabused of that notion in early August when Grimes threw a temper tantrum upon being taken out of a game. It was apparently not the first problem with the Brooklyn right-hander's behavior, and the outburst cost him a $200 fine and suspension without pay.[25] Ebbets appropriately let Grimes twist in the wind for a few days before summoning him to a face-to-face meeting where, according to Tom Rice, Grimes got "the stiffest talking-to" of his professional career. Nor did Ebbets let it go at that, giving Grimes a letter, which the Brooklyn magnate later released to the press, laying out strict conditions for the pitcher's reinstatement. Grimes, however reluctantly, recognized that he had no choice and agreed to the conditions. Reportedly there were no further problems for the rest of the 1922 season.[26] Although Brooklyn played .500 ball over the last two months of the season, it wasn't enough to overcome the horrific July road trip, and Ebbets' club again finished in the second division, this time a notch lower in sixth place.

The Grimes incident was just one example of the high-stress world of baseball executives which, after so many years, seemed to be getting to Ebbets, since the latest rumors of him selling his Brooklyn stock provoked him to claim, "I have had enough baseball."[27] Perhaps so, but Tom Rice of the *Eagle* scoffed at the notion of Ebbets selling his interest in the Dodgers, predicting that if he were out of baseball, Ebbets couldn't handle the "obscurity" and "not having his say upon important questions." More seriously, the *Eagle* writer noted how even in more "ordinary" businesses, older men who retire while they were "still going strong," without some "definite object" in mind, put their lives in danger. Someone like Ebbets, Rice believed, in the more "conspicuous position" of a baseball magnate, was even more at risk, and the writer worried that if Ebbets stepped down, he would "fret himself to death in two years."[28] Ebbets at least took a break from the trials and tribulations of baseball, leaving with Grace right after the December owners meeting on an "extensive tour of Europe." Apparently forgetting his 1911 trip to Puerto Rico, the Brooklyn magnate claimed that the trip was "his first real vacation in 40 years of big league baseball."[29]

Whether or not Ebbets was sick of baseball, what was far less debatable was that the Brooklyn magnate was a sick man. According to Ebbets, when he left on his European trip, he was unable "to walk twenty-five yards without breathing heavily."[30] After he returned, it was disclosed that Ebbets was going to build a bungalow near the club's spring training site in Clearwater, Florida, at a cost over $30,000. The news confirmed Ebbets' plans to become a winter resident of Florida since the warmer climate was better for his "neuritis and bronchitis." The seriousness of the neuritis wasn't revealed, but the paper indicated that Ebbets had suffered from "bronchial troubles" for a number of years, especially during the cold Northern winters.[31] Pictures of the Brooklyn magnate depict someone carrying more than a few extra pounds, which combined with his breathing difficulties wasn't a good sign. Particularly alarming was that even after an in-season vacation to Clearwater in August of 1923, Ebbets' bronchial problems resurfaced almost as soon as he returned north. Even Rice acknowledged the increased probability that Ebbets' declining health would force him to retire from baseball.[32]

In preparation for the 1923 season, Ebbets and Robinson made one major deal, to some degree in recognition of the changing nature of baseball. In mid–February, Brooklyn sent first baseman Ray Schmandt and long-time outfielder Hi Myers to St. Louis for first baseman Jack Fournier. Although Myers had hit over .300 on multiple occasions for the Dodgers, he had little or no power, while Fournier was a consistent double-digit home run hitter who was expected to do even better with Ebbets Field's short right field fence. Fournier made the deal look good in 1923, hitting 22 home runs with a .351 batting average, second only to Wheat's career-high .375. Sparked by the two heavy hitters and almost 40 wins between Grimes and Vance, Brooklyn was in second place on June 4, but that was the Dodgers' 1923 high-water mark.[33] Brooklyn was a .500 club through mid–August, but ten straight losses at the end of the month doomed them and their fans to a third straight second-division finish.[34]

Considering Ebbets' age and ill health, the long-time baseball executive should have been thinking about what would happen to his ownership position in the club after his death. Whatever concerns Ebbets had on this score, they were further magnified by Charles Jr.'s problems. As the 1923 season began, the *Eagle* reported that the younger Ebbets had been away since January, recovering from illness at Bill Brown's Physical Cultural Farm, reportedly a place for "building up broken down business men." While Charles Jr. had returned to Brooklyn, he was not at Ebbets Field due to some "differences with the other officials," specifically Steve McKeever.[35] Although the paper expressed hope that the differences might be resolved, things went from bad to worse in August when Ebbets Jr. sued Steve McKeever and the club for $20,000 after he was ejected from Ebbets Field on two occasions. Although the younger Ebbets had resigned his position as club secretary, he believed he should be allowed to attend games, especially since he was still a shareholder and club secretary. Doubtless trying to limit public discussion, Ebbets Sr., claimed the dispute had nothing to do with him, since his son was over 21 and "must handle his affairs in his own way."[36]

If Charles Jr. wasn't the best prospect to take over his father's interest in the Dodgers, another possibility was Charles Ebbets III, who reportedly aspired not just to be an owner, but also a player.[37] Unfortunately, the situation with Charles Jr. continued to deteriorate when Ebbets' son sued the club a second time in mid–July of 1924 for $4,270 in back pay. To make matters even worse, the lawsuit revealed a split within the club's directors, since both Ebbets and his long time attorney, Barney York (also a director of the club), believed the money should be paid, while the McKeevers were opposed. As the *Eagle* noted, the lawsuit "gives surface indications of a deep-seeded row among the club's officials," never a good sign, especially considering the three men's ages and their equal ownership of the club.[38]

At least in the last years of his baseball career, Ebbets no longer had to worry about his club's finances. Early in the 1923 season, the *Eagle* analyzed the Dodgers' financial condition to see if the team had enough money to acquire new talent. While the paper projected an annual net profit in the $335,000 range, it was based upon home attendance of just over 770,000, when according to *Total Baseball*, the actual 1921 and 1922 figures were lower at 613,245 and 498,865 respectively. Although the $335,000 figure was probably overstated, many years later the Cellar Committee reported profits in the $150,000 range for both years. Since he probably wouldn't be believed if he attempted to make corrections, Ebbets said the paper's account was "slightly exaggerated, but not so much."[39] What the figures did confirm was that after seeing his club at death's door more than once, Ebbets had finally achieved his long-time goal of putting his club on a firm financial basis.

Although Ebbets headed south for the winter, he returned for the December 1923 National League meetings in Chicago, where an issue especially close to his heart was on the agenda. Founded in 1876, the National League was approaching its golden anniversary, a record for longevity not just in baseball but in the history of organized sports. Proud of his almost 35 years in the National League, Ebbets moved that 1925 be celebrated as the senior circuit's Jubilee Year. It was, Ebbets said, "particularly pleasing to me, because when the league was born on Broadway, at the old place where now stands the Grand Central Hotel, I lived but a dozen blocks from there." In approving the motion, Ebbets and Barney Dreyfuss, the two senior owners, were appointed to a planning committee along with representatives of the league's two surviving founding clubs, Boston and Chicago.[40] Whatever Ebbets' faults, a lack of institutional loyalty wasn't one of them.

Before he went south in November, Ebbets told the media that few

Ebbets' and Grace's 1922 passport photograph, one of the few surviving pictures of Grace (www.ancestry.com).

1924 player contracts had been signed because he had simply "been too ill to think of business," which had been the case "for many months." Having lost "upward of 30 pounds" and with blood pressure normal for his age, the 64-year-old baseball magnate claimed that he felt much better.[41] Spending the winter in Florida led to further improvement, and Ebbets was even more bullish about his health by mid–February, claiming that team Doctor Herbert Casey had given him a "clean bill of health, except as to the heart." That was not, however, a minor qualification, and Ebbets was warned to avoid getting "all het up over any subject."[42] Still, the reports of improved health, another of which appeared in *Eagle* just before Opening Day, suggested a turn for the better.[43]

In addition to taking longer than usual to sign the returning players, Ebbets and Robinson failed to make any significant off-season roster changes, giving Dodgers fans little reason for optimism about the 1924 season. Even so, Brooklyn had two solid hitters in the starting lineup, Fournier at first base and Wheat in left field, reminiscent of the 1916 pennant-winning roster, when Wheat was paired with Jake Daubert. In addition, while the pitching rotation wasn't as deep as the two pennant-winning squads, Brooklyn had two future Hall of Famers in Burleigh Grimes and Dazzy Vance. Although Dodgers management wasn't active during the off-season, Ebbets and Robinson made in-season moves which improved the club, especially the addition of pitcher Bill Doak, who went 11–5 with a 3.07 ERA.

After playing a little over .500 ball for the first three months of the season, the Dodgers were third on June 30, eight games out. The eight-game deficit was primarily due to poor play against the defending champion Giants, who won 12 of the first 15 games between the two clubs. By the end of July, however, Brooklyn had fallen into fourth place and dropped even further behind in August. On August 9, the Dodgers were a distant 13 games behind New York, but Ebbets' club went on a run similar to the far better known streak of the 1951 Giants. Over the next three weeks, Brooklyn won 16 of 20 games, closing the gap to a mere four games heading into four straight doubleheaders, all on the road (three in Philadelphia, the other in Boston). Incredibly, Brooklyn swept all four doubleheaders, a record which stands to this day, putting the Dodgers just percentage points behind New York with over four weeks left in the season.[44]

The race became so close that on September 6, first place changed hands twice on one day. At 4:00 p.m., Brooklyn passed the Giants to move into first place by defeating Boston in the first game of a doubleheader while the Giants lost to Philadelphia. Only three hours later, however, the

Dodgers fell not just out of the top spot, but into third place as they lost their second game while New York won.[45] Caught up in the tight race, more than 30,000 people tried to cram their way into Ebbets Field for the next day's Dodgers-Giants game, including some fans who went so far as to break down the center field gate.[46] Unfortunately, the Dodgers lost, putting them 1½ games out, but the Dodgers won the following day at the Polo Grounds to move back into a virtual tie. Over the next few weeks, the teams were never more than a 1½ games apart, and on September 22, with only four games left, the Dodgers and Giants were once again tied for first.

Play resumed with the Giants hosting third-place Pittsburgh while Brooklyn took on the fifth-place Cubs at Ebbets Field. With Dazzy Vance (27–5) on the mound, Brooklyn fans had good reason to be optimistic, especially after the Dodgers took an early 3–0 lead. However, the Brooklyn right-hander was working with only two days' rest, which may explain why after giving up only 11 home runs all season, he allowed three in this one game.[47] It was a close game, but Brooklyn lost, 5–4, in ten innings, while the Giants not only won that day but also took their next two contests, clinching the 1924 pennant when Brooklyn could do no better than a split. Even with the disappointment of coming so close only to lose out, it was an exhilarating and profitable year, leading Ebbets, late in the season, to ask the sports writers to "tell the fans that I am in baseball until I die."[48]

After close pennant races in both leagues, the magnates and still relatively new commissioner Judge Kenesaw Mountain Landis probably hoped the horrors of 1919 were behind them, but such was not the case. Prior to the Giants' pennant-clinching win on September 27, New York's Jimmy O'Connell offered Phillies shortstop Heinie Sand $500 to "not bear down," an incident Sand reported and which O'Connell freely admitted to Landis. The commissioner's investigation also uncovered the involvement of Giants coach "Cozy" Dolan, and the two men were banned from organized baseball for life. Feeling he had addressed the issue, Landis bid the World Series go on, but American League president Ban Johnson and Pirates owner (and third-place finisher) Barney Dreyfuss argued that it should be cancelled. The owner with the most to gain if the Giants were disqualified was Charles Ebbets, but as historian Reed Browning noted, the Brooklyn owner made the "sanest public remark," saying that Landis acted correctly and the Series should proceed.[49]

Having completed a successful season both on the field and at the box office, it's no surprise that the writers thought Ebbets looked in the "pink of condition" at an October dinner he hosted before leaving for

Florida. As ready as Ebbets was for rest and relaxation, however, he never stopped thinking about how the game, or in this case the World Series, could be improved. At the time, the leagues alternated hosting the first six games, with the site of the seventh game decided by a coin toss. Ebbets' idea, which he proposed at the December owners meeting, was to go to a 2–3–2 format so that, if needed, the deciding contest would alternate between the two leagues. Unlike some of Ebbets' ideas which took a long time to gain acceptance, the National League magnates immediately saw the benefits and passed the proposal, which was adopted in due course by the American League.[50] First used in 1925, Ebbets' system remained in use for almost 80 years until 2003, when the All-Star Game first determined World Series home field advantage.

The highlight of the National League owners meetings in February of 1925 was the celebration of the league's golden anniversary, but sadly, Ebbets, the league's senior magnate, was missing. Although the Brooklyn owner may have appeared to be in good health in October, the *New York Times* reported in January that Ebbets was sick at his new Florida home.[51] In a telegram read at the dinner, Ebbets claimed that his health was "improving rapidly," but his doctor "strongly objects" to his traveling to "severe weather conditions" which could put him at risk of pneumonia. Fondly remembering that the "good old National League" was founded within a half-mile of where he "learnt the first rudiments of baseball," Ebbets praised the league's founders' (all but one of whom he claimed to have met) "courage to tear the control of the game from the gambling element."[52] Even though he wasn't there in the flesh, Ebbets also filed a report on funds donated to support Willie Keeler in his last years, demonstrating that both his sense of responsibility and his concern for old-time players continued regardless of his own health.[53]

Ebbets' decision to build his winter home near his club's spring training site in Clearwater allowed the new season to come to him, but sadly, Ebbets' last days in the game he loved were spent on one of the least enjoyable tasks, salary negotiations. Signing Zack Wheat for 1925 wasn't a problem, but Burleigh Grimes was joined by fellow ace Dazzy Vance as another demanding and tough negotiator. In early March, Ebbets thought he had Vance signed to a three-year, contract estimated at $50,000, almost doubling Vance's 1924 salary ($9,000) and making him one of the National League's highest-paid players. Grimes, according to Ebbets, was unsigned, but the Brooklyn magnate considered him "morally tied up" by an option for 1925.[54]

The announcement of an agreement with Vance proved, however, to be more than a little premature. The Brooklyn magnate claimed that when he and Vance realized they were only $5,000 apart, they agreed to split the difference. Since Ebbets had only one contract form with him, the two men agreed to postpone the signing until the next day, but the Brooklyn president took the precaution of having Vance sign "an agreement containing the salary figures and such." When Vance saw the formal contract, however, he supposedly "went wild," demanding both a no-trade provision and the elimination of the ten-day clause, which Ebbets refused to do.[55] The Brooklyn owner was also making no progress with Grimes and, while he had no proof, Ebbets claimed that the two players were using common arguments, suggesting they were in collusion. Outraged by the very possibility, Ebbets declared, "the limit has been reached in the cases of Vance and Grimes," leading the *Eagle* to report, "the Squire's coat is off and he is in the ring fighting."[56]

Ebbets' frustration was so great that he went public with the details of both negotiations. Vance's initial demand was $30,000 a year for three years, which Ebbets bargained down to $47,500 for three years (almost $16,000 a year), but the no-trade and ten-day clause issues were not yet resolved.[57] While there was also some back and forth with Grimes, the major issue was the pitcher's insistence that Ebbets originally offered $15,000 a year for two years, while the Brooklyn owner claimed it was $14,000 per year.[58] The imbroglio with Vance was resolved first, when the pitcher reportedly gave in on his non-salary demands in exchange for a $5,000 salary advance and some loosely defined help on real estate investments.[59] Probably not surprisingly given the stubbornness of both Grimes and Ebbets, neither man would compromise, and Grimes ultimately applied to Commissioner Landis, who ruled in Ebbets' favor.[60] Even after Landis' decision, Grimes continued to drag things out, saying at the end of March that he wouldn't sign until he met with Ebbets in Brooklyn for one more attempt to convince the Brooklyn owner that he (Grimes) was correct.[61] The conversation never took place.

An unanswerable question is why Ebbets, who was obviously not in good health, handled these intense negotiations himself instead of turning over at least part of the responsibility to the McKeevers. Even if neither man was as good a negotiator as Ebbets, overpaying either player wouldn't have hurt the club financially. The most likely explanation is that Ebbets was simply too stubborn to ask for help. That same stubbornness was also in plain view when the ailing Ebbets hosted a visit by Judge Landis against his doctor's orders. Ebbets tried to visit the park again the next day but couldn't leave his car, which the *Eagle* blamed on his neuritis (nerve inflammation). Even more ominously, the paper noted, "Trouble with leading players has been a handicap to his return to health," and only a few days later, Ebbets was described as "seriously ill" and "confined to his bed."[62]

Equally surprising, and never explained, was Ebbets' decision to leave Florida for the harsher climate of the North at the beginning of the 1925 season. Regardless of the reasons, by April 7, the Brooklyn owner was at the Waldorf Astoria, reportedly "seriously ill." Attended by two doctors and nurses, it was hoped that Ebbets would get well enough to be moved to a sanatorium at Watkins Glen, New York, for a long-term recovery.[63] Although Ebbets was first reported to be improving, the situation rapidly deteriorated, with an ominous report on April 17 that the Brooklyn owner had "taken a turn for the worse."[64] The turn couldn't be reversed, and Ebbets died at 6:05 a.m. on April 18.[65] The late magnate hadn't neglected his funeral plans and was to be buried in Brooklyn's Green-Wood Cemetery some 700 feet from his friend, the Father of Baseball, Henry Chadwick.[66] The funeral took place on Tuesday, April 21, at The Church of the Holy Trinity in Brooklyn, and all National League games scheduled that day were cancelled.[67]

Not only had Ebbets chosen his final resting place, he had given considerable thought to the division of his accumulated wealth among two wives and four children, some of whom were at odds with their father. When the will was filed for probate on May 6, it provided housing for both Minnie and Grace, confirmed the alimony arrangement with Minnie, and gave Charles Jr. a $2,000 annual annuity, thereby effectively ending his involvement with the Dodgers. Ebbets also remembered his friends, leaving a $5,000 trust fund with the income to pay for an annual dinner on his birthday. Finally, Ebbets addressed his most valuable assets. The balance of the estate, which consisted primarily of Ebbets' interests in the Dodgers and Ebbets Field (two separate corporations) was divided into 15 equal parts bequeathed to Grace, Ebbets' three daughters and his one daughter-in-law, Charles Jr.'s wife, plus any surviving grandchildren. Anticipating family disputes thanks to his messy private life, Ebbets gave every beneficiary sufficient incentive to honor his wishes by stipulating that anyone who opposed the will would have their interest revoked.[68]

Completely missing was any succession planning for the Brooklyn baseball club. At the time of Ebbets' death, he owned 50 percent of both corporations, with the two McKeevers holding 25 percent apiece. The lack of a majority owner was a problem, exacerbated by the replacement of Ebbets' single voice with the multiple voices of his heirs. Perhaps there was an unwritten understanding that the surviving partner would buy out the deceased partner's interests so the heirs could receive cash rather than stock in the club. Not long after Ebbets' death, Steve McKeever seemed to allude to such possibility, speaking without his younger brother Ed, who was ill with the "grippe."[69] Sadly the illness, apparently caught while standing in the cold rain at Ebbets' funeral, proved fatal, and only a few days after Steve's comments, Edward McKeever was not only out of baseball, but life itself. The two deaths so close together, along with the lack of succession planning, set the stage for civil war between the two families, which erupted almost immediately in a fight over who would replace Ebbets as club president.[70]

Shortly after Ebbets' death, Tom Rice of the *Eagle* reflected on the man he had known for 15 years, in both the best and worst of times. Rice claimed that Ebbets was the regular target of ridicule, "much of which was vicious," and the Brooklyn owner was so "abused in language both libelous and inexcusable" that he was "totally unappreciated by the general public." Calling Ebbets "the most farseeing man in the sport," Rice argued that he was "in many respects both the ablest and the most remarkable [man] in baseball history." In almost every case, Rice claimed, Ebbets had to overcome the opposition of the other owners if only because for some reason it was fashionable to oppose the Brooklyn magnate.[71] Thinking of Ebbets and others from the old baseball generation now passing away, William McGeehan of the *New York Herald Tribune* wrote that if the "men who now have the game in their keeping" valued it as much as the Brooklyn magnate did, "the game will be safe."[72] Charles Ebbets himself couldn't and wouldn't have asked for any better eulogy.

CHAPTER XV

"The good squire of Flatbush"

Although Charles Ebbets spent over 25 years at the top of his chosen profession, he was not a tycoon or captain of industry. Throughout Ebbets' long career, major league baseball franchises were small, highly seasonal businesses, requiring little management attention during the off-season. At the same time, however, major league baseball clubs were also something more than small local businesses because of the game's geographic reach and national following. Unlike, for example, the theater business, major league games weren't just local entertainment offered to a limited clientele. Rather, major league baseball was the ultimate level of the country's national game, commanding attention and exciting passions from coast to coast even among the many who had never seen a major league game in person.

Successfully running a business, limited in size but not significance, wasn't easy, especially for Ebbets, who started out with little money and literally had to climb the corporate ladder from game-day employee to club president. Nor were years that saw four baseball trade wars, a World War plus repeated efforts by more powerful owners to force Brooklyn out of the National League a time for the faint of heart to be a baseball magnate. Yet when death finally ended Ebbets' baseball career (the only way he would leave baseball), he had built a successful franchise while making important, lasting contributions to the game itself. Ebbets' strengths, including his intelligence, penchant for hard work and commitment, were the driving forces behind his accomplishments. Sadly, however, Ebbets also had his share of weaknesses which threatened what he had built and could have destroyed it. How did one man build a successful major league baseball club while simultaneously sowing the seeds for its possible destruction?

Two major factors in Ebbets' success were his deep, lifelong love of baseball and his extensive community involvement in Brooklyn. While

baseball has no single birthplace, the organized game got its start in Manhattan, not far from where Ebbets grew up, and, as we saw in Chapter I,
members of his family played for the pioneering Knickerbocker club.
While Ebbets seems never to have mentioned his personal connection to
organized baseball's early days, it would have been unusual for a young
man, growing up in post–Civil War New York, not to like what was rapidly
becoming the national game. There was, of course, nothing unique in that,
but Ebbets' youthful enthusiasm grew into a lifetime passion lasting long
after most of his peers had put away such seemingly childish things. Passion for one's work doesn't guarantee success, but no matter the profession,
it's hard to envision anyone climbing from the bottom to the top of the
ladder without it. Ebbets' interest in baseball was not limited to just his
own club, but to the game itself, which he worked tirelessly to improve
even when there was little direct benefit to himself or the Dodgers.

Ebbets' love for baseball certainly wasn't unique among club owners,
but few of his peers could match his level of community involvement.
Born with roots going back centuries in his native Manhattan, baseball
drew Ebbets across the East River, where he not only took up residence,
but became deeply involved in his new hometown. As we have seen, especially in Chapter II, Ebbets became a member and leader of multiple bowling clubs, fraternal orders and social organizations, not to mention
successfully seeking his fellow Brooklynites' votes for elected office. Without question, the relationships Ebbets formed throughout Brooklyn helped
his ball club many times, in many ways, especially in building his two ballparks. But Ebbets' active participation in Brooklyn organizations also
showed he cared deeply about his adopted community, which contributed
to the loyalty which developed between the team and its fans, loyalty that
was far from a one-way street. In spite of years of losing baseball, the fans
kept coming, and Ebbets, even when he desperately needed money,
refused to transfer games or sell players. And when Brooklynites saw
Ebbets fight against powerful owners like Andrew Freedman and John
Brush to keep National League baseball in the City of Churches, the
Dodgers became Brooklyn's team in a special and unique way.

No matter how great his commitment to both baseball and his local
community, however, Ebbets must be judged on his success in carrying
out a baseball club owner's two most important responsibilities, providing
accessible and attractive ballparks and developing winning teams. Working
in very different situations, Ebbets built two new ballparks in Brooklyn,
both times hampered by insufficient funds. In 1898, as described in Chapter III, Ebbets took over a second-division club, playing at an inconvenient

location just months before Opening Day. Short of both time and money, Ebbets, instead of asking for patience, built a new and far more convenient park in just 45 days, using little of the club's money in the process. Negotiating with little to offer local transportation company executives beyond community pride and potential passenger traffic, Ebbets convinced them to fund the new ballpark. Once it was built, Ebbets continued to upgrade Washington Park, investing in two major renovations in less than a decade, including an innovative modification allowing fans more convenient access to their seats.

By the time Ebbets made his final renovations to Washington Park, however, construction of a new, and far more expensive, generation of ballparks was underway. Unable or unwilling to buy his current site, Ebbets faced the additional challenge of finding and acquiring an accessible location. As told in Chapter IX, Ebbets showed exceptional vision in choosing a site others had difficulty even visualizing as a ballpark. Working in great secrecy, the Brooklyn magnate then successfully completed an acquisition process far more complicated than any encountered by his peers. Nor did the process get any easier, since the combination of complex site preparation and unfavorable weather made construction difficult and expensive.[1] Once again, Ebbets lacked sufficient funds, which in this case led to some serious mistakes, but in the end, he gave Brooklyn a state-of-the-art ballpark, no small accomplishment for a chronic second-division team and a cash-poor owner.

Although Ebbets was, without question, proficient at building ballparks, at first glance it may seem difficult to consider him similarly successful at developing pennant-winning teams. On closer examination, however, the Brooklyn magnate outperformed the majority of his peers. During Ebbets' 27-year tenure as Dodgers president, only two teams, the Giants (ten) and the Cubs (five) won more National League pennants. Next come Ebbets and Barney Dreyfuss of Pittsburgh, tied at four apiece. None of the other four clubs won more than a single league championship, with St. Louis unable to capture even one. One possible reason Ebbets' achievements are discounted is because his first two championship clubs were tainted by the use of syndicate ball. In 1899, Ebbets was a minority shareholder, so it isn't clear if he had any choice when majority owner Ferdinand Abell opted for the quick fix of syndication, but there's also no reason to believe Ebbets opposed the idea. Syndicate ball was a questionable practice even at the time, but joint ownership of multiple clubs wasn't prohibited by league rules and, while they may not have used the same model, the Pittsburgh and New York championship clubs of the early 20th century were built through deals that were far from arm's length transactions.[2]

Brooklyn's 1899–1900 championship teams were destroyed by defections to the new American League, leaving Ebbets with a rebuilding process which dragged out over 15 years, a very long time for even the most patient fan base. Although it shouldn't have taken that long, a lengthy rebuilding period was necessary because, as seen in Chapter III, attendance in the 1899–1900 pennant-winning seasons was below expectations, leading at least one contemporary observer to claim that the club's fans were at best ambivalent about the 19th century equivalent of "rented stars." When Ebbets' team finally broke through in 1916, it was a club built through a combination of minor league purchases and the acquisition of veteran major league pitchers believed by some to be past their prime. Brooklyn fans could identify with both groups, considering minor league acquisitions like Zack Wheat and Jake Daubert as "home grown" while also taking a positive view of veterans making a comeback.

The minor leagues proved to be an especially fertile source of talent after Ebbets wisely hired Larry Sutton as the club's lead scout, even though Sutton had few, if any, credentials for the job. The hiring was a dual blessing since not only could Sutton find talent, he did so at low prices, something of no small importance to the cash-strapped Ebbets. Similarly, when it came to acquiring major league players, Ebbets' choice of Wilbert Robinson as manager was excellent, since the Brooklyn skipper could both evaluate talent and help veteran pitchers regain their form. Over the course of his career, Ebbets hired four managers, and once he found the right one, he was smart enough to keep him. Having seen how a talented club could be destroyed by a baseball war, Ebbets also deserves credit for convincing his rebuilt team, at no small financial cost, not to succumb to the temptations of the upstart Federal League.

Although the 1916 team didn't come close to repeating, future Hall of Fame outfielder Zack Wheat, reliable catcher Otto Miller and the ubiquitous Jimmy Johnston formed the nucleus of the 1920 pennant-winning team and finished a close second four years later. Ebbets and Robinson added new talent to the remnant of the 1916 club through prudent transactions, especially the acquisitions of Burleigh Grimes, Ed Konetchy and the extremely fortuitous signing of future Hall of Famer Dazzy Vance. Neither Brooklyn nor any other team could match the dominant Giants clubs of the early 1920s, but Ebbets, assisted by Robinson and Sutton, built teams that gave Brooklyn competitive baseball often enough to keep the fan base engaged.

By the end of Ebbets' tenure, the Dodgers were also a financial success, and not solely because of competitive teams and a state-of-the-art ballpark. To some degree, the improved finances were due to the dramatic post–World War I growth of fan interest in baseball, something beyond Ebbets' control. More important locally, however, was Sunday baseball, which Ebbets tried to bring to Brooklyn for years, until in 1919, his goal of offering major league baseball on the one day most people could attend was finally realized. It was a victory for the fans, but also for Ebbets and the McKeevers, because Sunday baseball finally put the club on a sound financial basis.[3] When Ebbets died in 1925, his estate, which consisted primarily of his one-half interest in the Brooklyn club, was valued at over $1 million, a far cry from the club's initial $20,000 capitalization.[4] And while increased monetary returns certainly benefited the owners and their families, it also gave the club the financial wherewithal to stay competitive, no small change from years of little on-the-field success and even less money to do anything about it.

While Ebbets' primary responsibility was his own club, the Brooklyn magnate never neglected his role as a steward of the game. A review of over 25 years of owners meeting transcripts indicates that Ebbets, more than any other participant, made regular recommendations to improve the game for the benefit of all, not just his own team. Some of Ebbets' ideas, such as fair and efficient schedule making, decent visiting locker rooms, and structured pre-game practice times, made baseball more "professional." The Brooklyn club president never stopped trying to improve the game, making a final contribution, not long before his death, when he convinced owners in both leagues to adopt the 2–3–2 World Series format, which has been used ever since. Nor did Ebbets ignore the fans, developing and gaining approval for a standard ticket with a rain check, ending the confusion that often accompanied rainouts.

Above all, perhaps because his club had been at the bottom so often, Ebbets tried to make the league more competitive by helping chronic second-division finishers, who all too often had limited financial resources. And while Ebbets had more than sufficient self-interest to stop free pass abuse, secure adequate remuneration from Western Union, and institute crude revenue sharing mechanisms, he also supported those ideas when they no longer meant as much to his own team. This was especially true of his most important contribution to professional sports, the reverse order draft, allowing the worst teams first chance to improve their rosters. Today, it's such a fundamental part of all sports, it's taken for granted. Tom Rice, who knew Ebbets well, said it was the "fashion" for other owners to reject Ebbets' ideas just because they were his, but in the end, they usually saw the light, a tribute to both the Brooklyn man's wisdom and his tenacity.[5]

Why then are Ebbets' achievements not more widely recognized? It's at least partially because of the enduring image or caricature of Ebbets as a good-natured, clownish bumbler who even in his finest moments provided ammunition for those more than ready to laugh at him.[6] Just one example is the enduring myth that in building Ebbets Field, the Brooklyn magnate overlooked the media.[7] Without question the original park had no press box, but it's not because Ebbets or his architect forgot to include one. Rather, after consulting the working sportswriters, Ebbets provided them with designated seating in the upper deck, accommodations praised by those who actually worked there.[8] While there is doubtless some factual basis for the caricature, it has also detracted from Ebbets' many accomplishments as a baseball magnate.

Nor does Ebbets' cheapskate reputation help his image. Unappealing incidents like arguing over money with a washerwoman, supposedly gouging fans on World Series ticket prices, and complaining that he was the only owner too poor to afford a car were recorded by the media and have been repeated ever since.[9] Yet to some degree the cheapskate label simply went with (and may still go with) being an owner. Branch Rickey, Connie Mack and Charles Comiskey are just three of Ebbets' peers tarred with the same brush, but the label didn't prevent them from being elected to the Hall of Fame.[10] Also, as noted in Chapter I, Ebbets' generation was raised with a very different attitude towards money, placing far more importance on small amounts. It was an attitude shared by far wealthier men, such as John D. Rockefeller, a comparison Tom Rice made at the time of Ebbets' death.[11] The problem was, however, that like Rockefeller, Ebbets sometimes lost his sense of proportion, such as arguing late in his career that the players should pay their own travel, hotel and meal expenses during the World Series.[12] His reasoning that since the bulk of the proceeds for the first four or five games went to the players, their expenses should come from the gate receipts, not the owners' pockets, has some logic to it. But similar to Rockefeller's micro-management of small amounts of money while one of the richest men in the world, the seeming lack of any sense of proportion puts Ebbets in a bad light.[13]

More importantly, however, Ebbets' accomplishments don't get sufficient attention because they failed to endure, and he bears much of the responsibility for that failure. Ebbets' death, followed shortly thereafter by that of Ed McKeever, left ownership divided between two families who were quickly at loggerheads with no mechanism in place to resolve such deadlocks. Nor was any leadership forthcoming from the surviving partner, Steve McKeever, who at one of his first meetings as lead Brooklyn owner managed to offend league president John Heydler and the other magnates.[14] Much of the blame lies with Ebbets (and the McKeevers) for setting up a 50/50 ownership arrangement without some means of deadlock resolution and, even more importantly, for the lack of succession planning, especially when Ebbets' health began to fail. The Brooklyn magnate prepared a detailed, carefully thought-out will, but never paid the same level of attention to the future of the club. It's just one example of Ebbets' biggest shortcoming—his inability or unwillingness to face the long-term implications of short-term decisions and actions. The flaw was evident in his personal life, where his part in premarital sex led to a pregnancy and marriage neither party may have wanted, and then years later when he deserted his wife for another woman, wreaking havoc on his relationship with his children. Similarly, Ebbets took huge risks in embarking on the construction of Ebbets Field without the financing in place, risks which could have bankrupted him and/or the club and did lay the grounds for the deadlocked ownership situation.

The stage was set for a disaster, which when it came, brought the club once again to the brink of bankruptcy. Also suffering was Ebbets' lasting monument, the ballpark that bore his name, because of years of deferred maintenance and neglect. Yet at least one thing Ebbets helped build endured, the close bond between Brooklyn and its ball club, a relationship so strong that when competent leadership took over, the people of Brooklyn embraced the team in a special and unique way. The end result was something so powerful that although the Brooklyn Dodgers and Ebbets Field are gone forever, they will never die. And it never would have happened without Charles Ebbets, "the good squire of Flatbush."[15]

Chapter Notes

Chapter I

1. *New York Times*, May 20, 1925, 18.
2. *Brooklyn Daily Eagle*, October 3, 1920, 17; 1920 United States Census; forgotten-ny. com/2013/02/avenue-g-flatbush/; Ebbets' "snug little home" was located at 1466 Avenue G (today's Glenwood Road) and for census purposes, he was listed as a "boarder" in the home of Grace Slade. At the time of the census in January 1920, Ebbets was still legally married to Minnie, his first wife.
3. Edward E. Steele, *Ebbets: The History and Genealogy of a New York Family* (Revised Edition, 2013), 3–4; *New Amsterdam Gazette*, Volume 3, No. 10, May 31, 1886, 7.
4. Steele, *Ebbets: New York Family*, 10, 17, 36–37, 84; *New York Gazette*, June 20, 1821, 2; *Evening Post*, July 12, 1822, 2; *Spectator*, November 7, 1798, 1; *Centinel of Freedom*, June 26, 1810, 3; *New Amsterdam Gazette*, Volume 3, No. 10, May 31, 1886, 7.
5. Steele, *Ebbets: New York Family*, 84–87, 146; 1850 and 1860 United States Census; *Doggett's City Directory, 1850–51*; Trowbridge's *New York City Directory for the Year ended May 1, 1859*.
6. *Manual of the Corporation of the City of New York, for 1859*, by D. T. Valentine, 442; https://ephemeralnewyork.wordpress. com/tag/laurens-street-nyc/; *New York Herald*, September 11, 1860, 3; *Report of the Council of Hygiene and Public Health of the Citizen's Association of New York upon the Sanitary Conditions of the City*, 1865, 34, 37–38.
7. 1860 and 1870 United States Census; Steele, *Ebbets: New York Family*, 84; *Report of the Council of Hygiene and Public Health*, 67; *Trow's New York City Directory for the Year Ended May 1, 1870*, 320.
8. Edwin G. Burrows and Mike Wallace, *Gotham: A History of New York City to 1898* (New York: Oxford University Press, 1999), 876, 881, 883; http://www.taxhistory.org/ www/website.nsf/web/THM1861?Open Document.
9. Mark Sullivan, *Our Times: The United States, Volume II, 1900–1925, America Finding Herself* (New York: Scribner's, 1927), 2–3, 188; Steele, *Ebbets: New York Family*, 146.
10. Sullivan, *Our Times*, 7, 18, 20, 44–45.
11. *Brooklyn Daily Eagle*, April 19, 1925, 8.
12. Ron Chernow, *Titan: The Life of John D. Rockefeller Sr.* (New York: Random House, 1998), 312, 320, 505.
13. Sullivan, *Our Times*, 45, 94; *Brooklyn Daily Eagle*, April 19, 1925, 8; Ronald C. White, Jr., *Lincoln's Greatest Speech: The Second Inaugural* (New York: Simon & Schuster, 2002), 76.
14. Peter Morris, William J. Ryczek, Jan Finkel, Leonard Levin and Richard Malatzky, *Baseball Founders: The Clubs, Players and Cities of the Northeast That Established the Game* (Jefferson, NC: McFarland, 2013), 22, 27, 67; Steele, *Ebbets: New York Family*, 43–44, 88; Charles Ebbets to John Heydler, National League Owners Meeting Minutes, February 2, 1925, 5, National League Meetings, Conferences, Minutes and Financial Ledgers, 1899–1995, BA-MSS 55, National Baseball Hall of Fame Library, Cooperstown, New York, hereafter BA-MSS 55, HOF; e-mail from Ted Steele, January 8, 2017.
15. 1860 United States Census; *Standard Union*, April 9, 1913; Steele, *Ebbets: New York Family*, 84, 146.
16. *Goulding's New York City Directory for 1875–76*, 392; *Trow's New York City Directory for the Year Ended May 1, 1876*, 371; Steele, *Ebbets: New York Family*, 149–150, 155.
17. *Brooklyn Daily Eagle*, October 3, 1920, 17; Quick family tree provided by Edward E. Steele; *New York Times*, March 24, 1895, 12; *New York Herald*, August 29, 1871, 3; http:// daytoninmanhattan.blogspot.de/2013/07/ the-lost-metropolitan-hotel-no-578.html.
18. *Goulding's Business Directory of New York For the Year Ending May 1st, 1873* 58;

http://new-york-city.yodelout.com/new-york-city-printers-and-booksellers/; *American Bookseller*, October 15, 1881, 237; J. Randolph Cox, *The Dime Novel Companion: A Source Book* (Westport, CT: Greenwood Press, 2000), 85–86; Carol Nackendorf, *The Fictional Republic: Horatio Alger and American Political Discourse* (New York: Oxford University Press, 1994), 188; http://www.accessible-archives.com/collections/frank-leslies-weekly.

19. Steele, *Ebbets: New York Family*, 155.

Chapter II

1. William Shakespeare, *Julius Caesar*, 4.3, 218–19.

2. *New York Times*, August 31, 1864, and December 25, 1866, 2; *Eastern State Journal*, January 13, 1906, 3; *New York Herald*, March 8, 1876, 8; *New York Tribune*, September 22, 1871, 1; *The Sporting News*, January 20, 1906, 2. Doyle and Byrne were brothers-in-law, while Abell and Doyle likely knew each other from both gambling and politics. Although Abell is better known as a gambling house operator, multiple newspaper accounts like the above suggest significant Tammany Hall involvement.

3. Ellen M. Snyder-Grenier, *Brooklyn: An Illustrated History* (Philadelphia: Temple University Press, 1996), 10.

4. *The Sporting News*, January 20, 1906; *New York Clipper*, December 23, 1882, 647, and January 20, 1883, 711.

5. Steele, *Ebbets: New York Family*, 155; Charles Ebbets, November 16, 1922, passport application; *Trow's New York City Directory for the Year Ended May 31, 1883*, 457; *New York Clipper*, April 16, 1892, 89.

6. *Brooklyn Daily Eagle*, January 18, 1913, 23.

7. T. J. Stiles, *Custer's Trials: A Life on the Frontier of a New America* (New York: Alfred Knopf, 2015), 344–45.

8. *Brooklyn Daily Eagle*, March 8, 1883, 3.

9. Harold Seymour and Dorothy Seymour Mills, *Baseball: The Early Years* (New York: Oxford University Press, 1960), 194.

10. *Brooklyn Daily Eagle*, October 20, 1886, 1, and January 18, 1913, 23.

11. Robert F. Burk, *Never Just a Game: Players, Owners & American Baseball to 1920* (Chapel Hill: University of North Carolina Press, 1994), 243.

12. *Brooklyn Daily Eagle*, August 9, 1894, 2, and April 26, 1896, 15.

13. *Sporting Life*, January 8, 1898, 3.

14. *New York Clipper*, May 19, 1883, 135;

Brooklyn Daily Eagle, June 1, 1883, 2, and April 17, 1883, 3.

15. *Brooklyn Daily Eagle*, March 9, 1897, 10, April 29, 1897, 4, and May 1, 1897, 4.

16. *New York Sun*, January 5, 1898, 4; *Brooklyn Daily Eagle*, April 26, 1896, 15.

17. *Brooklyn Daily Eagle*, April 26, 1896, 15; *Sporting Life*, quoted in the *Brooklyn Daily Eagle*, March 6, 1897, 4.

18. *New York Clipper*, July 28, 1883, 302; *Brooklyn Daily Eagle*, July 24, 1883, 3, and September 30, 1883, 3; Seymour and Seymour Mills, *Early Years*, 160, 163–64.

19. *Brooklyn Daily Eagle*, October 8, 1887, 6, November 2, 1887, 4, and November 30, 1887, 6.

20. *Cincinnati Enquirer*, quoted in the *Brooklyn Daily Eagle*, September 27, 1888, 1.

21. The final pieces in the puzzle were Hub Collins, "Oyster" Burns, "Pop" Corkhill and Tim Lovett.

22. Seymour and Seymour Mills, *Early Years*, 160, 163–64.

23. *Brooklyn Daily Eagle*, December 12, 1884, 1, and January 23, 1913, 19.

24. *Brooklyn Daily Eagle*, January 20, 1889, 7.

25. *Brooklyn Daily Eagle*, March 4, 1888, 16.

26. *Trenton Evening Times*, March 6, 1892, 3; *New York Clipper*, April 16, 1892, 89; National League Owners Meeting, Minutes, December 9, 1919, 258, BA-MSS 55, HOF.

27. *Brooklyn Daily Eagle*, March 8, 1889, 1.

28. *Brooklyn Daily Eagle*, January 18, 1891, 8.

29. *Brooklyn Daily Eagle*, March 5, 1891, 6.

30. *Brooklyn Daily Eagle*, December 27, 1891, 8.

31. *New York Clipper*, January 23, 1892, 766.

32. *Brooklyn Daily Eagle*, February 21, 1892, 9.

33. *Brooklyn Daily Eagle*, March 4, 1892, 1.

34. *Brooklyn Daily Eagle*, October 9, 1893, 8.

35. *New York Clipper*, July 7, 1894, 280.

36. *Brooklyn Daily Eagle*, February 26, 1896, 10.

37. *Brooklyn Daily Eagle*, October 20, 1895, 24.

38. *Brooklyn Daily Eagle*, May 20, 1889; *New York Tribune*, May 20, 1889, 3.

39. *Brooklyn Daily Eagle*, May 21, 1889, 1.

40. *Brooklyn Daily Eagle*, May 21, 1889, 1.

41. *Brooklyn Daily Eagle*, May 28, 1889, 6

42. *Brooklyn Daily Eagle*, June 2, 1889, 6.

43. *Brooklyn Daily Eagle*, May 31, 1889, 1.
44. *Brooklyn Daily Eagle*, May 21, 1889, 1.
45. Burk, *Never Just a Game*, 94–102.
46. *Ibid.*, 104–106.
47. Charles Alexander, *Turbulent Seasons: Baseball in 1890–91* (Dallas: Southern Methodist University Press, 2011), 54.
48. *New York Herald*, November 15, 1889, 8; *Sporting Life*, November 20, 1889, 2.
49. *Brooklyn Daily Eagle*, December 6, 1889, 6.
50. *Brooklyn Daily Eagle*, December 11, 1889, 1, and February 17, 1893, 3.
51. *Brooklyn Daily Eagle*, December 11, 1889, 1.
52. *Brooklyn Daily Eagle*, December 12, 1889, 6.
53. Burk, *Never Just a Game*, 110; Alexander, *Turbulent Seasons*, 48.
54. David Nemec, *The Beer and Whiskey League* (Lyons, CT: Guilford Press, 2004), 192, 197.
55. Burk, *Never Just a Game*, 108.
56. *Brooklyn Daily Eagle*, April 27, 1890, 18.
57. Seymour and Seymour Mills, *Early Years*, 238; Burk, *Never Just a Game*, 111.
58. Nemec, *Beer and Whiskey*, 199.
59. *Sporting Life*, November 22, 1890, 6.
60. Seymour and Seymour Mills, *Early Years*, 244–45.
61. *New York Clipper*, October 25, 1890, 521.
62. *Brooklyn Daily Eagle*, November 13, 1890, 6, November 14, 1890, 6, and January 7, 1891, 6; *New York Clipper*, October 25, 1890, 521, and January 17, 1891, 713.
63. *New York Herald*, January 6, 1891, 8, and January 28, 1891, 9; *New York Sun*, January 7, 1891, 4; *Brooklyn Daily Eagle*, January 8, 1891, 6, January 23, 1891, 6, and January 31, 1891; *New York Clipper*, January 17, 1891, 713.
64. *Brooklyn Daily Eagle*, December 11, 1899, 16.
65. National League Owners Meeting, Minutes, December 13, 1899, 40, BA-MSS 55, HOF.
66. *Brooklyn Daily Eagle*, October 31, 1890, and November 2, 1890.
67. Peter Morris, *A Game of Inches: The Stories Behind the Innovations That Shaped Baseball* (Chicago: Ivan R. Dee, 2006), 419.
68. *Brooklyn Daily Eagle*, March 20, 1889, and March 30, 1889. For a more detailed description and pictures of the old and new Brooklyn scorecards, see http://amanlypastime.blogspot.com/2016/01/hey-get-your-scorecard.html
69. *Brooklyn Daily Eagle*, October 4, 1891, 8, and November 4, 1892, 7.
70. *Brooklyn Daily Eagle*, April 2, 1893, 3, and October 12, 1893, 8; *New York Clipper*, October 4, 1890, 473.
71. http://www.bowlingmuseum.com/Visit/History-of-Bowling.
72. *Brooklyn Daily Eagle*, August 31, 1894, 2.
73. *Brooklyn Daily Eagle*, April 4, 1890, 4, September 30, 1894, 11, June 10, 1894, 10, and January 26, 1902, 42.
74. *Brooklyn Daily Eagle*, November 15, 1894, 4.
75. *Brooklyn Daily Eagle*, December 12, 1894, 4, and January 8, 1896, 10.
76. *Brooklyn Daily Eagle*, January 21, 1894, 3.
77. *Brooklyn Daily Eagle*, October 8, 1885, 1, January 18, 1887, 4, and January 9, 1897, 3.
78. http://www.brownstoner.com/blog/2010/10/walkabout-club/.
79. *Brooklyn Daily Eagle*, September 1, 1897, 10.
80. *Brooklyn Daily Eagle*, August 26, 1897, 2.
81. *Lain's Brooklyn Street Guide*, 1895, 362; other residences from Brooklyn street guides and directories found at www.ancestry.com.
82. *Brooklyn Daily Eagle*, October 20, 1895, 24; *Brooklyn Daily Eagle Almanac*, 1895, 223.
83. *Brooklyn Daily Eagle*, October 9, 1895, 10, and October 28, 1895, 14.
84. *Brooklyn Daily Eagle*, October 20, 1895, 23.
85. *Brooklyn Daily Eagle*, November 3, 1895, 22.
86. *Brooklyn Daily Eagle*, December 20, 1895, 9.
87. Burrows and Wallace, *Gotham*, 1228–229, 1233.
88. *Brooklyn Daily Eagle*, March 10, 1896, 1; Burrows and Wallace, *Gotham*, 1234.
89. *Brooklyn Daily Eagle*, April 22, 1896, 1.
90. Andy McCue, *Mover and Shaker: Walter O'Malley, The Dodgers, & Baseball's Western Expansion* (Lincoln: University of Nebraska Press, 2014), 128–140.
91. *Brooklyn Daily Eagle*, September 29, 1896, 4.
92. *Brooklyn Daily Eagle*, November 7, 1896, 5.
93. *Brooklyn Daily Eagle*, October 5, 1897, 7.
94. *Brooklyn Daily Eagle*, November 29, 1897, 1.
95. *Brooklyn Daily Eagle*, June 27, 1898, 16, July 11, 1898, 14, January 20, 1899, 11, and January 28, 1899, 9.

96. *Brooklyn Daily Eagle*, January 15, 1892, 6, and October 13, 1892, 2; *New York Clipper*, December 24, 1892, 678.

97. *Brooklyn Daily Eagle*, November 14, 1893, 9, November 13, 1894, 4, and November 13, 1895, 10; *Sporting Life*, January 8, 1898, 5.

98. *New York Tribune*, February 8, 1894, 12, and February 12, 1894, 16.

99. *Brooklyn Daily Eagle*, November 11, 1891, 1; *New York Herald*, November 11, 1891, 11.

100. *Brooklyn Daily Eagle*, January 12, 1892; *New York Herald*, November 11, 1891, 11.

101. *New York Tribune*, February 8, 1894, 12.

102. *Brooklyn Daily Eagle*, February 8, 1894, 8.

103. *Brooklyn Daily Eagle*, January 4, 1895, 4.

104. *Brooklyn Daily Eagle*, January 5, 1897, 4.

105. *Brooklyn Daily Eagle*, September 1, 1897, 10.

106. *Brooklyn Daily Eagle*, September 4, 1897, 4.

107. *Brooklyn Daily Eagle*, October 10, 1897, 8.

Chapter III

1. *Sporting Life*, January 8, 1898, 5; *Brooklyn Daily Eagle*, January 27, 1898, 5. In a letter to his players, reprinted in the *Eagle*, Ebbets put the 1898 loss at over $10,000. *Sporting Life*, in an interview with Ferdinand Abell, said it was $14,000.

2. *Brooklyn Daily Eagle*, February 13, 1898, 9. The $56,000 appears to be money advanced by the owners, primarily Byrne and Abell, in the form of loans rather than additional equity. As such in a bankruptcy and liquidation, it would be repaid before the stockholders got any of their money back.

3. *Brooklyn Daily Eagle*, May 1, 1897, 4, and May 12, 1897, 4. Hot Springs, Virginia, should not be confused with the popular Deadball training area of the same name in Arkansas.

4. *Brooklyn Daily Eagle*, May 29, 1897, 4, and July 4, 1897, 4.

5. *Brooklyn Daily Eagle*, August 3, 1897, 5.

6. *Brooklyn Daily Eagle*, October 9, 1897, 4, November 8, 1897, 10.

7. *Brooklyn Daily Eagle*, November 19, 1897, 4.

8. *Brooklyn Daily Eagle*, December 11, 1897, 1.

9. *Brooklyn Daily Eagle*, January 4, 1898, 16.

10. *Brooklyn Daily Eagle*, March 2, 1898, 1.

11. *Brooklyn Daily Eagle*, January 4, 1898, 16.

12. *New York Sun*, January 3, 1898, 8.

13. *Sporting Life*, January 8, 1898, 5; *Brooklyn Daily Eagle*, January 2, 1898, 22.

14. *Brooklyn Daily Eagle*, January 2, 1898, 22; *New York Sun*, January 3, 1898, 8; *Sporting Life*, January 8, 1898, 5.

15. *Brooklyn Daily Eagle*, March 5, 1898, 5; *New York Times*, June 19, 1894, 12.

16. Frank Graham, *The Brooklyn Dodgers: An Informal History* (New York: G. P. Putnam's Sons, 1945), 7–8.

17. *Brooklyn Daily Eagle*, January 3, 1912, 22.

18. *Brooklyn Daily Eagle*, December 12, 1928, 3.

19. *Brooklyn Daily Eagle*, January 3, 1912, 22.

20. *Howard's Practice Reports in the Supreme Court and Court of Appeals of the State of New York*, Volume 66, 1884, 184–86; *New York Herald*, May 20, 1886, 9; *New Amsterdam Gazette*, Volume 3, No. 10, May 31, 1886, 7. For a summary of the lawsuit, the property sale and Ebbets' share of the bequest, see http://amanlypastime.blogspot.com/2016/02/till-lower-manhattan-comes-to-brooklyn.html.

21. United States Census 1900; *Brooklyn Daily Eagle*, January 3, 1912, 22; *Lain and Healey's Brooklyn Directory for the Year Ended May 1st 1897*, 399.

22. *Sporting Life*, January 8, 1898, 5.

23. *Brooklyn Daily Eagle*, January 12, 1898, 1.

24. *Brooklyn Daily Eagle*, January 2, 1898, 22; *New York Sun*, January 4, 1898, 8.

25. *New York Sun*, January 3, 1898, 8, and January 4, 1898, 8.

26. *New York Sun*, January 4, 1898, 8.

27. *Brooklyn Daily Eagle*, January 3, 1898, 4; *New York Sun*, January 3, 1898, 8.

28. *Brooklyn Daily Eagle*, January 7, 1898, 4.

29. *New York Sun*, February 2, 1898, 4.

30. *Brooklyn Daily Eagle*, January 21, 1898, 5.

31. Burt Solomon, *Where They Ain't: The Fabled Life and Untimely Death of the Original Baltimore Orioles, the Team that Gave Birth to Modern Baseball* (New York: Doubleday, 1999), 133.

32. Mark L. Armour and Daniel R. Levitt, *In Pursuit of Pennants: Baseball Operations from Deadball to Moneyball* (Lincoln: University of Nebraska Press, 2015), 5–6; William

F. Lamb, "A Fearsome Collaboration: The Alliance of Andrew Freedman and John T. Brush," *Baseball: A Journal of the Early Game* 3, no. 2 (Fall 2009): 5, 9–11; Seymour and Seymour Mills, *Early Years*, 298.

33. William Lamb, "Andrew Freedman: A Different Take on Turn-of-the-Century Baseball's Most Hated Team Owner," SABR 19th Century Base Ball Committee Lecture.

34. Lamb, "A Fearsome Collaboration," 7; Solomon, *Where They Ain't*, 179; Lamb, "The Brush Family Women," SABR Baseball Biography Project, http://sabr.org/node/26334.

35. Solomon, *Where They Ain't*, 178–79.

36. Armour and Levitt, *In Pursuit of Pennants*, 21.

37. *Brooklyn Daily Eagle*, January 7, 1898, 4, and March 2, 1898, 4.

38. *Brooklyn Daily Eagle*, January 23, 1898, 10.

39. *Brooklyn Daily Eagle*, October 9, 1897, 4; *The Sporting News*, March 26, 1898, 6.

40. *New York Sun*, March 16, 1898, 4; Alexander, *Turbulent Seasons*, 29, 109.

41. *New York Sun*, January 18, 1898, 4; *Brooklyn Daily Eagle*, January 19, 1898, 5, and January 23, 1898, 10.

42. *Brooklyn Daily Eagle*, February 13, 1898, 9.

43. *Brooklyn Daily Eagle*, February 23, 1898, 16; *New York Sun*, January 30, 1898, 8.

44. *New York Sun*, January 30, 1898, 8.

45. *New York Sun*, March 16, 1898, 4; *Brooklyn Daily Eagle*, March 15, 1898, 16.

46. *Brooklyn Daily Eagle*, February 23, 1898, 16.

47. *Brooklyn Daily Eagle*, March 16, 1898, 5; *The Sporting News*, March 26, 1898, 6; *New York Sun*, Mary 16, 1898, 4.

48. *Sporting Life*, March 26, 1898, 6; Hannah Frishberg, "Eight Long Lost Islands That Used to Be Part of New York," Curbed New York (website), December 3, 2014, accessed November 28, 2017, http://ny.curbed.com/2014//12/3/10016116/8-long-lost-islands-that-used-to-be-part-of-new-york-city. Barren Island was connected to Brooklyn with landfill in 1930.

49. *Brooklyn Daily Eagle*, March 16, 1898, 5.

50. *Brooklyn Daily Eagle*, January 10, 1896, 10, and October 9, 1897, 4; *New York Sun*, March 16, 1898, 4; *New York Clipper*, January 18, 1896, 731.

51. *New York Sun*, March 16, 1898, 4; *New York Times*, March 20, 1898, 16.

52. *Brooklyn Daily Eagle*, March 15, 1898, 16, and March 16, 1898, 5. The March 15 article indicates that the total seating was 12,000, but then lists stands made up of 5,000, 3,000

and 3,200 respectively, so total capacity of 11,200 is used in the text for consistency.

53. *Brooklyn Daily* Eagle, March 16, 1898, 5.

54. *Brooklyn Daily Eagle*, March 15, 1898, 16, and March 25, 1898, 13.

55. *Brooklyn Daily Eagle*, March 24, 1898, 3.

56. *Brooklyn Daily Eagle*, April 4, 1898, 4.

57. *Brooklyn Daily Eagle*, April 11, 1898, 4.

58. *Brooklyn Daily Eagle*, January 27, 1898, 5.

59. *Brooklyn Daily Eagle*, February 13, 1898, 9

60. *Brooklyn Daily Eagle*, February 25, 1898, 4, March 11, 1894, 4, and March 17, 1898, 5.

61. *Brooklyn Daily Eagle*, January 21, 1898, 5, and May 1, 1898, 33.

62. *Brooklyn Daily Eagle*, May 1, 1898, 33.

63. *New York Times*, May 15, 1898, 17.

64. *Brooklyn Daily Eagle*, May 19, 1898, 5.

65. *Brooklyn Daily Eagle*, May 25, 1898, 5.

66. *Brooklyn Daily Eagle*, May 19, 1898, 5.

67. *Brooklyn Daily Eagle*, April 8, 1898, 5, and May 6, 1898, 5.

68. *Brooklyn Daily Eagle*, May 6, 1898, 5.

69. *Brooklyn Daily Eagle*, June 3, 1898, 5.

70. *Brooklyn Daily Eagle*, June 6, 1898, 5.

71. *Brooklyn Daily Eagle*, June 7, 1898, 5.

72. *Brooklyn Daily Eagle*, June 11, 1898, 4.

73. *New York Sun*, August 28, 1898, 8.

74. *Sporting Life*, October 1, 1898, 6.

75. *Ibid.*

76. *Brooklyn Daily Eagle*, September 20, 1898, 16, and November 15, 1898, 10.

77. *Sporting Life*, November 19, 1898, 4.

78. John Thorn, Pete Palmer, Michael Gershman and David Pietrusza, *Total Baseball: The Official Encyclopedia of Major League Baseball*, 6th ed. (New York: Total Sports, 1999), 106.

79. *The Sporting News*, November 12, 1898, 6.

80. *Brooklyn Daily Eagle*, September 3, 1898, 4.

81. *New York Sun*, August 28, 1898, 8.

82. *Brooklyn Daily Eagle*, August 30, 1898, 5.

83. *Sporting Life*, September 17, 1898, 6.

84. *Brooklyn Daily Eagle*, September 20, 1898, 16.

85. *Sporting Life*, November 19, 1898, 4.

86. *New York Sun*, September 9, 1898, 5.

Chapter IV

1. *Brooklyn Daily Eagle*, April 28, 1899, 14.

2. *Sporting Life*, September 17, 1898, 6.

3. Seymour and Seymour Mills, *Early Years*, 303.

4. Armour and Levitt, *In Pursuit of Pennants*, 4.

5. *Brooklyn Daily Eagle*, December 16, 1898, 2.

6. Solomon, *Where They Ain't*, 129, 133, 149.

7. Thorn, *Total Baseball*, 106.

8. Solomon, *Where They Ain't*, 38–40, 133.

9. *Ibid.*, 25, 44–45, 90–91, 125, 133–34.

10. *Brooklyn Daily Eagle*, December 16, 1898, 2, and December 17, 1898, 1.

11. Solomon, *Where They Ain't*, 146, 149.

12. *Brooklyn Daily Eagle*, December 16, 1898, 2.

13. *Ibid.*, and December 18, 1898, 32.

14. *Brooklyn Daily Eagle*, December 18, 1898.

15. *Brooklyn Daily Eagle*, December 19, 1898, 11.

16. *Brooklyn Daily Eagle*, January 16, 1899, 3, and January 21, 1899, 3.

17. *Brooklyn Daily Eagle*, January 21, 1899, 3.

18. *Brooklyn Daily Eagle*, January 21, 1899, 3. No confirmation has been found of this, and it seems unlikely that Ebbets worked an entire year without drawing a salary.

19. *Brooklyn Daily Eagle*, January 19, 1899, 12.

20. *Brooklyn Daily Eagle*, January 20, 1899, 10.

21. *New York Sun*, January 22, 1899, 8.

22. *Brooklyn Daily Eagle*, February 3, 1899, 12. Byrne said he told Ebbets the stock was available to him, but the price was still $10,000, clearly beyond Ebbets' resources.

23. *Brooklyn Daily Eagle*, February 5, 1899, 30.

24. *Brooklyn Daily Eagle*, February 8, 1899, 12, February 9, 1899, 12, February 11, 1899, 12, and February 21, 1899, 1.

25. *Brooklyn Daily Eagle*, February 28, 1899, 12.

26. *Brooklyn Daily Eagle*, February 7, 1899, 12.

27. *Brooklyn Daily Eagle*, March 8, 1899, 16.

28. *Brooklyn Daily Eagle*, April 9, 1899, 31, February 25, 1900, 11.

29. Baltimore acquired Dahlen from Chicago in an off-season trade for Gene DeMontreville before the 1899 season, so the star shortstop never actually played in Baltimore.

30. *Brooklyn Daily Eagle*, April 16, 1899, 10.

31. *New York Times*, July 12, 1899, 12.

32. *New York Tribune*, June 28, 1899, 3, August 3, 1899, 1.

33. *New York Tribune*, August 3, 1899, 3; *New York Times*, August 10, 1899, 1.

34. *New York Times*, August 10, 1899, 1.

35. *New York Sun*, September 6, 1899, 3.

36. *New York Times*, July 12, 1899, 12.

37. *New York Times*, August 16, 1899, 1; *New York Tribune*, August 17, 1899, 3.

38. Anna Mary Lanahan, "Brooklyn's Political Life, 1898–1916" (PhD diss., St. John's University, 1977), 317.

39. *Brooklyn Daily Eagle*, April 11, 1900, 15.

40. *Brooklyn Daily Eagle*, October 22, 1899, 8.

41. Thorn, *Total Baseball*, 106.

42. *Brooklyn Daily Eagle*, December 11, 1899, 2.

43. *Brooklyn Daily Eagle*, February 13, 1898, 9; *Sporting Life*, January 13, 1900, 6.

44. *Sporting Life*, November 4, 1899, 8.

45. *Ibid.*

46. *Sporting Life*, January 6, 1900, 6.

47. Seymour and Seymour Mills, *Early Years*, 302.

48. *Brooklyn Daily Eagle*, December 10, 1899, 37.

49. *Brooklyn Daily Eagle*, September 20, 1899, 14.

50. *Ibid.*; National League Board of Directors Meeting, December 13, 1899, 47, BA-MSS 55, HOF.

51. National League Board of Directors Meeting, December 13, 1899, 52, BA-MSS 55, HOF; *Brooklyn Daily Eagle*, September 20, 1899, 14, September 25, 1899, 14, October 11, 1899, 16, and October 14, 1899, 13.

52. *Brooklyn Daily Eagle*, October 11, 1899, 16, and October 14, 1899, 13. At the time, teams didn't always play the same number of games, so the pennant was decided by winning percentage. Hanlon managed things so Wrigley played in six wins and six losses; removing all those games increased Brooklyn's winning percentage. Hanlon wasn't called "Foxy Ned" for nothing.

53. National Board of Arbitration Minutes, December 12, 1899, 1, 32, 66, BA-MSS 55, HOF; *Brooklyn Daily Eagle*, October 14, 1899, 13.

54. James D. Hardy, *The New York Giants Base Ball Club: The Growth of a Team and a Sport*, 1897–1900 (Jefferson, NC: McFarland, 1996), 154–56.

55. Seymour and Seymour Mills, *Early Years*, 238.

56. Hardy, *New York Giants*, 158; Lamb, "Fearsome Collaboration," 5.

57. Hardy, *New York Giants*, 159–64; Lamb, "Fearsome Collaboration," 10–11.

58. Hardy, *New York Giants*, 165; Thorn, *Total Baseball*, 106.

59. Lamb, "Fearsome Collaboration," 10.

60. Hardy, *New York Giants*,165; Lamb, "Fearsome Collaboration," 19, note 37.

61. Lamb, "Fearsome Collaboration," 5, 9, 10; Solomon, *Where They Ain't*, 179; John Saccoman, "John T. Brush," SABR Baseball Biography Project, http://sabr.org/bioproj/person/a46ef165.

62. Lamb, "Fearsome Collaboration," 5; Solomon, *Where They Ain't*, 179.

63. Lamb, "Fearsome Collaboration," 12.

64. Lamb, "Fearsome Collaboration," 5.

65. Hardy, *New York Giants*, 167; Lamb, "Fearsome Collaboration," 12.

66. *Brooklyn Daily Eagle*, December 10, 1899, 37; Hardy, *New York Giants*, 166.

67. *Democrat and Chronicle*, December 13, 1899, 15.

68. *Ibid.*

69. National Board of Arbitration Minutes, December 12, 1899, 32–33, BA-MSS 55, HOF.

70. *Ibid.*, 53.

71. *Ibid.*

72. National League Board of Directors Minutes, December 13, 1899, 24–25, 51, 53, 64, 66, BA-MSS 55, HOF.

73. *Brooklyn Daily Eagle*, December 14, 1899, 3; *The World*, December 14, 1899, 9.

74. National League Board of Directors Minutes, December 14, 1899, 26, 28–30, 32–33, 36; National League Owners Meeting, Minutes, December 15, 1899, 30, 42, BA-MSS 55.

75. National League Owners Meeting Minutes, December 15, 1899, 31–33, 41, 43, 45, 67–69, BA-MSS 55, HOF.

76. *Brooklyn Daily Eagle*, December 17, 1899, 10.

77. *Brooklyn Daily Eagle*, December 28, 1899, 14, and January 4, 1900, 13; *New York Clipper*, December 23, 1899, 901

78. National League Owners Meeting Minutes, December 16, 1899, 70–75, 80, BA-MSS 55, HOF.

79. Hardy, *New York Giants*, 165–66; Lamb, "Fearsome Collaboration," 19, Footnote 37.

80. *Brooklyn Daily Eagle*, December 15, 1899, 2.

81. Solomon, *Where They Ain't*, 179–80.

82. National League Owners Meeting Minutes, March 8, 1900, 11–13, 17–18, 20, 56, 61, 66, BA-MSS 55, HOF.

83. *Ibid.*, 85–87.

84. *Ibid.*, 107–111.

85. *Ibid.*, 113–14, 116, 120–21.

86. Lamb, "Fearsome Collaboration," 12.

87. *Brooklyn Daily Eagle*, March 9, 1900, 18.

88. *Brooklyn Daily Eagle*, March 12, 1900, 14.

89. *Brooklyn Daily Eagle*, October 13, 1900, 17.

90. *Brooklyn Daily Eagle*, March 12, 1900, 14.

91. *Brooklyn Daily Eagle*, October 13, 1900, 17.

Chapter V

1. "The Fifth Avenue Hotel: Opulence Atop a Potter's Field and Accommodations for Heated Republican Power-Brokering," Bowery Boys History (website), January 6, 2012, accessed November 28, 2017, http://www.boweryboyshistory.com/2012/01/fifth-avenue-hotel-opulence-atop.html.

2. Seymour and Seymour Mills, *Early Years*, 309–10.

3. Burk, *Never Just a Game*, 62–64, 101.

4. Hearing Given by the League Committee to the Committee of the Players Association, Held at the Fifth Avenue Hotel, December 12, 1900, 48, 52–57, 61–63, BA-MSS 55, HOF.

5. Seymour and Seymour Mills, *Early Years*, 310–11.

6. *Ibid.*, 311.

7. National League Owners Meeting, Minutes, December 14, 1900, 185, 211–17, 220, 222, BA-MSS 55, HOF.

8. Seymour and Seymour Mills, *Early Years*, 307.

9. *Ibid.*, 307–09.

10. *Ibid.*, 309, 311–14.

11. *Brooklyn Daily Eagle*, January 8, 1901, 14.

12. *Brooklyn Daily Eagle*, January 3, 1901, 16.

13. *Brooklyn Daily Eagle*, January 8, 1901, 14.

14. *Brooklyn Daily Eagle*, January 11, 1901, 14.

15. *Brooklyn Daily Eagle*, January 13, 1902, 17.

16. *Brooklyn Daily Eagle*, January 23, 1902, 17.

17. *Brooklyn Daily Eagle*, January 26, 1902, 42.

18. *Brooklyn Daily Eagle*, September 30, 1902, 8.

19. *Brooklyn Daily Eagle*, November 6, 1901, 13.
20. *Brooklyn Daily Eagle*, March 13, 1901, 3.
21. *Brooklyn Daily Eagle*, March 14, 1901, 3.
22. *Brooklyn Daily Eagle*, March 15, 1901, 10.
23. *Ibid.*
24. *Brooklyn Daily Eagle*, October 9, 1901, 5.
25. *Brooklyn Daily Eagle*, November 6, 1901, 13.
26. Seymour and Seymour Mills, *Early Years*, 313.
27. National League Owners Meeting, Minutes, December 14, 1900, 232, 234–36, BA-MSS 55, HOF.
28. Meeting between Mr. Zimmer representing the Players Protective Association and the committee of the National League appointed to confer with Mr. Zimmer, consisting of Messers. Soden, Brush and Hart, February 26, 1901, 15, BA-MSS 55, HOF.
29. *Ibid.*, 15–33.
30. *Ibid.*, 16–17, 79–80, National League Owners Meeting, Minutes, February 26, 1901, 141, 147, BA-MSS 55, HOF.
31. National League Owners Meeting, Minutes, February 26, 1901, 141, 145–49, BA-MSS 55, HOF.
32. *Ibid.*, 143.
33. Seymour and Seymour Mills, *Early Years*, 313.
34. *Ibid.*
35. *Brooklyn Daily Eagle*, April 17, 1901, 12, and April 22, 1901, 17.
36. Don Doxsie, *Iron Man McGinnity: A Baseball Biography* (Jefferson, NC: McFarland, 2009), 57–58.
37. *Brooklyn Daily Eagle*, June 14, 1905, 17.
38. Solomon, *Where They Ain't*, 221.
39. Tim Hornbaker, *Turning the Black Sox White: The Misunderstood Legacy of Charles A. Comiskey* (New York: Sports Publishing, 2014), 120.
40. *Brooklyn Daily Eagle*, October 5, 1902, 48.
41. *Brooklyn Daily Eagle*, October 6, 1902, 7.
42. Lyle Spatz, *Willie Keeler: From the Playgrounds of Brooklyn to the Hall of Fame* (Lanham, MD: Rowman and Littlefield, 2015), 179.
43. Spatz, *Willie Keeler*, 187, 189.
44. Norman L. Macht, *Connie Mack and the Early Days of Baseball* (Lincoln: University of Nebraska Press, 2007), 209.
45. Thorn, *Total Baseball*, 106.

46. Matthew 10:36.
47. *Brooklyn Daily Eagle*, July 29, 1901, 11.
48. *The Sporting News*, August 10, 1901, 1.
49. Hardy, *New York Giants*, 175; Seymour and Seymour Mills, *Early Years*, 318.
50. Seymour and Seymour Mills, *Early Years*, 318; Hardy, *New York Giants*, 175–76.
51. Hardy, *New York Giants*, 175.
52. Seymour and Seymour Mills, *Early Years*, 318.
53. National League Owners Meeting, Minutes, December 12, 1901, 220, BA-MSS 55, HOF.
54. *Ibid.*, 244–45.
55. *Ibid.*, December 10, 1901, 61.
56. *Ibid.*, December 10, 1901, 28, 30.
57. *Ibid.*, 32–34; Hardy, *New York Giants*, 177.
58. National League Owners Meeting, Minutes, December 12, 1901, 125–27, BA-MSS 55, HOF.
59. *Ibid.*, 224–25.
60. *Ibid.*, December 13, 1901, 301–307.
61. Seymour and Seymour Mills, *Early Years*, 321.
62. *Brooklyn Daily Eagle*, December 15, 1900, 22, and December 8, 1901, 17.
63. *Brooklyn Daily Eagle*, December 11, 1901, 2.
64. *Sporting Life*, February 15, 1902.
65. National League Owners Meeting, Minutes, April 1, 1902, 6–10, BA-MSS 55, HOF.
66. *Ibid.*, April 2, 1902, 18–53, 59–63, 81.
67. *Ibid.*, 64–65.
68. *Ibid.*, 116.
69. *Ibid.*, 104–06.
70. *Ibid.*, 120–23, 142–51.
71. *Ibid.*, 122, 141–42.
72. *Ibid.*, April 3, 1902, 152, 159–69, Seymour and Seymour Mills, *Early Years*, 321.
73. National League Owners Meeting, Minutes, April 3, 1902, 153–55, 172–73.
74. *Ibid.*, December 13, 1901, 254–55; Lamb, "Fearsome Collaboration," 15.
75. National League Owners Meeting, Minutes, September 24, 1902, 1–2, BA-MSS 55, HOF.
76. *Ibid.*, 2–3, December 10, 1902, 2–3.
77. *Ibid.*, April 2, 1902, 91, and December 12, 1902, 7.
78. *Sporting Life*, January 24, 1903, 4.
79. *Brooklyn Daily Eagle*, January 11, 1903, 50, and January 22, 1903, 13.
80. *Sporting Life*, January 24, 1903, 4.
81. *The Sporting News*, January 11, 1903, 2.
82. National League Owners Meeting, Minutes, January 20, 1903, 15–17, and January 21, 1903, 20–22, BA-MSS 55, HOF.

83. *Ibid.*, January 21, 1903, 41; *Brooklyn Daily Eagle*, January 25, 1903, 44.
84. National League Owners Meeting, Minutes, January 21, 1903, 41–42, and December 8, 1903, 10, BA-MSS 55, HOF.
85. Thorn, *Total Baseball*, 106.
86. National League Owners Meeting, Minutes, December 9, 1903, 20–21, BA-MSS 55, HOF.
87. *Brooklyn Daily Eagle*, October 23, 1903, 3, and December 11, 1903, 21.

Chapter VI

1. Thorn, *Total Baseball*, 106.
2. Charles Bevis, *Sunday Baseball: The Major Leagues' Struggle to Play Baseball on the Lord's Day, 1876–1934* (Jefferson, NC: McFarland, 2003), 52–55, 77–78.
3. Ebbets to Herrmann, January 5, 1904, Box 99, Folder 12, August "Garry" Herrmann Papers, BA MSS-12, Baseball Hall of Fame Library, Cooperstown, New York. Hereafter cited as Herrmann Papers, BA-MSS 12, HOF.
4. Seymour and Seymour Mills, *Early Years*, 323.
5. *Brooklyn Daily Eagle*, January 7, 1904, 13.
6. Ebbets to Herrmann, January 6, 1904, Box 99, Folder 12, Herrmann Papers, BA-MSS 12, HOF.
7. *Ibid.*, Herrmann to Ebbets, January 7, 1904.
8. *Ibid.*, Pulliam to Herrmann, January 12, 1904; *Brooklyn Daily Eagle*, February 7, 1904, 50.
9. *Ibid.*, Ban Johnson to Herrmann, January 9, 1904.
10. *Ibid.*, Herrmann to Pulliam, January 18, 1904.
11. *Ibid.*, Ebbets to National League owners, January 7, 1904.
12. *Ibid.*, Ebbets to Herrmann, January 30, 1904.
13. *Brooklyn Daily Eagle*, February 14, 1904, 7, and March 4, 1904, 15.
14. Bevis, *Sunday Baseball*, 153–54, 156, 175–76.
15. *Ibid.*, 54.
16. *Brooklyn Daily Eagle*, January 2, 1898, 22.
17. Bevis, *Sunday Baseball*, 153–54.
18. *Brooklyn Daily Eagle*, April 18, 1904, 7.
19. Bevis, *Sunday Baseball*, 154–59.
20. *Ibid.*, 157.
21. *Ibid.*, 158.
22. *Brooklyn Daily Eagle*, April 24, 1905, 6.

23. *Brooklyn Daily Eagle*, May 1, 1905, 6.
24. Bevis, *Sunday Baseball*, 160.
25. *Sporting Life*, June 23, 1906, 2.
26. Bevis, *Sunday Baseball*, 160.
27. *Brooklyn Daily Eagle*, April 14, 1906, 1.
28. *Brooklyn Daily Eagle*, April 16, 1906, 6.
29. *Brooklyn Daily Eagle*, May 7, 1906, 7; Bevis, *Sunday Baseball*, 160–61.
30. Bevis, *Sunday Baseball*, 161.
31. *Brooklyn Daily Eagle*, June 9, 1906, 1.
32. *Brooklyn Daily Eagle*, June 18, 1906, 2; Bevis, *Sunday Baseball*, 162–63.
33. *Brooklyn Daily Eagle*, December 14, 1903, 15; Lyle Spatz, *Bad Bill Dahlen: The Rollicking Life and Times of an Early Baseball Star* (Jefferson, NC: McFarland, 2004), 119.
34. *Brooklyn Daily Eagle*, January 5, 1904, 13.
35. *Brooklyn Daily Eagle*, July 2, 1904, 3.
36. *Brooklyn Daily Eagle*, August 21, 1904, 43.
37. *The Sporting News*, August 6, 1904, 1; *Sporting Life*, June 23, 1906, 2.
38. *The Sporting News*, August 6, 1904, 1.
39. *Brooklyn Daily Eagle*, September 2, 1904, 7, September 12, 1904, 18, and September 28, 1904, 14.
40. *The Sporting News*, November 26, 1904, 5, and April 29, 1905, 2.
41. National League Board of Directors Meeting, Minutes, October 13, 1904, 3–4, December 13, 1904, 2, BA-MSS 55, HOF.
42. *New York Sun*, September 29, 1904, 3; *Brooklyn Daily Eagle*, October 5, 1904, 13, November 9, 1904, 2.
43. *Brooklyn Daily Eagle*, October 12, 1904, 4.
44. *Brooklyn Daily Eagle*, October 25, 1904, 1.
45. *Brooklyn Daily Eagle*, November 7, 1904, 5.
46. *The Sporting News*, November 14, 1904, 5.
47. *Brooklyn Daily Eagle*, November 9, 1904, 2, 14.
48. *Brooklyn Daily Eagle*, March 1, 1905, 11.
49. *Ibid.*
50. *Brooklyn Daily Eagle*, March 18, 1905, 8.
51. *Brooklyn Daily Eagle*, February 5, 1899, 30, February 28, 1899, 12, March 17, 1905, 2, March 18, 1905, 8, and November 3, 1907, 64. The exact mathematical breakdown isn't clear. While most accounts claimed Abell and von der Horst owned 40 percent each with Ebbets and Hanlon holding ten percent apiece, it appears that those were round numbers, and there were a few others, direc-

tors and officers, who held a small number of shares. If, for example, Ebbets owned ten percent and Medicus bought 38 percent from von der Horst, then the small holdings of others who were Ebbets' friends and associates could easily have pushed them over the 51 percent mark.

52. *American Cabinet Maker and Upholsterer* 71, no. 1, October 15, 1904; *Brooklyn Daily Eagle*, March 17, 1905, 2, March 18, 1905, 8, and December 12, 1906, 6.

53. Solomon, *Where They Ain't*, 245–46.

54. *Brooklyn Daily Eagle*, March 20, 1905, 2.

55. *Brooklyn Daily Eagle*, March 21, 1905, 11; *The Sporting News*, November 26, 1904, 5.

56. *Brooklyn Daily Eagle*, June 14, 1905, 17.

57. *Brooklyn Daily Eagle*, June 17, 1905, 5; *Sporting Life*, June 17, 1905, 11.

58. *Brooklyn Daily Eagle*, October 3, 1905, 12, and October 9, 1905, 12.

59. *Brooklyn Daily Eagle*, September 19, 1905, 12, September 20, 1905, 12, and October 9, 1905, 12.

60. *Brooklyn Daily Eagle*, October 9, 1905, 12.

61. *Sporting Life*, November 4, 1905.

62. *Brooklyn Daily Eagle*, December 14, 1905, 13; *Sporting Life*, December 30, 1905, 9.

63. *Sporting Life*, December 23, 1905, 11.

64. *Ibid.*

65. *Brooklyn Daily Eagle*, March 22, 1906, 11.

66. *Brooklyn Daily Eagle*, January 3, 1905, and January 17, 1905, 15.

67. *Brooklyn Daily Eagle*, April 3, 1906, 13, and August 7, 1906, 6.

68. *Sporting Life*, October 13, 1906, 16.

Chapter VII

1. *Brooklyn Daily Eagle*, August 16, 1905, 6.

2. National League Owners Meeting, Minutes, February 14, 1906, 7, BA-MSS 55, HOF.

3. *Brooklyn Daily Eagle*, February 28, 1908, 24; National League Owners Meeting, Minutes, December 13, 1905, 10, BA-MSS 55, HOF.

4. National League Owners Meeting, Minutes, February 14, 1906, 7–8, and February 15, 1906, 13, BA-MSS 55, HOF.

5. *Ibid.*, June 19, 1906, 3–4.

6. *The Sporting News*, November 3, 1906, 5.

7. *Brooklyn Daily Eagle*, March 1, 1906, 11.

8. *Brooklyn Daily Eagle*, May 7, 1906, 16, June 3, 1906, 18, and July 21, 1906, 3.

9. *Sporting Life*, June 23, 1906, 2.

10. *Brooklyn Daily Eagle*, October 7, 1906, 18; *The Sporting News*, October 13, 1906, 4.

11. *Sporting Life*, October 20, 1906, 9.

12. *The Sporting News*, January 20, 1906, 1.

13. *Chicago Sunday Tribune*, November 18, 1906, 4.

14. Solomon, *Where They Ain't*, 250–51; *New York Tribune*, November 13, 1906, 10.

15. Solomon, *Where They Ain't*, 251.

16. *Evening Star*, November 24, 1906, 2.

17. *Brooklyn Daily Eagle*, January 3, 1907, 19.

18. *Brooklyn Daily Eagle*, January 22, 1907, 20.

19. *Brooklyn Daily Eagle*, February 2, 1907, 10.

20. National League Owners Meeting, Minutes, February 23, 1907, 32–34, 38, 45, 52, 55, BA-MSS 55, HOF, *Brooklyn Daily Eagle*, February 27, 1907, 12.

21. *Brooklyn Daily Eagle*, February 27, 1907, 12.

22. *Brooklyn Daily Eagle*, January 3, 1907, 19.

23. Solomon, *Where They Ain't*, 252.

24. *Brooklyn Daily Eagle*, February 20, 1907, 11.

25. *The Sporting News*, March 16, 1907, 3; *Brooklyn Daily Eagle*, April 30, 1907, 22.

26. *Brooklyn Daily Eagle*, April 30, 1907, 22.

27. *Brooklyn Daily Eagle*, January 31, 1907, 12; *New York Sun,* February 1, 1907, 5.

28. *Sporting Life*, January 12, 1907, 9; *Brooklyn Daily Eagle*, January 14, 1907, 10.

29. *Brooklyn Daily Eagle*, June 25, 1907, 22.

30. *Brooklyn Daily Eagle*, April 27, 1907, 14.

31. *Sporting Life*, April 6, 1907, 6.

32. *Brooklyn Daily Eagle*, July 7, 1907, 50.

33. *New York Sun*, November 3, 1907, 11.

34. *New York Times*, January 21, 1912, 45; *Brooklyn Daily Eagle*, November 3, 1907, 64.

35. *Brooklyn Daily Eagle*, November 3, 1907, 64; *New York Times*, January 21, 1912, 45.

36. *New York Times*, January 21, 1912, 45.

37. *Brooklyn Daily Eagle*, December 8, 1906, 12.

38. *Brooklyn Daily Eagle*, November 3, 1907, 64.

39. *Brooklyn Daily Eagle*, May 10, 1907, 22.

40. *Brooklyn Daily Eagle*, May 6, 1898, 5.
41. National League Owners Meeting, Minutes, February 28, 1901, 297–98, BA-MSS 55, HOF.
42. *Ibid.*, December 9, 1908, 183–84, 222–23, 229.
43. *Ibid.*, December 9, 1908, 184.
44. *Ibid.*, December 8, 1908, 92.
45. *Ibid.*, December 14, 1915, 22–23.
46. *Ibid.*, December 14, 1915, 23–66.
47. *Ibid.*, February 8, 1916, 144–46.
48. The pass issue was discussed in detail by the owners in February of 1908 (National League Owners Meeting, Minutes, February 27, 1908, 119–143), December of that year (National League Owners Meeting, Minutes, December 8, 1908, 89–104, December 9, 1908, 183–234), December 1915 (December 14, 1915, 23–66), and February of 1916 (National League Owners Meeting, Minutes, February 8, 1916, 73–153), BA-MSS 55, HOF.
49. *Ibid.*, National League Owners Meeting, Minutes, December 8, 1908, 101.
50. *Brooklyn Daily Eagle*, January 5, 1908, 44.
51. *Brooklyn Daily Eagle*, January 13, 1908, 24.
52. *Brooklyn Daily Eagle*, February 9, 1908, 45, and April 20, 1908, 24.
53. *Brooklyn Daily Eagle*, January 5, 1908, 44.
54. *Brooklyn Daily Eagle*, June 19, 1908, 22.
55. *Brooklyn Daily Eagle*, January 12, 1908, 47.
56. National League Owners Minutes, Minutes, February 26, 1908, 6–8, 35–38, 57–58, BA-MSS 55, HOF.
57. *Ibid.*, February 26, 1908, 59–74, and February 27, 1908, 82–101.
58. *Ibid.*, February 26, 1908, 75.
59. *Brooklyn Daily Eagle*, March 10, 1908, 24.
60. *Brooklyn Daily Eagle*, June 15, 1908, 22.
61. *Ibid.*
62. *Brooklyn Daily Eagle*, June 17, 1908, 21, and June 21, 1908, 14.
63. *Brooklyn Daily Eagle*, April 21, 1908, 22, January 27, 1909, 24, and March 28, 1910, 6, 19.
64. *Washington Post*, October 6, 1908, 8; National League Board of Directors Meeting, Minutes, October 5, 1908, BA-MSS 12, Herrmann Papers, Series XVIII, Box 46, Folders 2 and 3, 13, 18.
65. *Cincinnati Enquirer*, October 7, 1908, 4; National League Board of Directors Meeting, Minutes, October 5, 1908, BA-MSS 12, Herrmann Papers, Series XVIII, Box 46, Folders 2 and 3, 30, 88–89, 92–94.
66. *Sporting Life*, January 23, 1909, 3.
67. *Sporting Life*, October 24, 1908, 12; *Brooklyn Daily Eagle*, November 11, 1908, 22.
68. *Brooklyn Daily Eagle*, November 19, 1908, 1, and December 5, 1908, 24.
69. *New York Evening World*, November 14, 1908, 3; *Brooklyn Daily Eagle*, November 14, 1908, 16; On Ebbets' November 6, 1922, passport application, Grace stated that she had known Ebbets for 20 years, which would put their meeting a year earlier than the newspaper accounts.
70. National League Meeting Owners Meeting, Minutes, December 8, 1908, 53–54, 64–65, 69, 73–74, BA-MSS 55, HOF.
71. *Ibid.*, December 10, 1908, 254.
72. *Ibid.*, December 9, 1908, 153–55, 157.
73. *Ibid.*, December 11, 1908, 326–332.
74. *Ibid.*, 349–50, 353–358.
75. *Ibid.*, 375.
76. *Ibid.*, 380–81.
77. *Ibid.*, 384, 408, 412–13; *Brooklyn Daily Eagle*, December 12, 1908, 24. The investigation and the appointment of Brush as chair have received a lot of attention in accounts of the 1908 season. See Maury Klein's *Stealing Games: How John McGraw Transformed Baseball with the 1911 New York Giants*, 301–305 for a summary of the differing viewpoints. Klein's own reading of the Brush appointment, also based primarily on the meeting transcripts, is similar to my own.
78. *Brooklyn Daily Eagle*, January 9, 1909, 5.
79. *Brooklyn Daily Eagle*, December 5, 1908, 24, and December 8, 1908, 2.
80. *Brooklyn Daily Eagle*, January 8, 1909, 22.
81. *New York Evening World*, January 9, 1909, 7.
82. National League Owners Meeting, Minutes, February 16, 1909, 38, 40–44, BA-MSS 55, HOF.
83. *Ibid.*, 13–14, 19, 22, 24–30, 38, 43, 45.
84. *Ibid.*, February 17, 1909, 101–18, 134, and February 18, 1909, 314–16.
85. *Ibid.*, February 16, 1909, 65–69, 76–78, and February 18, 1909, 250–51, 257.
86. *Ibid.*, February 16, 1909, 79–80, 82–83, 94, and February 18, 1909, 252, 255–57, 261, 267–89, 299–301, 312, 320–328.

Chapter VIII

1. *Brooklyn Daily Eagle*, April 26, 1909, 22.
2. National League Owners Meeting, Minutes, June 4, 1909, 5, 7, BA-MSS 55, HOF.
3. *Ibid.*, 7–10, 32–33, 47, 56–57.

4. *Ibid.*, 48.

5. *Ibid.*, August 2, 1909, 2.

6. *Sporting Life*, June 26, 1909, 6.

7. *Ibid.*, July 3, 1909, 6.

8. *Brooklyn Daily Eagle*, July 25, 1909, 45.

9. *Brooklyn Daily Eagle*, June 30, 1910, 26.

10. *Brooklyn Daily Eagle*, September 18, 1910, 60.

11. *Brooklyn Daily Eagle*, August 21, 1909, 16.

12. *Brooklyn Daily Eagle*, December 27, 1909, 24.

13. *Sporting Life*, August 21, 1909, 6, and September 11, 1909, 3.

14. *Sporting Life*, October 27, 1909, 28.

15. *Brooklyn Daily Eagle*, December 7, 1909, 15.

16. National League Owners Meeting, Minutes, December 16, 1909, 135–37, BA-MSS 55, HOF.

17. *Ibid.*, December 16, 1909, 138, 180–84.

18. *Chicago Tribune*, November 28, 1909, 27.

19. National League Owners Meeting, Minutes, December 16, 1909, 199–201, and December 17, 1909, 215, 221–22, 224–31, 236–240, 245–51, 253–258, BA-MSS 55, HOF.

20. *Ibid.*, December 17, 1909, 256, 285–286, and December 18, 1909, 326–27, 333–334.

21. Graham, *Brooklyn Dodgers*, 27; *Brooklyn Daily Eagle*, December 16, 1909, 26; *Philadelphia Inquirer*, December 17, 1909, 10; *Pittsburgh Press*, December 19, 1909, 16. The *Eagle* makes no mention of the comment, much less its causing an uproar and, of course, Graham provides no source. There was, however, considerable newspaper mention in the week that followed, of which the *Inquirer* and *Press* are just two examples.

22. National League Owners Meeting, Minutes, December 18, 1909, 346–50, BA-MSS 55, HOF.

23. Ebbets to Herrmann, January 3, 1910, Herrmann Papers, Box 43, Folder 15, BA-MSS 12, HOF.

24. *Sporting Life*, January 22, 1910, 14.

25. National League Owners Meeting, Minutes, February 15, 1910, 12, BA-MSS 55, HOF.

26. *Brooklyn Daily Eagle*, January 11, 1910, 26.

27. *Ibid.*

28. Dreyfuss to Ebbets, January 12, 1910, Herrmann Papers, Box 42, Folder 15, BA-MSS 12, HOF.

29. *Ibid.*, Ebbets to Dreyfuss, January 15, 1910; Dreyfuss to Ebbets, January 17, 1910.

30. *Brooklyn Daily Eagle*, January 13, 1910, 28, and January 15, 1910, 24.

31. Johnson to Herrmann, January 18, 1910, Dreyfuss to Herrmann, February 1, 1910, Herrmann Papers, Box 43, Folder 15, BA-MSS 12, HOF.

32. National League Owners Meeting, Minutes, February 15, 1910, 22–23, BA-MSS 55, HOF.

33. Johnson to Herrmann, January 29, 1910, Dreyfuss to Herrmann, February 1, 1910, Herrmann Papers Box 43, Folder 15, BA-MSS 12, HOF.

34. National League Owners Meeting, Minutes, February 18, 1910, 87.

35. *Brooklyn Daily Eagle*, February 19, 1910, 16.

36. *Sporting Life*, December 31, 1910, 8.

37. Ebbets to Dreyfuss, January 15, 1910, Herrmann Papers, Box 43, Folder 15, BA-MSS 12, HOF.

38. *Ibid.*, Dreyfuss to Herrmann, February 5, 1910; *Brooklyn Daily Eagle*, March 2, 1910, 23.

39. *Ibid.*, March 2, 1910, 23.

40. *Ibid.*, April 5, 1910, 24.

41. *Ibid.*, May 8, 1910, 58, and May 29, 1910, 52.

42. *Ibid.*, April 30, 1910, 23, and May 1, 1910, 57.

43. *Ibid.*, May 2, 1910, 23.

44. *Sporting Life*, October 15, 1910, 6, and October 22, 1910, 17; *Brooklyn Daily Eagle*, December 23, 1910, 12.

45. *Sporting Life*, June 25, 1910.

46. National League Board of Directors Meeting, Minutes, December 13, 1910, 10–14, BA-MSS 55, HOF.

47. National League Owners Meeting, Minutes, December 14, 1910, 40–79, BA-MSS 55, HOF.

48. National League Owners Meeting, Minutes, February 18, 1910, 88.

49. National League Owners Meeting, Minutes, December 14, 1910, 81–83, 85–87, 108–109, 127, and December 16, 1910, 252–265.

50. National League Owners Meeting, Minutes, December 16, 1910, 245.

51. *Brooklyn Daily Eagle*, January 3, 1911, 25.

52. *Brooklyn Daily Eagle*, February 14, 1911, 18.

53. National League Owners Meeting, Minutes, February 14, 1911, 5, 26–27; National League Schedule Meeting, Minutes, February 15, 1911, 3, BA-MSS 55, HOF.

54. *Ibid.*; National League Owners Meet-

ing, Minutes, December 13, 1911, 31–32; *The Sporting News*, December 14, 1911.

55. *Brooklyn Daily Eagle*, January 5, 1911, 9.

56. *Brooklyn Daily Eagle*, February 16, 1911, 23.

57. National League Owners Meeting, Minutes, February 14, 1911, 19–20, BA-MSS 55, HOF.

58. *The Sporting News*, February 23, 1911, 2; *Brooklyn Daily Eagle*, February 26, 1911, 52.

59. *Brooklyn Daily Eagle*, April 19, 1911, 2.

60. *The Sporting News*, July 27, 1911, 3.

61. *Brooklyn Daily Eagle*, May 26, 1911, 27, and July 23, 1911, 44.

62. *Brooklyn Daily Eagle*, June 10, 1911, 23; *Evening World*, June 21, 1911, 10.

63. *Brooklyn Daily Eagle*, September 3, 1911, 48.

64. *Brooklyn Daily Eagle*, September 1, 1911, 10.

65. *Brooklyn Daily Eagle*, August 27, 1911, 46.

66. *Sporting Life*, November 4, 1911, 6.

67. *Brooklyn Daily Eagle*, November 28, 1911, 23.

68. National League Owners Meeting, Minutes, February 14, 1911, 15–17, BA-MSS 55, HOF.

69. National League Owners Meeting, Minutes, December 12, 1911, 8–14, and December 14, 1911, 266–285.

70. National League Owners Meeting, Minutes, December 13, 1911, 77–79.

71. Morris, *Game of Inches*, 346; Burk, *Never Just a Game*, 122, 162.

72. Ebbets to owners, November 27, 1911, Herrmann Papers, Box 77, Folder, 17, BA-MSS 12, HOF; National League Owners Meeting, Minutes, December 14, 1911, 168–71, BA-MSS 55, HOF.

73. National League Owners Meeting, Minutes, December 14, 1911, 174–75, 179–181, 186–87, BA-MSS 55, HOF.

74. *Brooklyn Daily Eagle*, December 17, 1911, 69.

Chapter IX

1. *Brooklyn Daily Eagle*, January 3, 1912, 22.

2. *Brooklyn Standard Union*, January 3, 1912.

3. *Brooklyn Daily Eagle*, January 2, 1912, 22; *Brooklyn Citizen*, January 3, 1912; *Brooklyn Daily Times*, January 3, 1912.

4. *Brooklyn Daily Times*, January 3, 1912; *New York Tribune*, January 3, 1912, 8.

5. *New York Tribune*, January 3, 1912, 8; *Brooklyn Standard Union*, January 3, 1912.

6. *Brooklyn Daily Eagle*, January 3, 1912, 22.

7. *Brooklyn Daily Times*, January 3, 1912.

8. *Brooklyn Daily Eagle*, January 3, 1912, 22.

9. *Brooklyn Citizen*, January 3, 1912; *Brooklyn Standard Union*, January 3, 1912; *Brooklyn Daily Times*, January 3, 1912.

10. *Brooklyn Daily Times*, January 3, 1912; *Brooklyn Daily Eagle*, January 3, 1912, 22.

11. *Brooklyn Daily Eagle*, January 3, 1912, 22.

12. Ron Selter, *Ballparks of the Deadball Era: A Comprehensive Study of Their Dimensions, Configurations and Effects on Batting 1901–1919* (Jefferson, NC: McFarland, 2006), 42.

13. *Ibid.*, 42; *Brooklyn Daily Eagle*, January 3, 1912, 21–22.

14. Selter, *Ballparks*, 39, 42–43.

15. Bob McGee, *The Greatest Ballpark Ever: Ebbets Field and the Story of the Brooklyn* Dodgers (New Brunswick, NJ: Rutgers University Press, 2006), 49.

16. *Brooklyn Daily Eagle*, April 19, 1913, 18.

17. *New York Tribune*, January 3, 1912, 8; *Brooklyn Daily Eagle*, January 3, 1912, 22.

18. *Brooklyn Daily Eagle*, January 3, 1912, 22.

19. *Ibid.*

20. *Ibid.*

21. Ebbets to Herrmann, May 12, 1912, Herrmann Papers, Box 47, Folder 29, BA-MSS 12, HOF.

22. John and Paul Zinn, *Ebbets Field: Essays and Memories of Brooklyn's Historic Ballpark, 1913–1960* (Jefferson, NC: McFarland, 2014), 18–19.

23. *Brooklyn Citizen*, January 3, 1912.

24. *Brooklyn Daily Times*, January 3, 1912.

25. *Brooklyn Daily Times*, January 5, 1912.

26. *Brooklyn Standard Union*, January 5, 1912.

27. *Brooklyn Citizen*, January 3, 1912.

28. *Brooklyn Daily Eagle*, January 4, 1912, 20.

29. *Brooklyn Daily Eagle*, January 7, 1912, 62.

30. *Brooklyn Daily Eagle*, February 1, 1912, 22.

31. *Brooklyn Daily Eagle*, January 17, 1912, 3.

32. *Brooklyn Daily Eagle*, January 10, 1912, 23, February 10, 1912, 1, and February 19, 1912.

33. *Brooklyn Daily Eagle*, February 4, 1912, 49.

34. Donald G. Lancaster, "Forbes Field Praised as a Gem When It Opened," *Baseball Research Journal* 15 (1986): 26–29.

35. *Brooklyn Daily Eagle*, March 5, 1912, 21.

36. *Brooklyn Daily Eagle*, January 10, 1912, 12, and January 27, 1912, 20.

37. *Brooklyn Daily Eagle*, July 26, 1913, 1.

38. *Brooklyn Daily Times*, April 18, 1912.

39. *Brooklyn Daily Eagle*, April 29, 1913, 21.

40. Ebbets to Herrmann, May 12, 1912, Herrmann Papers, Box 47, Folder 29, BA-MSS 12, HOF.

41. National League Owners Meeting, Minutes, February 13, 1912, 38, and February 14, 1912, 170–73, 176–77, 186, 203, 207–09, BA-MSS 55, HOF; *Brooklyn Daily Eagle*, February 14, 1912, 22.

42. *Brooklyn Daily Eagle*, March 3, 1912, 54.

43. *New York Sun*, April 12, 1912, 8; Selter 39.

44. *Brooklyn Daily Eagle* April 12, 1912, 22; *Evening World*, April 11, 1912, 2.

45. *Brooklyn Daily Eagle*, April 12, 1912, 22.

46. *New York Tribune*, April 12, 1912, 1.

47. *Brooklyn Daily Eagle*, April 12, 1912, 22.

48. *New York Sun*, April 12, 1912, 8; *New York Tribune* April 12, 1912, 1.

49. Ebbets to Herrmann, January 26, 1912, and January 29, 1912, Herrmann Papers, Box 49, Folder 27, BA-MSS 12, HOF.

50. *Brooklyn Daily Eagle*, May 2, 1912, 22.

51. *Brooklyn Standard Union*, April 18, 1912.

52. *Brooklyn Daily Eagle*, March 20, 1912, 1.

53. *Brooklyn Daily Eagle*, March 21, 1912, 1; *Brooklyn Daily Times*, March 25, 1912, 25.

54. *Brooklyn Standard Union*, May 2, 1912; *Brooklyn Daily Eagle*, July 18, 1912, 17.

55. *Brooklyn Daily Eagle*, April 3, 1913, 8.

56. *Brooklyn Daily Eagle*, August 15, 1912, 2; *Brooklyn Citizen*, August 16, 1912.

57. *Brooklyn Daily Times*, July 6, 1912.

58. *Brooklyn Daily Eagle*, July 6, 1912, 2; *Brooklyn Daily Times*, July 6, 1912.

59. *Brooklyn Daily Eagle*, July 1, 1912, 18.

60. *Brooklyn Daily Eagle*, July 6, 1912, 2.

61. Fleischmann to Herrmann, August 3, 1912, Herrmann Papers, BA-MSS 12, HOF.

62. *Brooklyn Daily Eagle*, August 20, 1912, 18.

63. *Brooklyn Daily Eagle*, August 29, 1912, 20.

64. Ebbets to Herrmann, May 12, 1912, Herrmann Papers, BA-MSS 12, HOF; *Brooklyn Daily Eagle*, March 2, 1910, 23. The 1910 *Eagle* account quoted information provided by Ebbets that Charles Jr. owned ten percent, in his letter to Herrmann, Ebbets probably meant that he controlled the rest, including his son's shares.

65. *Brooklyn Daily Eagle*, January 7, 1912, 62.

66. *New York Tribune*, September 26, 1912, 10.

67. Disagreement among the three men became public over the handling of Charles Ebbets, Jr.'s position with the club (see Chapter XIV), and after Ebbets' death, William Baker of the Phillies told the other owners that Ebbets had had problems with Steve McKeever, at least in the last two years of his life, National League Owners Meeting, Minutes, December 9, 1925, 124, BA-MSS 55, HOF; *Brooklyn Daily Eagle*, July 16, 1924, 1.

68. *Brooklyn Daily Eagle* April 9, 1913, 26.

69. *Brooklyn Daily Eagle*, May 1, 1925, 24.

70. *Brooklyn Daily Eagle*, May 21, 1898, 1, 3.

71. *Brooklyn Daily Eagle*, February 24, 1894, 1.

72. *Brooklyn Daily Eagle*, August 29, 1912, 20.

73. *Brooklyn Daily Times*, September 21, 1912; *Brooklyn Daily Eagle*, October 21, 1912, 20.

74. *New York Sun*, August 10, 1912, 8; *Brooklyn Daily Eagle*, November 9, 1912, 16.

75. *New York Sun*, September 21, 1912, 10; *Brooklyn Daily Eagle*, September 21, 1912, 18, and December 6, 1912, 20.

76. *Brooklyn Daily Eagle*, December 12, 1912, 27.

77. National League Owners Meeting, Minutes, December 10, 1912, 33, 74–76, BA-MSS 55, HOF.

78. *Brooklyn Daily Eagle*, December 28, 1912, 16.

79. *Brooklyn Daily Eagle*, December 29, 1912, 52.

80. *Brooklyn Daily Eagle*, January 4, 1913, 11.

81. National League Schedule Meeting, Minutes, February 12, 1913, 69–75, BA-MSS 55, HOF.

82. National League Schedule Meeting, Minutes, January 3, 1913, 20, March 11, 1913, 20, and March 13, 1913, 22.

83. National League Schedule Meeting, Minutes, March 17, 1913, 20.

84. *New York Times*, April 6, 1913, 58–59; *New York Sun*, April 6, 1913, 15; *Morning Telegraph*, April 6, 1913.

85. *New York American*, April 6, 1913; *Brooklyn Daily Times*, April 3, 1913; *Brooklyn Standard Union*, April 6, 1913.

86. *Brooklyn Standard Union*, April 6, 1913; *Brooklyn Daily Eagle*, April 5, 1, and April 6, 1913, 1; *New York Evening Mail*, April 5, 1913; *Brooklyn Daily Times*, April 5, 1913; *New York Times*, April 6, 1913, 58–59.

87. *New York Evening Mail*, April 5, 1913; *New York Times*, April 6, 1913, 58–59; *New York Herald*, April 6, 1913; *Brooklyn Standard Union*, April 6, 1913; *New York Sun*, April 6, 1913, 15; *New York American*, April 6, 1913; *New York Morning Telegraph*, April 6, 1913; *Brooklyn Daily Eagle*, April 6, 1913, 1.

88. *New York Evening Mail*, April 5, 1913; *Brooklyn Standard Union*, April 6, 1913; *New York Morning Telegraph*, April 6, 1913; *New York Tribune*, April 6, 1913, 13; *New York Times*, April 6, 1913, 58–59; *New York Herald*, April 6, 1913; *New York American* April 6, 1913.

89. *Brooklyn Standard Union*, April 6, 1913; *Brooklyn Daily Eagle*, April 6, 1913, 1.

90. *Brooklyn Daily Eagle*, April 6, 1913, 1; *Standard Union*, April 6, 1913; *New York World*, April 6, 1913; *New York Times*, April 6, 1913, 58–59; *Morning Telegraph*, April 5, 1913; *New York American*, April 1, 1913; *New York Sun*, April 6, 1913, 15; *Brooklyn Daily Times*, April 5, 1913.

91. *Brooklyn Standard Union*, April 10, 1913; *Philadelphia Inquirer*, April 10, 1913, 10; *New York Herald*, April 10, 1913; *Brooklyn Daily Times*, April 10, 1913; *New York Sun*, April 10, 1913, 12; *New York Evening Journal*, April 10, 1913; *New York Evening Mail*, April 9, 1913.

92. *Brooklyn Daily Eagle*, April 5, 1913, 18.

93. *Brooklyn Daily Eagle*, April 11, 1913, 2.

94. *Brooklyn Daily Eagle*, April 12, 1913, 18, and April 14, 1913, 3.

95. *Brooklyn Daily Eagle*, May 9, 1913, 28.

96. *Brooklyn Daily Eagle*, May 11, 1913, 1, 5.

97. *Brooklyn Daily Eagle*, April 27, 1913, 1; Selter, *Ballparks of the Deadball Era*, 43.

98. *Sporting Life*, October 25, 1913, 17.

99. *Brooklyn Daily Eagle*, November 17, 1913, 20.

100. *Brooklyn Daily Eagle*, November 18, 1913, 1.

101. *Brooklyn Daily Eagle*, November 21, 1913, 20.

Chapter X

1. Daniel Levitt, *The Battle That Forged Modern Baseball: The Federal League Challenge and Its Legacy* (Lanham, MD: Ivan R.

Dee, 2012), 5–6; Ebbets to Herrmann, October 31, 1913, Herrmann Papers, Box 47, Folder 30, BA-MSS 12, HOF.

2. National League Owners Meeting, Minutes, December 11, 1913, 339, 344–48, BA-MSS 55, HOF.

3. *Sporting Life*, December 20, 1913, 14.

4. *Brooklyn Daily Eagle*, February 18, 1914, 33.

5. National League Owners Meeting, Minutes, February 9, 1916, 203, 211–12, 219, BA-MSS 55, HOF.

6. *New York Times*, February 18, 1916, 8; Fred Lieb, undated article, Herrmann Papers, Box 77, Folder 10, BA-MSS 12, HOF.

7. John Tener to Garry Herrmann, January 11, 1917, March 10, 1917, Herrmann Papers, Box 77, Folder 10, BA-MSS 12, HOF; *New York Evening Mail*, December 29, 1916; National Commission Minutes, 1916–1920, Herrmann Papers, BA-MSS 12, HOF.

8. Harold Seymour and Dorothy Seymour Mills, *Baseball: The Golden Age* (New York: Oxford University Press, 1971), 406.

9. *Brooklyn Daily Eagle*, October 17, 1922, 3.

10. *Brooklyn Daily Eagle*, December 6, 1913, 20, December 7, 1913, 33, December 10, 1913, 2, and December 11, 1913, 1; Levitt, *Battle That Forged*, 3–4, 7.

11. *New York Sun*, December 13, 1913, 13.

12. *Ibid.*

13. *Brooklyn Daily Eagle*, December 15, 1913, 22, December 16, 1913, 20.

14. Ebbets to Tinker, December 14, 1913, Tinker Federal League Case Affidavit, *The Federal League of Professional Baseball Clubs v. the National League, the American League et al*, before Judge Kenesaw Mountain Landis. Hereafter: Landis Case.

15. Tinker Affidavit, Landis Case, 8.

16. *Brooklyn Daily Eagle*, December 19, 1913, 22.

17. Tinker Affidavit, Landis Case, 9.

18. National League Owners Meeting, Minutes, February 12, 1914, 378–381, BA-MSS 55, HOF.

19. Ebbets to Tinker, December 23, 1913; Tinker Affidavit, Landis Case.

20. *Brooklyn Daily Eagle*, December 24, 1913, 16.

21. *Brooklyn Daily Eagle*, December 30, 1913, 18.

22. Tinker affidavit, Landis Case, 10.

23. *Brooklyn Daily Eagle*, January 4, 1914, 71.

24. *Brooklyn Daily Eagle*, January 22, 1914; 20; Ebbets to Tinker, January 26, 1914, Tinker Affidavit, Landis Case.

25. *Sporting Life*, December 19, 1914, 4;

National League Board of Directors Meeting, Minutes, June 10, 1914, 15, BA-MSS 55, HOF.

26. Levitt, *Battle That Forged*, 32, 37–38, 42–43, 86–88, 90.

27. *Brooklyn Daily Eagle*, January 22, 1914, 20; National League Owners Meeting, Minutes, February 12, 1914, 383, BA-MSS 55, HOF.

28. Charles Alexander, *The Miracle Braves, 1914–1916* (Jefferson, NC: McFarland, 2015), 29–31.

29. National League Owners Meeting, Minutes, February 11, 1914, 131, 227, 230, 241, BA-MSS 55, HOF.

30. Alexander, Miracle Braves, 32.

31. National League Owners Meeting, Minutes, February 11, 1914, 291–293, BA-MSS 55, HOF.

32. National League Owners Meeting, Minutes, February 12, 1914, 374.

33. National League Owners Meeting, Minutes, February 10, 1914, 108–110.

34. *Brooklyn Daily Eagle*, February 12, 1914, 18.

35. *Ibid.*; Levitt, *Battle That Forged*, 109; National League Owners Meeting, Minutes, February 10, 1914, 121–22, BA-MSS 55, HOF.

36. Heydler to National Commission, May 12, 1914, Herrmann Papers, Box 102, Folder 15, BA-MSS 12, HOF; *Brooklyn Daily Eagle*, April 15, 1914, 22.

37. Levitt, *Battle That Forged*, 121, 145; Thorn, *Total Baseball*, 106; http://www.baseballchronology.com/Baseball/Years/1914/Attendance.asp.

38. Levitt, *Battle That Forged*, 145; *New York Sun*, June 30, 1914, 10.

39. *Brooklyn Daily Eagle*, June 10, 1914, 1, August 16, 1914, 6, and November 19, 1914, 18; Zinn and Zinn, *Ebbets Field: Essays and Memories*, 101–23.

40. Ebbets to Herrmann, September 20, 1914, Herrmann Papers, Box 47, Folder, 30, BA-MSS 12, HOF.

41. Ebbets to Heydler, December 3, 1915, National League Owners Meeting, Minutes, December 8, 1914, 6, BA-MSS 55, HOF.

42. Ebbets to Herrmann, February 1, 1916, and February 27, 1916, Herrmann Papers, Box 99, Folder 15, BA-MSS 12, HOF.

43. *Ibid.*

44. Ebbets to Heydler, December 3, 1914, National League Owners Meeting, Minutes, December 8, 1914, 6, BA-MSS 55, HOF.

45. Levitt, *Battle That Forged*, 74–75, 138.

46. *Brooklyn Daily Eagle*, January 4, 1915, 18.

47. National League Owners Meeting, Minutes, June 1914. 76, BA-MSS 55, HOF.

48. Levitt, *Battle That Forged*, 147, 160.

49. Tener to Club Presidents, January 29, 1915, Herrmann Papers, BA-MSS 12, HOF; Treasurer's Report to National League Board of Directors, December 14, 1915, 2, BA-MSS 55, HOF.

50. *Brooklyn Daily Eagle*, February 4, 1915, 20, and February 18, 1915, 18.

51. *Brooklyn Daily Eagle*, February 18, 1915, *18*; *New York Tribune*, February 19, 1915, 10.

52. *Brooklyn Daily Eagle*, June 4, 1920, 2; President's Report to National League Board of Directors, December 14, 1915, 1, BA-MSS 55, HOF.

53. *Brooklyn Daily Eagle*, April 15, 1915, 15; Brooklyn Claim Against Newark Club Franchise, Herrmann Papers, Box 99, Folder 15, BA-MSS 12, HOF.

54. Brooklyn Claim Against Newark Club Franchise, Ebbets to Herrmann, February 27, 1916, Herrmann Papers, Box 99, Folder 15, BA-MSS 12, HOF.

55. Brooklyn Claim Against Newark Club Franchise, Barrow to Herrmann, January 26, 1916, Herrmann Papers, Box 99, Folder 15; Johnson to Herrmann, May 25, 1916, Box 99, Folder 16; Ebbets to Herrmann, April 9, 1918, Herrmann Papers, Box 99, Folder 16, BA-MSS 12, HOF.

56. Thorn, *Total Baseball*, 106; Ebbets to Herrmann, June 21, 1915, Herrmann Papers, Box 102, Folder 15, BA-MSS 12, HOF; Levitt, *Battle That Forged*, 220.

57. *Sporting Life*, October 30, 1915, 8.

58. Levitt, *Battle That Forged*, 227–28.

59. National League Owners Meeting, Minutes, December 14, 1915, 211, BA-MSS 55, HOF.

60. Alexander, *Miracle Braves*, 46, 48, 49–50, 53, 58, 63.

61. *Sporting Life*, July 4, 1914, 2.

62. *Brooklyn Daily Eagle*, January 19, 1915, 20.

63. Ebbets to Herrmann, September 4, 1914; Herrmann to Ebbets, September 5, 1914; Ebbets to Herrmann, September 22, 1914; Johnson to Herrmann, September 25, 1914; Johnson to Herrmann, October 1, 1914; Herrmann to Ebbets, October 2, 1914; Ebbets to Herrmann, October 3, 1914; Ebbets to Herrmann, October 22, 1914; and Fultz to Herrmann, May 7, 1915. From the Herrmann Papers, Box 140, Folder 22, BA-MSS 12, HOF.

64. *Brooklyn Daily Eagle*, July 2, 1915, 16.

65. *Brooklyn Daily Eagle*, July 10, 1915, 14.

66. *Brooklyn Daily Eagle*, July 12, 1915, 16.

67. *Brooklyn Daily Eagle*, September 9, 1915, 22.

Chapter XI

1. National League Owners Meeting, Minutes, December 14, 1915, 85, BA-MSS 55, HOF.
2. www.retrosheet.org.
3. Johnston Complaint to the National Commission and Johnston Deposition to the National Commission, March 4, 1916, Herrmann Papers, Series, Box 127, Folder 30, BA-MSS 12, HOF.
4. Ebbets to Johnston, November 24, 1915; Johnston Complaint, March 4, 1915, Hermann Papers; Fultz to Herrmann, March 6, 1916; Johnson to Herrmann, March 18, 1916; Ebbets to Herrmann, March 22, 1916. From Herrmann Papers, Box 127, Folder, 30, BA-MSS 12, HOF.
5. Johnston to Herrmann, March 25, 1916, Herrmann Papers, BA-MSS 12, HOF.
6. *Brooklyn Daily Eagle*, February 17, 1916, 18.
7. Burk, *Never Just a Game*, 243.
8. Fultz Brief in support of Johnston Complaint, Herrmann Papers, Box 127, Folder 30, BA-MSS 12, HOF.
9. Paul G. Zinn and John G. Zinn, *The Major League Pennant Races of 1916: "The Most Maddening Baseball Melee in History"* (Jefferson, NC: McFarland, 2009), 24–25.
10. *The Sporting News*, April 13, 1916, 5.
11. Zinn and Zinn, *1916 Pennant Races*, 24–25.
12. *Brooklyn Daily Eagle*, February 7, 1916, 18.
13. Zinn and Zinn, *1916 Pennant Races*, 30.
14. *Brooklyn Daily Eagle*, April 13, 1916, 20, and April 1, 1889, 1.
15. Zinn and Zinn, *1916 Pennant Races*, 103; *Brooklyn Daily Eagle*, June 22, 1916, 22.
16. Zinn and Zinn, *1916 Pennant Races*, 107; *Brooklyn Daily Eagle*, June 25, 1916, 33.
17. *Brooklyn Daily Eagle*, July 9, 1916, 33.
18. Zinn and Zinn, *1916 Pennant Races*, 112–13.
19. *Ibid.*, 117–18.
20. *Brooklyn Daily Eagle*, July 14, 1916, 14.
21. Zinn and Zinn, *1916 Pennant Races*, 113.
22. *Brooklyn Daily Eagle*, July 8, 1916, 14, and July 12, 1916, 20.
23. *Brooklyn Daily Eagle*, July 18, 1916, 20.
24. *Brooklyn Daily Eagle*, July 20, 1916, 20.
25. *Brooklyn Daily Eagle*, July 29, 1916, 14.
26. Zinn and Zinn, *1916 Pennant Races*, 128.
27. *Brooklyn Daily Eagle*, August 13, 1916, 25.
28. *Brooklyn Daily Eagle*, August 26, 1916, 10.
29. Zinn and Zinn, *1916 Pennant Races*, 162–67.
30. *Ibid.*, 167–80.
31. *Ibid.*, 225–28.
32. *Ibid.*, 228–31.
33. *Ibid.*, 231–32.
34. *Ibid.*, 232–39.
35. *Coshocton (OH) Morning Tribune*, October 8, 1916, 8.
36. Ebbets to Herrmann, September 22, 1916, Herrmann Papers, Box 89, Folder 10, BA-MSS 12, HOF.
37. *Brooklyn Daily Eagle*, October 5, 1916, 25.
38. *New York Sun*, September 22, 1916, 12.
39. 1916 World's Series Bulletin, Herrmann Papers, Box 89, Folder 10, BA-MSS 12, HOF.
40. *New York Sun*, September 22, 1916, 12, and September 23, 1916, 12. The players received the bulk of the gate receipts for the first four games, so the participating club owners didn't see any real financial return until the fifth game.
41. *Brooklyn Daily* Eagle, September 22, 1916, 22; Ebbets to Herrmann, September 16, 1916, Herrmann Papers, Box 89, Folder 10, BA-MSS 12, HOF.
42. *Brooklyn Daily Eagle*, September 22, 1916, 22; *New York Sun*, September 23, 1916, 12.
43. *Brooklyn Daily Eagle*, September 22, 1916, 22.
44. Lannin to Ban Johnson, September 25, 1916, Herrmann Papers, Box 89, Folder 10, BA-MSS 12, HOF.
45. *Brooklyn Daily Eagle*, October 6, 1916, 1–2; Zinn and Zinn, *1916 Pennant Races*, 245.
46. *Brooklyn Daily Eagle*, October 6, 1916, 1–2.
47. *Brooklyn Daily Eagle*, October 7, 1916, 8.
48. Zinn and Zinn, *1916 Pennant Races*, 244, 246.
49. *Ibid.*, 247–49.
50. *Bristol (PA) Daily Courier*, October 9, 1916, 1.
51. *Washington Post*, October 9, 1916, 8.
52. Zinn and Zinn, *1916 Pennant Races*, 250–52.
53. *Ibid.*, 253, *Brooklyn Daily Eagle*, October 11, 1916, 25.
54. Zinn and Zinn, *1916 Pennant Races*, 253–55.
55. *Ibid.*, 255–57.
56. Bruce to Herrmann, Johnson and Tener, November 1, 1916, Herrmann Papers, Box 90, Folder 2, BA-MSS 12, HOF.
57. Zinn and Zinn, *1916 Pennant Races*, 258–59.

58. *Sporting Life*, November 18, 1916, 6; Bruce to Herrmann, Johnson and Tener, November 1, 1916, Herrmann Papers, Box 90, Folder 2, BA-MSS 12, HOF; Thorn, *Total Baseball*, 106; Ebbets to National League owners, July 8, 1916, Herrmann Papers, BA-MSS12, HOF.

59. *Brooklyn Daily Eagle*, October 17, 1916, 1; *Evening World*, October 4, 1916, 12; *New York Tribune*, November 12, 1916, 12.

Chapter XII

1. National League Owners Meeting, Minutes, December 1916, 252, 254–55, 257, 262, BA-MSS 55, HOF.

2. *New York Times*, February 25, 1917, 74.

3. *Ibid.*; *Brooklyn Daily Eagle*, February 13, 1917, 20.

4. *Brooklyn Daily Eagle*, January 21, 1917, 37.

5. *Brooklyn Daily Eagle*, January 22, 1917, 22, and February 13, 1917, 20.

6. *Brooklyn Daily Eagle*, January 11, 1918, 20.

7. *Brooklyn Daily Eagle*, January 20, 1917, 14, and February 13, 1917, 20.

8. *Brooklyn Daily Eagle*, February 13, 1917, 20.

9. *Brooklyn Daily Eagle*, March 18, 1917, 33, March 21, 1917, 20, and March 27, 1917, 27.

10. Michael Haupert, Professional Baseball Player Salary Database, accessed in 2016 and 2017. Hereafter: Haupert Database.

11. *Brooklyn Daily Eagle*, January 20, 1917, 14.

12. *Brooklyn Daily Eagle*, February 11, 1917, 33.

13. *Brooklyn Daily Eagle*, March 1, 1917, 13.

14. *Brooklyn Daily Eagle*, March 9, 1917, 20, and March 20, 1917, 22.

15. *Brooklyn Daily Eagle*, March 22, 1917, 22, and March 23, 1917, 22.

16. WAR, or wins above replacement, offers a measure of a player's value by estimating the number of games his team won because he was in the lineup instead of his replacement, http://www.baseball-reference.com/about/war_explained.shtml, http://www.baseball-reference.com/leagues/NL/1916.shtml

17. Haupert Database.

18. *Brooklyn Daily Eagle*, April 16, 1917, 1, and February 15, 1918, 15.

19. *New York Times*, February 12, 1918, 8; National League Owners Meeting, Minutes, December 11, 1917, 118–130, BA-MSS 55, HOF.

20. *New York Tribune*, February 1, 1918, 12.

21. *Brooklyn Daily Eagle*, March 22, 1918, 1.

22. *Brooklyn Daily Eagle*, March 24, 1918, 37.

23. *Brooklyn Daily Eagle*, April 30, 1918, 22. The 1917 salary was previously stated as $5,300 plus a possible bonus, so it seems that Wheat earned the bonus, which now became part of his salary, Haupert Database.

24. *New York Sun*, July 27, 1918, 11.

25. *Brooklyn Daily Eagle*, July 20, 1918, 4.

26. *Brooklyn Daily Eagle*, September 14, 1918, 16.

27. *New York Sun*, October 6, 1918, 3.

28. *New York Tribune*, November 20, 1918, 13.

29. *Brooklyn Daily Eagle*, December 7, 1918, 8.

30. *New York Tribune*, August 30, 1919, 10.

31. *Brooklyn Daily Eagle*, June 13, 1916, 22; *New York Tribune*, October 21, 1916, 15.

32. *New York Sun*, June 24, 1917, 2.

33. *Brooklyn Daily Eagle*, July 6, 1917, 1, and September 24, 1917, 1.

34. *Brooklyn Daily Eagle*, August 21, 1917, 2.

35. *Brooklyn Daily Eagle*, September 13, 1917, 22, September 15, 1917, 22, September 16, 1916, 14, and September 17, 1917, 18.

36. *Brooklyn Daily Eagle*, November 23, 1917, 18.

37. *New York Sun*, September 28, 1917, 11.

38. *Brooklyn Daily Eagle*, April 10, 1918, 22.

39. *New York Sun*, September 28, 1917, 11.

40. *Brooklyn Daily Eagle*, January 9, 1918, 20.

41. *Brooklyn Daily Eagle*, January 11, 1918, 20.

42. *Brooklyn Daily Eagle*, February 7, 1918, 20.

43. Thorn, *Total Baseball*, 106.

44. *New York Times*, January 16, 1919, 10.

45. National League Owners Meeting, Minutes, January 15, 1919, 13–14, BA-MSS 55, HOF.

46. *New York Sun*, January 16, 1919, 13.

47. National League Owners Meeting, Minutes, January 17, 1919, 10, BA-MSS 55, HOF.

48. *New York Sun*, August 18, 1919, 17.

49. Bevis, *Sunday Baseball*,174, 188, 190–91, 193–94.

50. *New York Tribune*, April 14, 1919, 15, and April 21, 1919, 19.

51. *Brooklyn Daily Eagle*, May 5, 1919, 18.

52. National League Owners Meeting, Minutes, May 13, 1919, 1–3, BA-MSS 55, HOF.

53. *New York Sun*, April 20, 1919, 2.

54. Thorn, *Total Baseball*, 106.
55. *Brooklyn Daily Eagle*, December 24, 1918, 13.
56. *Brooklyn Daily Eagle*, December 26, 1918, 2.
57. *Brooklyn Daily Eagle*, September 6, 1919, 1.
58. J. Herbie DiFonzo and Ruth C. Stern, "Addicted to Fault: Why Divorce Reform Has Lagged in New York," *Pace Law Review* 27, no. 4 (Summer 2007): 559, 566.
59. *Brooklyn Daily Eagle*, October 22, 1919, 16.
60. *New York Sun*, October 18, 1919, 18.
61. *Chicago Daily Tribune*, August 14, 1923, 14.
62. *New York Sun*, October 28, 1919, 24.
63. *Brooklyn Daily Eagle*, November 3, 1919, 1.
64. *Ibid.*, December 26, 1919, 1, and January 9, 1920, 2.
65. *New York Tribune*, January 12, 1922, 6; *Brooklyn Daily Eagle*, January 10, 1922, 19, and January 27, 1922, 2; DiFonzo and Stern, "Addicted to Fault," 571. Since adultery was the only grounds for divorce in New York state, a ploy was developed where typically, the estranged wife, a process server and a detective "caught" the adulterous husband sitting next to a "scantily clad" woman apparently hired for the occasion. The process was so standardized that the participants "performed their scripted roles in the courtroom." It appears that the Ebbets' family had some prior experience with this process, although whether it was a ploy or not isn't clear. In early 1914, Charles Jr. "caught" Frank Hendricks, his sister Lydia's estranged husband, in a compromising position in a Manhattan hotel, leading to her obtaining a divorce (*Brooklyn Daily Eagle*, February 11, 1914, 18, and February 17, 1914, 2).
66. *Brooklyn Daily Eagle*, May 9, 1922, 2.

Chapter XIII

1. National League Owners Meeting, Minutes, February 10, 1920, 7–10, BA-MSS 55, HOF.
2. *Brooklyn Daily Eagle*, February 22, 1920, 24.
3. *Brooklyn Daily Eagle*, February 11, 1920, 18.
4. National League Owners Meeting, Minutes, February 10, 1920, 68–72, 85–87, BA-MSS 55, HOF.
5. *New York Sun and New York Herald*, February 1, 1920, 54.

6. *Brooklyn Daily Eagle*, February 20, 1920, 18.
7. *Brooklyn Daily Eagle*, March 4, 1920, 20.
8. *Brooklyn Daily Eagle*, February 5, 1920, 22.
9. *Brooklyn Daily Eagle*, March 29, 1920, 22, and October 4, 1920, 18.
10. *Brooklyn Daily Eagle*, April 2, 1920, 18.
11. Ebbets to Lane, March 22, 1920, F. C. Lane Papers, BA-MSS 36, National Baseball Hall of Fame Library, Cooperstown, New York.
12. *Brooklyn Daily Eagle*, April 13, 1920, 18.
13. *Brooklyn Daily Eagle*, April 16, 1920, 20.
14. *Brooklyn Daily Eagle*, April 19, 1920, 18, and April 26, 1920, 18.
15. *Brooklyn Daily Eagle*, May 2, 1920, 67, and May 3, 1920, 18.
16. *Brooklyn Daily Eagle*, May 3, 1920, 18.
17. *Brooklyn Daily Eagle*, May 4, 1920, 20.
18. *Brooklyn Daily Eagle*, June 2, 1920, 18.
19. *Brooklyn Daily Eagle*, June 8, 1920, 22, and June 13, 1920, 59.
20. Charles Alexander, *John McGraw* (Lincoln: University of Nebraska Press, 1988), 219.
21. *Ibid.*, 218, 220.
22. *Brooklyn Daily Eagle*, July 23, 1920, 10.
23. *New York Sun* and *New York Herald*, August 8, 1920, 30.
24. *Ibid.*
25. *Brooklyn Daily Eagle*, August 31, 1920, 18.
26. *Brooklyn Daily Eagle*, September 4, 1920, 10.
27. *Brooklyn Daily Eagle*, September 10, 1920, 22.
28. *Brooklyn Daily Eagle*, September 13, 1920, 18.
29. *Brooklyn Daily Eagle*, September 12, 1920, 56.
30. *Brooklyn Daily Eagle*, September 14, 1920, 20.
31. *Brooklyn Daily Eagle*, October 4, 1920, 18.
32. Alexander, *John McGraw*, 225–226.
33. *Brooklyn Daily Eagle*, September 29, 1920, 1.
34. *New York Tribune*, September 30, 1920, 1; *Brooklyn Daily Eagle*, October 1, 1920, 2.
35. Joe Niese, *Burleigh Grimes: Baseball's Last Legal Spitballer* (Jefferson, NC: McFarland, 2013), 68.
36. *Brooklyn Daily Eagle*, September 21, 1920, 20.
37. *Brooklyn Daily Eagle*, October 3, 1920, 64.

38. *Brooklyn Daily Eagle*, October 6, 1920, 22.
39. *Brooklyn Daily Eagle*, October 8, 1920, 24.
40. Larry D. Mansch, *Rube Marquard: The Life and Times of a Baseball Hall of Famer* (Jefferson, NC: McFarland, 1998), 183–84, 186.
41. *Brooklyn Daily Eagle*, October 11, 1920, 1.
42. *New York Sun* and *The New York Herald*, September 27, 1920, 8.
43. *Brooklyn Daily Eagle*, October 11, 1920, 1; Mansch, 186–87.
44. *Brooklyn Daily Eagle*, October 10, 1920, 1.
45. *Brooklyn Daily Eagle*, October 11, 1920, 20.
46. *Brooklyn Daily Eagle*, October 13, 1920, 22.
47. Thorn, *Total Baseball*, 106
48. *Brooklyn Daily Eagle*, October 21, 1920, 20.
49. *Ibid.*; *Organized Baseball*, Hearings Before the Subcommittee on [the] Study of Monopoly Power of the Committee of the Judiciary, House of Representatives, 82nd Congress, 1st Session, Serial Nol. 1, Part 6 (Washington, DC: Government Printing Office, 1952), 1600, hereafter Celler Committee Report; Thorn, *Total Baseball*, 106.

Chapter XIV

1. *New York Tribune*, February 13, 1921, 17.
2. *Brooklyn Daily Eagle*, February 9, 1921, 20.
3. *Brooklyn Daily Eagle*, March 6, 1921, 89.
4. *Brooklyn Daily Eagle*, March 9, 1921, 22.
5. *Brooklyn Daily Eagle*, March 17, 1921, 22.
6. Ebbets to Herrmann, October 27, 1921, Herrmann Papers, BA-MSS 12, HOF.
7. *Brooklyn Daily Eagle*, December, 20, 1922, 26; Haupert has Wheat making $8,300 in 1922; the $500 difference is not significant enough to make a difference in evaluating the unreasonableness of Ebbets' position.
8. *Brooklyn Daily Eagle*, February 18, 1923, 38.
9. *Brooklyn Daily Eagle*, March 30, 1923, 24.
10. *Brooklyn Daily Eagle*, March 31, 1923, 5.
11. Haupert Database; www.baseball-reference.com.

12. *Brooklyn Daily Eagle*, March 9, 1921, 22.
13. *Brooklyn Daily Eagle*, March 17, 1921, 22, April 1, 1921, 24.
14. Haupert Database; *Brooklyn Daily Eagle*, April 13, 1921, 22; Niese, *Burleigh Grimes*, 75. Niese's source is the *Eagle* article, which lists no salary figure.
15. *Brooklyn Daily Eagle*, March 13, 1922, 22.
16. *Brooklyn Daily Eagle*, March 15, 1922, 26.
17. *Brooklyn Daily Eagle*, February 25, 1924, 24.
18. *Ibid.*; Haupert Database; www.baseball-reference.com. Alexander and Rixey, like Grimes, are Hall of Famers. Although largely forgotten today, Wilbur Cooper won 106 games for Pittsburgh from 1920 to 1924.
19. *Brooklyn Daily Eagle*, June 19, 1921, 45.
20. *Brooklyn Daily Eagle*, November 6, 1921, 50.
21. Brian McKenna, "Sam Crane," SABR Baseball Biography Project, http://sabr.org/bioproj/person/232b9f0d.
22. National League Owners Meeting, Minutes, February 14, 1922, 11–13, 16–22, 27, 29–32, 74, 77, 87, BA-MSS 55, HOF.
23. John C. Skipper, *Dazzy Vance: A Biography of the Brooklyn Dodger Hall of Famer* (Jefferson, NC: McFarland, 2007), 31–32.
24. Niese, *Burleigh Grimes*, 86–87.
25. *Ibid.*, 86; *Brooklyn Daily Eagle*, August 13, 1922, 44.
26. *Brooklyn Daily Eagle*, August 14, 1922, 22, Niese, Grimes, 87.
27. *Brooklyn Daily Eagle*, December 13, 1922, 26.
28. *Brooklyn Daily Eagle*, January 17, 1923, 20.
29. *Brooklyn Daily Eagle*, December 16, 1922, 1.
30. *New York Times*, February 8, 1923, 22.
31. *Brooklyn Daily Eagle*, March 11, 1923, 42, and June 18, 1923, 20.
32. *Brooklyn Daily Eagle*, August 21, 1923, 22.
33. Niese, *Burleigh Grimes*, 91.
34. Skipper, *Dazzy Vance*, 49.
35. *Brooklyn Daily Eagle*, June 9, 1919, 18, and April 25, 1923, 22.
36. *Brooklyn Daily Eagle*, August 14, 1923, 1.
37. *Brooklyn Daily Eagle*, August 1, 1923, 23.
38. *Brooklyn Daily Eagle*, July 16, 1924, 1.
39. *Brooklyn Daily Eagle*, May 2, 1923, 26, and May 4, 1923, 26; Thorn, *Total Baseball*, 106; Celler Committee Report, 1600.

40. National League Owners Meeting, Minutes, December 10, 1923, 46–47, BA-MSS 55, HOF. While Ebbets' baseball career dates back to 1883, Brooklyn didn't join the National League until 1890.

41. *Brooklyn Daily Eagle*, November 2, 1923, 26.

42. *Brooklyn Daily Eagle*, February 15, 1924, 24.

43. *Brooklyn Daily Eagle*, April 10, 1924, 26.

44. Reed Browning, *Baseball's Greatest Season, 1924* (Amherst: University of Massachusetts Press, 2003), 95–96.

45. *Brooklyn Daily Eagle*, September 7, 1924, 40.

46. *Brooklyn Daily Eagle*, September 8, 1924, 20.

47. Browning, *Baseball's Greatest Season*, 107.

48. *Brooklyn Daily Eagle*, September 24, 1924, 24.

49. Browning, *Baseball's Greatest Season*, 112–15; *Brooklyn Daily Eagle*, October 4, 1924, 11.

50. *Brooklyn Daily Eagle*, October 18, 1924, 11, December 11, 1924, 26, February 4, 1925, 18, and February 11, 1925, 22.

51. *New York Times*, January 23, 1925, 15.

52. National League Owners Meeting, Minutes, February 2, 1925, 5–6, BA-MSS 55, HOF.

53. National League Owners Meeting, Minutes, February 3, 1925, 3–7, BA-MSS 55, HOF.

54. *Brooklyn Daily Eagle*, March 2, 1925, 20; Haupert Database.

55. *Brooklyn Daily Eagle*, March 5, 1925, 22.

56. *Brooklyn Daily Eagle*, March 7, 1925, 4.

57. *Ibid.*

58. *Brooklyn Daily Eagle*, March 8, 1925, 46.

59. *Brooklyn Daily Eagle*, March 11, 1925, 22.

60. *Brooklyn Daily Eagle*, March 19, 1925, 20.

61. *Brooklyn Daily Eagle*, March 31, 1925, 24.

62. *Brooklyn Daily Eagle*, March 15, 1925, 4, and March 20, 1925, 24.

63. *Brooklyn Daily Eagle*, April 7, 1925, 20.

64. *Brooklyn Daily Eagle*, April 10, 1925, 20, and April 17, 1925, 1.

65. *Brooklyn Daily Eagle*, April 19, 1925, 1.

66. *Brooklyn Daily Eagle*, April 20, 1925, 22.

67. *Ibid.*, 3, 22.

68. *Brooklyn Daily Eagle*, May 6, 1925, 1. The parts were not divided equally among the beneficiaries.

69. *Brooklyn Daily Eagle*, April 27, 1925, 3.

70. *Brooklyn Daily Eagle*, May 25, 1925, 1.

71. *Brooklyn Daily Eagle*, April 19, 1925, 8.

72. *New York Herald Tribune*, April 22, 1925, 20.

Chapter XV

1. Zinn and Zinn, *Ebbets Field*, 17–19.

2. Armour and Levitt, *In Pursuit of Pennants*, 14–15, 23.

3. *Brooklyn Daily Eagle*, May 2, 1923, 26.

4. *Brooklyn Daily Eagle*, March 8, 1883, 3, and May 6, 1925, 1.

5. *Brooklyn Daily Eagle*, April 19, 1925, 8.

6. See, among others, Frank Graham's *The Dodgers: An Informal History*.

7. McGee, *Greatest Ballpark*, 49.

8. *Brooklyn Daily Eagle*, April 19, 1913, 18; *Sporting Life*, May 11, 1912, 5.

9. Fred Lieb, *Baseball As I Have Known It* (Lincoln: University of Nebraska Press, 1996 reprint), 268.

10. Andy McCue, *Mover and Shaker*, 37; Norman Macht, *Connie Mack and the Early Years of Baseball*; Hornbaker, *Turning the Black Sox White*, 225.

11. *Brooklyn Daily Eagle*, April 19, 1925, 8.

12. National League Owners Meeting, Minutes, December 15, 1920, 31–32, BA-MSS 55, HOF.

13. Chernow, *Titan*, 505.

14. National League Owners Meeting, Minutes, December 9, 1925, 121–29, BA-MSS 55, HOF.

15. National League Owners Meeting, Minutes, December 9, 1925, 8.

Bibliography

Books and Articles

Alexander, Charles. *John McGraw*. Lincoln: University of Nebraska Press, 1988.
_____. *The Miracle Braves: 1914–16*. Jefferson, NC: McFarland, 2015.
_____. *Turbulent Seasons: Baseball in 1890–91*. Dallas: Southern Methodist University Press, 2011.

Armour, Mark L., and Daniel R. Levitt. *In Pursuit of Pennants: Baseball Operations from Deadball to Moneyball*. Lincoln: University of Nebraska Press, 2015.

Bernstein, Iver. *The New York City Draft Riots: Their Significance for American Society and Politics in the Age of the Civil War*. New York: Oxford University Press, 1990.

Bevis, Charlie. *Sunday Baseball: The Major Leagues' Struggle to Play Baseball on the Lord's Day, 1876–1934*. Jefferson, NC: McFarland, 2003.

Browning, Reed. *Baseball's Greatest Season, 1924*. Amherst: University of Massachusetts Press, 2003.

Burk, Robert F. *Never Just a Game: Players, Owners and American Baseball to 1920*. Chapel Hill: University of North Carolina Press, 1994.

Burrows, Edwin G. and Wallace, Mike. *Gotham: A History of New York City to 1898*. New York: Oxford University Press, 1999.

Chernow, Ron. *Titan: The Life of John D. Rockefeller Sr.* New York: Random House, 1998.

Cox, J. Randolph. *The Dime Novel Companion: A Source Book*. Westport, CT: Greenwood Press, 2000.

DiFonzo, J. Herbie, and Ruth C. Stern. "Addicted to Fault: Why Divorce Reform Has Lagged in New York." *Pace Law Review* 27, no. 4 (Summer 2007): 559–603.

Doxsie, Don. *Iron Man McGinnity: A Baseball Biography*. Jefferson, NC: McFarland, 2009.

"The Fifth Avenue Hotel: Opulence Atop a Potter's Field and Accommodations for Heated Republican Power-Brokering." Bowery Boys History (website), January 6, 2012, accessed November 28, 2017, http://www.boweryboyshistory.com/2012/01/fifth-avenue-hotel-opulence-atop.html.

Frishberg, Hannah. "Eight Long Lost Islands That Used to Be Part of New York." Curbed New York (website), December 3, 2014, accessed November 28, 2017, http://ny.curbed.com/2014//12/3/10016116/8-long-lost-islands-that-used-to-be-part-of-new-york-city.

Graham, Frank. *The Brooklyn Dodgers: An Informal History*. New York: G. P. Putnam's, 1984.

Hardy, James, D., Jr. *The New York Giants Baseball Club: The Growth of a Team and a Sport, 1870–1900*. Jefferson, NC: McFarland, 1996.

Hornbaker, Tim. *Turning the Black Sox White: The Misunderstood Legacy of Charles A. Comiskey*. New York: Sports Publishing, 2014.

Klein, Maury. *Stealing Games: How John McGraw Transformed Baseball with the 1911 New York Giants*. New York: Bloomsbury Press, 2016.

Lamb, William. "A Fearsome Collaboration." *Baseball: A Journal of the Early Game* 3, no. 2 (Fall 2009): 5–20.

_____. "The Brush Family Women." SABR Baseball Biography Project, http://sabr.org/node/26334.

Lancaster, Donald G. "Forbes Field Praised as a Gem When It Opened." *Baseball Research Journal* 15 (1986): 26–29.

Leib, Fred. *Baseball as I Have Known It.* Lincoln: University of Nebraska Press, 1996.

Levitt, Daniel R. *The Battle That Forged Modern Baseball: The Federal League Challenge and Its Legacy.* Lanham, MD: Ivan R. Dee, 2012.

Macht, Norman L. *Connie Mack and the Early Days of Baseball.* Lincoln: University of Nebraska Press, 2007.

Mansch, Larry D. *Rube Marquard: The Life and Times of a Baseball Hall of Famer.* Jefferson, NC: McFarland, 1998.

McCue, Andy. *Mover and Shaker: Walter O'Malley, the Dodgers and Baseball's Western Expansion.* Lincoln: University of Nebraska Press, 2014.

McGee, Bob. *The Greatest Ballpark Ever: Ebbets Field and the Story of the Brooklyn Dodgers.* New Brunswick, NJ: Rutgers University Press, 2005.

McKenna, Brian. "Sam Crane." SABR Baseball Biography Project, http://sabr.org/bioproj/person/232b9f0d.

Morris, Peter, William J. Ryczek, Jan Finkel, Leonard Levin, Richard Malatzky. *Baseball Founders: The Clubs, Players and Cities of the Northeast That Established the Game.* Jefferson, NC: McFarland, 2013.

Morris, Peter. *A Game of Inches: The Story Behind the Innovations That Shaped Baseball.* Chicago, IL: Ivan R. Dee, 2006.

Nackenoff, Carol. *The Fictional Republic: Horatio Alger and American Political Discourse.* New York: Oxford University Press, 1994.

Nemec, David. *The Beer and Whiskey League: The Illustrated History of the American Association—Baseball's Renegade Major League.* Guilford, CT: Lyons Press, 2004.

Niese, Joe. *Burleigh Grimes: Baseball's Last Legal Spitballer.* Jefferson, NC: McFarland, 2013.

Saccoman, John. "John T. Brush." SABR Baseball Biography Project, http://sabr.org/bioproj/person/a46ef165.

Selter, Ronald M. *Ballparks of the Deadball Era: A Comprehensive Study of Their Dimensions, Configurations and Effects on Batting, 1901–1919.* Jefferson, NC: McFarland, 2008.

Seymour, Harold, and Dorothy Seymour Mills. *Baseball: The Early Years.* New York: Oxford University Press, 1960.

_____. *Baseball: The Golden Age.* New York: Oxford University Press, 1971.

Skipper, John C. *Dazzy Vance: A Biography of the Brooklyn Dodger Hall of Famer.* Jefferson, NC: McFarland, 2007.

Snyder-Grenier, Ellen M. *Brooklyn! An Illustrated History.* Philadelphia: Temple University Press, 1996.

Solomon, Burt. *Where They Ain't: The Fabled Life and Untimely Death of the Original Baltimore Orioles, the Team That Gave Birth to Modern Baseball.* New York: Doubleday, 1999.

Spatz, Lyle. *Willie Keeler, From the Playgrounds of Brooklyn to the Hall of Fame.* Lanham, MD: Rowman and Littlefield, 2015.

_____. *Bad Bill Dahlen: The Rollicking Life and Times of an Early Baseball Star.* Jefferson, NC: McFarland, 2004.

Steele, Edward E. *Ebbets: The History and Genealogy of a New York Family.* Revised edition, Self-published, 2013.

Stiles, T. J. *Custer's Trials: A Life on the Frontier of a New America.* New York: Alfred Knopf, 2015.

Sullivan, Mark. *Our Times: The United States, 1900–1925.* Volume 2. New York: Scribner's, 1927.

Thorn, John, Pete Palmer, Michael Gershman and David Pietrusza. *Total Baseball: The Official Encyclopedia of Major League Baseball*, Sixth Edition. New York: Total Sports, 1999.

White, Ronald C., Jr. *Lincoln's Greatest Speech: The Second Inaugural.* New York: Simon & Schuster, 2002.

Voigt, David Quentin. *American Baseball: From the Gentleman's Sport to the Commissioner System.* State College: Pennsylvania State University, 1983.

Zinn, Paul G., and John G. Zinn. *The Major League Pennant Races of 1916:*

"The Most Maddening Baseball Melee in History." Jefferson, NC: McFarland, 2009.

_____. Ebbets Field: Essays and Memories of Brooklyn's Historic Ballpark, 1913–1960. Jefferson, NC: McFarland, 2013.

Newspapers

Bristol (PA) Daily Courier
Brooklyn Citizen
Brooklyn Daily Eagle
Brooklyn Daily Times
Brooklyn Standard Union
Chicago Daily Tribune
Coshocton (OH) Morning Tribune
Eastern State Journal (White Plains, NY)
New Amsterdam Gazette
New York American
New York Clipper
New York Evening Mail
New York Evening World
New York Herald
New York Morning Telegraph
New York Sun
New York Times
New York Tribune
New York World
Sporting Life
The Sporting News
Washington Post

Archival Collections

1899–1900 Brooklyn Dodger Financial Ledgers. Privately held.
August "Garry" Herrmann Papers, BA-MSS 12. Baseball Hall of Fame and Museum, Cooperstown, New York.

F. C. Lane Papers, 1911–1936, BA-MSS 36. Baseball Hall of Fame and Museum, Cooperstown, New York.
National League Meetings, Conferences, Minutes and Financial Ledgers, 1899–1995, BA-MSS 55. Baseball Hall of Fame and Museum, Cooperstown, New York.

Miscellaneous Other Sources

1850, 1860, 1870, 1880, 1900 and 1920 U.S. Censuses.
Dogget's City Directory, New York City.
Haupert Professional Baseball Player Salary Database. Accessed 2016–2017, courtesy of Michael Haupert.
Lanahan, Anna Maria. "Brooklyn's Political Life, 1898–1916." PhD diss., St. John's University, 1977.
Organized Baseball, Hearings Before the Subcommittee on [the] Study of Monopoly Power of the Committee of the Judiciary. House of Representatives, 82nd Congress, 1st Session, Serial No. 1, Part 6 (Washington, D.C.: Government Printing Office, 1952), 1600.
Trowbridge's New York City Directory.

Websites

www.baseballreference.com
www.retrosheet.org
www.sabr.org

Index

Numbers in *bold italics* indicate pages with illustrations

239